C000262907

Sunderland over Far Eastern Seas

Sunderland over Far Eastern Seas

An RAF Flying Boat Navigator's Story

Group Captain Derek K. Empson MBE

Pen & Sword
AVIATION

First published in Great Britain in 2010 by
Pen & Sword Aviation
an imprint of
Pen & Sword Books Ltd
47 Church Street
Barnsley
South Yorkshire
S70 2AS

Copyright © Derek K. Empson 2010

ISBN 978-1-84884-163-5

The right of Derek K. Empson to be identified as Author of this Work has
been asserted by him in accordance with the Copyright, Designs and
Patents Act 1988.

A CIP catalogue record for this book is available from the British Library.

All rights reserved. No part of this book may be reproduced or
transmitted in any form or by any means, electronic or mechanical
including photocopying, recording or by any information storage and
retrieval system, without permission from the Publisher in writing.

Typeset in 11.5pt Ehrhardt by
Mac Style, Beverley, E. Yorkshire

Printed and bound in the UK by the MPG Books Group

Pen & Sword Books Ltd incorporates the imprints of Pen & Sword
Aviation, Pen & Sword Maritime, Pen & Sword Military, Wharncliffe
Local History, Pen and Sword Select, Pen and Sword Military Classics and
Leo Cooper.

For a complete list of Pen & Sword titles please contact
PEN & SWORD BOOKS LIMITED
47 Church Street, Barnsley, South Yorkshire, S70 2AS, England
E-mail: enquiries@pen-and-sword.co.uk
Website: www.pen-and-sword.co.uk

Contents

Note
Colour maps are grouped in a section between pages 16–17.
Colour photographs are grouped in a section between pages 256–257.

Foreword

Air Vice-Marshal G.A. Chesworth CB, OBE, DFC
Former Chief of Staff No. 18 Group Royal Air Force

Operating flying boats has always been regarded as a mystique and the envy of those aviators who have not flown them. 'Being on boats' has been the ambition of aircrew, past and present, and those of us who have had the privilege of being 'boatmen' are still looked upon with some awe – even by today's Royal Air Force aircrew.

Derek Empson's account of Sunderland flying with the Far East Air Force Flying Boat Wing, the only formed Royal Air Force Unit assigned to the United Nations International Force during the Korean War, describes the variety of tasks undertaken, not just in the UN theatre, but throughout the vast area of responsibility of the Far East Air Force.

The Air Ministry did not want to allocate significant resources to the Korean conflict. The RAF was heavily committed to building up forces, from the limited Defence resources, to counter the Soviet threat to the NATO alliance. Supporting operations many thousands of miles from home, including the Malayan Communist Terrorist threat was, therefore, a very low priority and attracted very little public attention. Perhaps that is the reason so little has been written about the activities of Sunderlands in that theatre and why limited role information was available to aircrew before they left the UK on posting to the Flying Boat Wing.

Sunderland over Far Eastern Seas recounts the day-to-day experiences of the young Derek Empson, a navigator on his first operational tour. It describes the Sunderland, its crew, equipment and procedures, roles and operating conditions that will allow the reader to understand why the crews were pleased and proud to be 'boatmen'.

With five crews to five Sunderlands, the crew's lives revolved around the servicing schedules and availability of their own aircraft. I have always said, being a 'boatman' was not just a job; it was a way of life. This book explains why.

Preface

The author, then a flying officer navigator, working at the navigation table of a Sunderland in the Far East in 1952.

This is an autobiographical account of events that took place in the early 1950s when, initially as a newly qualified navigator just turned 21 years of age, I flew in Sunderland flying boats in the Far East. There are several reasons why I decided, rather late in life, to write this account. First, I wanted readers who are unfamiliar with flying boats to begin to understand why 'being on boats' was so special to those who flew them – to convey that sense of self-reliance and freedom that operating from, and mostly over, the sea gave to flying boat crews unconstrained by runways and airfield boundaries.

Secondly, May 2009 marked fifty years since the withdrawal of the Sunderland from RAF service that began in 1938 and continued though the Second World War until 20 May 1959. Far East Flying Boat Wing squadrons were the last RAF units to operate the Sunderland, so the Far East was where

RAF flying boat operations finally came to an end after forty-one years. Today, the RAF no longer operates routinely in any of the Far East areas where we flew daily in the 1950s. Many interested in military aviation therefore understandably have only a hazy idea of what it was like to operate from, and fly over, the eastern seas that we who were 'boatmen' came to know so well.

The third reason is that while many aviators agree that the Sunderland was an iconic aircraft, relatively few were lucky enough to fly in them. As one of the fortunate few, I feel – even after such a long interval – that I should try to recall and convey to others interested in flying boats, what a Sunderland was like to fly in, what equipment we had to work with, and how our operating techniques compared with and differed from those of landplanes. I also wanted to try to convey how different life in the Royal Air Force in the Far East was in those far-off days, compared with today.

And finally I wanted to write this book for my family, and for those with whom I flew in Sunderlands in the Far East in the early 1950s; to provide a written and visual record of some of the many memories I have cherished over the years of those momentous and happy 'flying boat days'.

Derek Empson
Knutsford, Cheshire

Footnote on AVM George Chesworth. *As many readers will know, Flying Officer George A. Chesworth – as he was in 1952/3 – had a very distinguished Royal Air Force career. He was one of the main driving forces behind the introduction of the Nimrod MR1 that replaced the Shackleton MR2/3 when he was serving at the Ministry of Defence as a wing commander. After further promotions and holding many senior and responsible appointments, thirty years later he was Air Vice-Marshal G.A. Chesworth CB, OBE, DFC, a highly respected air officer, most notably within No. 18 Group, of which he became Chief of Staff. After retiring from the Royal Air Force in 1984, George Chesworth was made Chief Executive of the Glasgow Garden Festival, a tremendously successful event due in large measure to his leadership. He has since become a Justice of the Peace and, most notably, was the Lord Lieutenant of Moray. Born in London, George and his wife Betty have permanently settled in Scotland, which they love.*

Acknowledgements

I offer my sincere thanks to several former Royal Air Force colleagues with whom I flew in Sunderland flying boats during the squadron tour I describe in this book. These include Air Vice-Marshal George Chesworth (who has kindly written the Foreword), David Germain, the late Sandy Innes-Smith (who sadly died on 30 April 2009), John Land and Stuart Holmes, all of whom helped me in various ways. Some confirmed for me their recollection of certain events at which we had both been present; others dug out old photographs. I wish to thank Tony Burt with whom I have often been in contact. We have periodically passed information to each other, and I have greatly valued his assistance. I want also to thank Brian Banks for his description of Song Song Range and Bidan; and Mike Reece for his recollections as an airman at Seletar. I am extremely grateful to David Croft who, over a long period, has gone to enormous lengths to locate and send me photographs taken by members of the RAF Seletar Association and the Butterworth and Penang Association. Many are included here, and wherever possible I have identified the individual photographers. Those whose photographs I have included are Dave Croft, David Germain, John Land, Tony Burt, 'Bob', the late Derek Lehrle, Jack Gretton, Brian Lavender, Joe Lockhart, the late Bill Whiter, Joe Manny, William Devine, Charles Ayres, Don Jones, Tony Feist, the late Bill Wilson, Sam Mold, Ted Wilkins, Don Jones, 'Ginge' Mills, Graham Horton, the late Peter Giddens, Alan Hills, Mike Rees, Bill Murray, A Carrie, Ron Bevan, 'Climpson', Boon Swee Low, 47 Air Navigation School, Queenstown South Africa, and others whom I could not identify. I have included a few examples of the work of the excellent cartoonist 'Kane', who was an engine fitter on Far East Flying Boat Wing. I am similarly grateful for photographs I downloaded from the former 88 Squadron Association website. I apologise sincerely to anyone whose name I have missed. All the above photographs and snippets of information – provided or confirmed to me by those whom I have been able to contact – have helped to piece together the jigsaw of events that, at this distance in time, it has not been easy to complete. I want to thank the Imperial War

Museum, especially Mr Craig Murray, the former Collections officer at Duxford Air Museum, who allowed me to photograph Sunderland ML796. This was a rare privilege to which I hope Appendix 4 does justice. I am also grateful to Ian Alder of the RAF Museum Reserve Collection for access to the 88 Squadron History Book, located there with the help of Tony Burt.

I thank, too, all RAF servicing and Marine Branch personnel at the bases from which we flew, who gave such unstinting support to Sunderland crews, twenty-four hours a day, no matter how hot, cold or wet were the conditions in which they had to work. I also wish to remember the members of staff at the officers' messes at Iwakuni, Kai Tak and Seletar, who saw to our every need with such courtesy and good humour. My thanks are also due to certain members of the United States Navy whose names I have quoted in the text. They served aboard the destroyer USS *De Haven* (DD-727) and contacted me last year to give their recollections and to send photographs of my aircraft following the ditching that our crew had to make in the Tsushima Strait in December 1953. These include Dale Harbin, Hal C. Smith, Jim Bussard, Scott Martin and Lloyd Gasway. USS *De Haven* came to our assistance, and our crew spent several days on board enjoying the hospitality of Captain Sigmund USN and his crew. I should at the same time like to thank and send greetings to those of the US Navy with whom we worked at Iwakuni as members of the United Nations Force engaged in operations during the Korean War. I include the operations staff and crews of US Navy Mariner and Privateer VP aircraft based at Iwakuni who flew the same missions as we did. I also wish to mention the RAF Unit at Iwakuni and members of the Royal Australian Air Force in whose officers' mess my fellow RAF officers and I were made most welcome. I include the RAAF weather forecasters who gave us excellent service, often at ungodly hours of the night.

I especially mention Michael R Haines who kindly contacted me recently. Michael is the son of the late Flight Sergeant R C Haines who, sadly, together with three other crewmen, was killed in the accident to Sunderland PP148 (F) while landing at Iwakuni on 25th March 1953, an accident I briefly recount in Chapter 3.

Finally, I thank my wife Margaret for her patience, for the numerous cups of tea, coffee and occasionally something stronger that she set down beside me at regular intervals during the many months I spent in front of my computer while this book was in the making. I hope she and the remainder of my family find something of interest herein – just as I hope this book will resurrect fond memories for those who, like me, were fortunate to have flown in 'boats', or who supported our operations from ashore.

Chapter One

Early Days in the Far East

Introduction

T his two-and-a-half-year journey began when I arrived at RAF Seletar on the north shore of Singapore. It was my first squadron posting. Before that, since May 1950, I had been on various RAF courses at Jurby IoM, Thorney Island, Swinderby and St Mawgan to train and qualify me as a navigator and to learn and practise the skills of maritime air operations. While at St Mawgan, I was told that my wish to join a flying boat squadron in the Far East had been granted. For three months before setting off for Singapore, ten of us – a crew – were sent on a Sunderland flying boat conversion course at historic RAF Calshot in the Solent. In the classroom we learned about the aircraft and its equipment, seamanship, how to use tide tables and knot ropes, take soundings, and identify buoys and lights. Our two pilots carried out numerous take-offs and landings. We practised 'slipping' the buoy, using the sea drogues, mooring and anchoring. We flew bombing, gunnery and navigation exercises in the Western Approaches and Bay of Biscay by day and at night. When I left England for Singapore, I was a young pilot officer, fresh from training and with only 450 flying hours – barely a hundred in the Sunderland. I had never been to the Far East and looked forward keenly to whatever might lie ahead.

My intention is to describe some of my main recollections of what happened at various times during the two and a half years that followed. This includes a variety of operations throughout the Far East as well as a journey from Singapore to the UK and back. I hope this will give the reader an insight into what it was like to be a member of a flying boat crew in the early 1950s. To put this account into context, perhaps I should remind readers that the strength of the RAF in 1952 was 270,000 men and women; today, it is about 41,000, an 85% contraction. In 1952 a pilot officer's pay was about £13 a week. In real terms this equates to about half of today's salary. Not only is it fifty years since the RAF ceased operating flying boats, but there are no RAF bases in any of the Far East locations from which we flew in 1952. As I am sure readers will understand, I would have found it impossible to write this book without having my official flying logbook as a source of reference. How I wish I had kept a daily diary. I can only hope that my recollections, various pieces of information provided or confirmed by friends, and constant reference to my logbook will enable me adequately to convey why RAF aircrew who flew Sunderland flying boats regard their experience as 'special'.

I was a navigator. I hope readers will forgive me, therefore, if from time to time I recount my thoughts and actions as the aircraft's navigator during some of the sorties I describe. In the same way that the two pilots were responsible for the safe handling of the aircraft, the navigator, whatever the weather or the presence or absence of navigation aids, was responsible for the safe navigation of the aircraft from take-off to landing. Consequently, my recollection of many sorties was clearest when navigation conditions were difficult and the safety of the aircraft and crew were to some extent at greater than usual risk. In any event, safe navigation always called for care and concentration. In the Far East, where there were few radio navigation aids, the navigator had to make the best use of the aircraft's own equipment and whatever outside navigation aids happened to be available. The safety of the crew and any passengers was as important in the 1950s as it is today, but a Sunderland's navigation equipment was, at best, rudimentary. Today's computer-enhanced navigation aids and flight-management systems effortlessly provide a quantum improvement in navigation accuracy, far greater than crews in 1952 – even in their wildest dreams – could ever have thought remotely possible, let alone wished for. Such are the technical capabilities and accuracy of today's navigation systems that a majority of aircraft no longer carry a specialist navigator. Hence, for the historical record and for those who would like to know more about a typical Far East Sunderland squadron tour, navigation, the Sunderland as an aircraft, its layout, equipment and flight performance, I cover these aspects in some detail in Appendices 1 to 4.

Arrival in Singapore

On my 21st birthday I took off from Lyneham as a passenger in an RAF Hastings transport aircraft bound for Singapore. Ten days later, on 24 June 1952, I reported to the Commanding Officer of 88 Squadron at RAF Seletar for my first tour of active duty in the Royal Air Force. The Headquarters of 88 Squadron was the 'basher hut' shown on the next page.

I had graduated as a navigator in September 1951 and been appointed to an eight-year Short Service Commission. My ambition to fly Sunderland flying boats went back to 1948 when I attended an Air Training Corps Summer Camp while at Tonbridge School. We stayed at RAF Calshot, on the Solent, for a week. Calshot was where RAF crews were trained to fly and

The headquarters of 88 Squadron was this 'basher hut'. *Author*

operate Sunderlands. During our stay there as ATC cadets we were fortunate to fly several times in the aircraft, and it left a lasting impression upon me. Two years later, when I joined the Royal Air Force and began to train as a navigator, I set my sights on the Sunderland. Even so, when my wish came true and I arrived at Seletar I had only a vague idea what the role of the aircraft actually was in the Far East. The CO soon told me that, although based in Singapore, '88' and the other two Sunderland squadrons there, 205 and 209, operated throughout the Far East – in Ceylon (now named Sri Lanka), Malaya, British North Borneo (now Sabah), French Indo-China (now Vietnam), Hong Kong, the Philippines and Japan (see maps 1 & 2).

The squadron commander was S/L Harold Francis DFC, a New Zealander in the RAF. He had only recently assumed command of the squadron from Mike Helme. '88' operated five four-engine Short Sunderland Mark Vs. The squadron had just one crew per aircraft. The CO told me I was to be the navigator of a crew captained by F/O 'Misty' Donaldson, an experienced former SNCO Sunderland pilot. That afternoon I met 'Misty', and he took me to the 'compass base', where he, another crew member and I were that afternoon to 'swing' the compasses of our aircraft PP155 (D-Dog).

Sunderland ML797 on its beaching legs and tail rolley outside one of the two Far East Flying Boat Wing hangars at RAF Seletar. The slipway into the water is to the left of the picture. *Derek Lehrle, RAF Seletar Association.*

This was to be the first-ever compass 'swing' for which I alone was fully responsible. I had better make a good job of it!

After completing the 'swing' (calibration) I went to Wing Headquarters to collect a set of maps, charts, and various documents. A reduced ('skeleton') crew put D-Dog into the water, moored and then refuelled her. Early the following morning I met the remainder of the crew. The co-pilot, F/O Len Stapleton, had been on the course with me at the School of Maritime Reconnaissance at St Mawgan and had converted onto the Sunderland at Calshot with me before being posted to Seletar; so I knew Len well. All the other members of our Calshot crew had been assigned to different crews or squadrons. The remainder of Misty's crew were new to me. I've no doubt they were wondering what sort of a navigator I'd turn out to be! I was well aware that having responsibility for the navigation of the aircraft and its crew over wide expanses of ocean and unfamiliar territories without quick-fixing navigation aids was very different from flying around the UK when an accurate Gee fix or a VHF QTE were usually instantly available.

We took off to 'air test' D-Dog, returning 3 hrs 20 min later with a long list of faults. The flight had included another 'first' for me – an airborne 'loop swing' – calibrating bearing errors in the aircraft's medium-frequency (MF) direction-finding (DF) loop aerial and drawing up a correction card. Like the compasses, I would frequently be reliant on this for navigation bearings in the coming weeks. The next day we tested a different aircraft, RN303, C-Charlie. It was then I learned that the following night, 27 June, we were to ferry over night to Hong Kong the Air Officer Commanding

AVM G.H. Mills, Air Officer Commanding Malaya, whom we flew in PP155 D-Dog from Seletar to Hong Kong on 27 June 1952. He is seen with No. 88 Squadron Commander, S/L Harold Francis.

Malaya, Air Vice-Marshal George Mills (later Sir George Mills). He was the officer in charge of all RAF units and stations in Malaya. From there he would be ferried by another aircraft to the RAF Detachment at Iwakuni, where he was to interview Permanent Commission candidates; I didn't know at that stage that I too would be interviewed, as a Permanent Commission candidate, by AVM Mills a year later. F/O Misty Donaldson told me that S/L Alec Barrell, the Flying Boat Wing navigation officer, would brief me on the route and help me collect the necessary flight-planning information needed for the outbound and return flights. As it was to be my first long-distance flight with 88 Squadron in the Far East – and no doubt because we would be carrying the AOC – S/L Barrell[1] said he would accompany me on the flight in case (as he put it) 'he could be of any help'. I felt reassured that he would be on board.

Overnight to Hong Kong
On 27 June at 22.20 hrs, we took off in darkness for Kai Tak, one of two RAF flying stations in what was then the British colony of Hong Kong.

Map 1. The southern area of Far East Flying Boat Wing operations, and the main bases from which Sunderlands operated. These were, from west to north-east: RAF China Bay, Trincomalee, Ceylon (Sri Lanka) – Seletar 1,448 nm; RAF Glugor, Penang – Seletar 327 nm; RAF Seletar, home base of the FEFBW, Nos 88, 205 and 209 Squadrons; Christmas Island, South of Java – Seletar 763 nm; RAF Labuan in former British North Borneo (Sabah) – Seletar 710 nm; Sandakan to Labuan 255 nm. Other bases: Jesselton, Kuching, Tawau and Lahad Datu. Cat Lai, near Saigon (Ho Chi Minh City),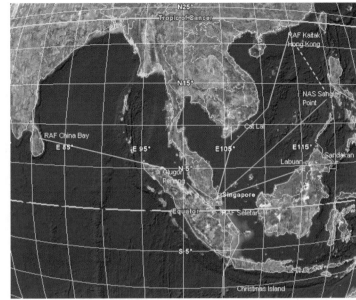
French Indo-China (Vietnam) – Seletar 583 nm. NAS Sangley Point, Manila Bay, Philippines – Seletar 1,393 nm. RAF Kai Tak, Kowloon, Hong Kong. Seletar 1,418 nm. Kai Tak, on the outskirts of Kowloon, was approximately in the centre of the Sunderland's total area of operations. Approximate flight times: to calculate the minimum and maximum likely flight times by Sunderland, divide distances by 137 knots (±12 knots). (*Google Earth image, with additional overlaid information drawn by the author*)

Map 2. The northern area of operations by FEFBW Sunderlands. RAF Kai Tak alighting area south of Kai Tak runway. Distance to Iwakuni 1,381 nm. NAS Sangley Point, Manila Bay, Philippines; alternative route to Iwakuni and diversion for Sunderlands flying to Kai Tak. Iwakuni 1,393 nm. Kai Tak 580 nm. Buckner Bay, US Navy Base near Naha, Okinawa. Emergency diversion for Sunderlands. Base for USN PB4Ys. Iwakuni 534 nm, Sangley Point 843 nm. (*Google Earth image, with additional overlaid information drawn by the author*)

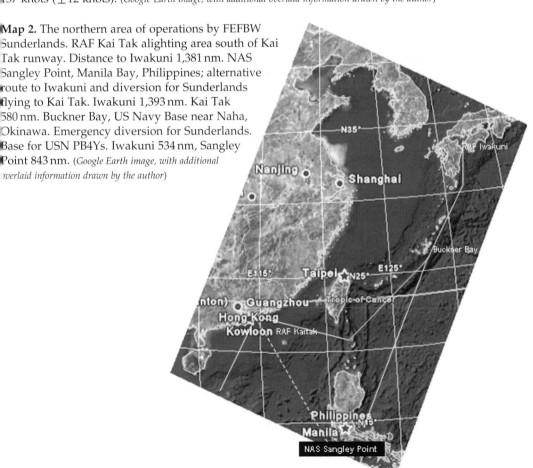

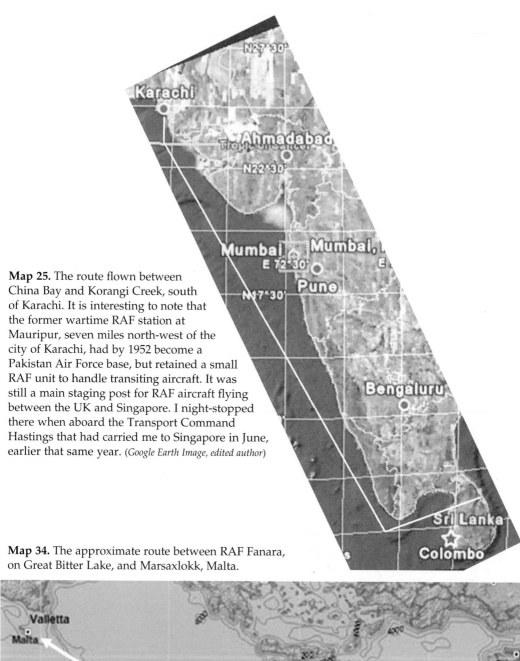

Map 25. The route flown between China Bay and Korangi Creek, south of Karachi. It is interesting to note that the former wartime RAF station at Mauripur, seven miles north-west of the city of Karachi, had by 1952 become a Pakistan Air Force base, but retained a small RAF unit to handle transiting aircraft. It was still a main staging post for RAF aircraft flying between the UK and Singapore. I night-stopped there when aboard the Transport Command Hastings that had carried me to Singapore in June, earlier that same year. (*Google Earth Image, edited author*)

Map 34. The approximate route between RAF Fanara, on Great Bitter Lake, and Marsaxlokk, Malta.

Map 35. The Marsaxlokk alighting area in 2008. The industrial development in the foreground and the dock area on the far shore were not there in 1952/3. The direction of view is south-west, the approximate direction in which we approached to land on 11 January 1953. (*Google Earth*)

Map 41. The map shows the approximate route flown on 8 March 1953 from RAF Pembroke Dock across France towards Malta, but diverting to Bizerte near Tunis due to adverse weather and sea conditions in Malta. The yellow dashed line from Bizerte shows our track south of Malta and towards the Suez Canal the following morning.

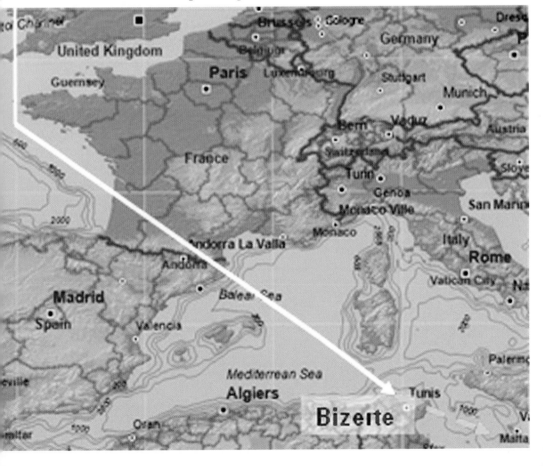

Map 42. The former flying boat alighting area then named Bizerte to the east of Ahmad military airfield. Bizerte town is to the north-east, out of view. (*Google Earth, edited author*)

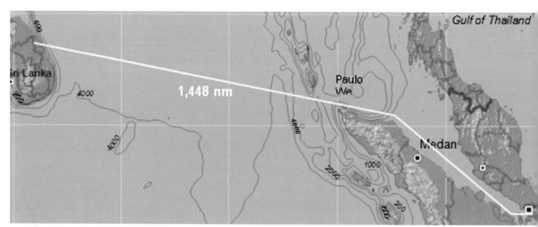

Map 45. The approximate route from China Bay to Seletar on 21 March 1953.

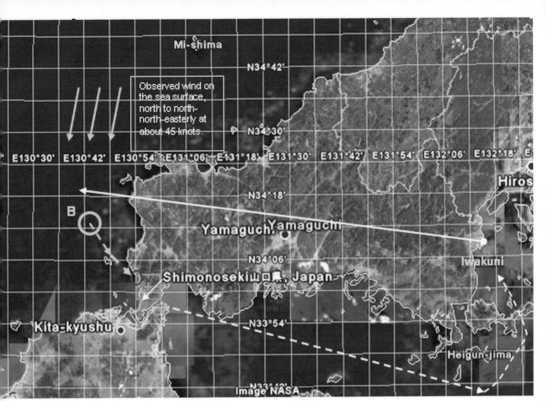

Map 48. This map shows my intended track (in white) from Iwakuni to the Sea of Japan, where I intended to break through the cloud base and alter course towards Shimonoseki. I had hoped then to fly along the white dashed track to Iwakuni if there was time before nightfall. The yellow circle 'B' was where we actually broke through the cloud base at 250–300 feet, 6 miles south of my intended track, blown there by storm force northerly winds during our descent. From 'B' we flew the yellow route to the red circle on the coastline, Yoshimi harbour, where we landed. (*Google Earth edited by the author*)

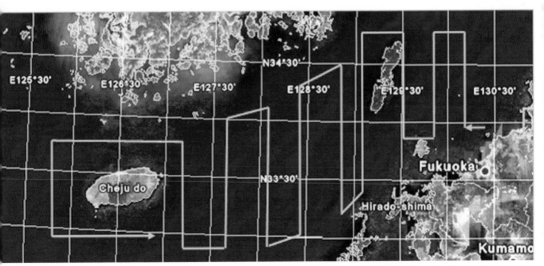

Map 50. ASP Tsushima. This map shows notional shipping surveillance patrol tracks flown by Sunderland and USN VP aircraft to cover the main west/east shipping routes throughout the Tsushima Strait. (*Google Earth, edited author*)

Map 52. Fox patrol tracks were orientated roughly north-north-west to south-south-east, linked at the ends by short 25–35-mile tracks. The area extended westwards in some places to within 15–20 nm of the coastline of Red China. At that time Communist Chinese forces were actively engaged in support of North Korea. Sortie durations varied between ten hours fifteen minutes and thirteen hours, depending on the Fox 'colour' and the number of ships encountered. We deviated as necessary from the ordered patrol tracks to intercept, reconnoitre and photograph all ships detected by radar, or visually by the pilots or nose, beam and tail gunners. (*Google Earth, edited author*)

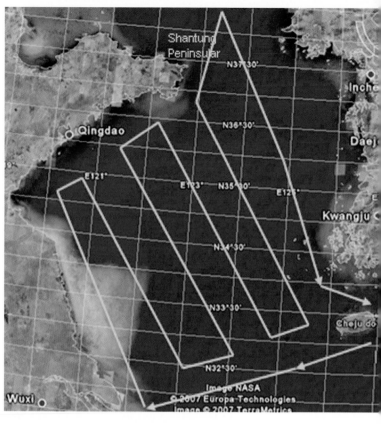

Map 54. *Minusinsk's* plotted position. (*Google Earth, edited author*)

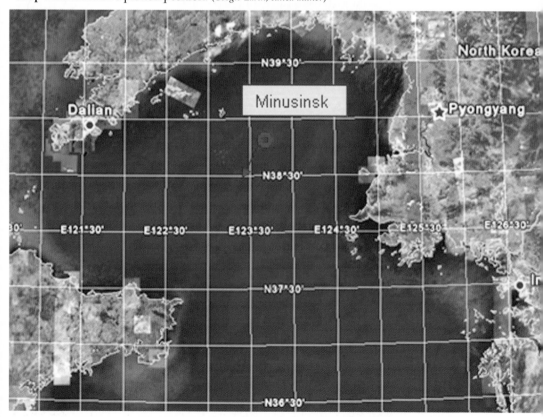

Map 123. Showing the position where we landed in Sunderland RN293 in the South China Sea beside a stranded motor launch. The red line indicates the approximate track we took as we towed it 38 nm back to Labuan, a journey that took some eight hours, the last two-and-a-half hours in darkness. (*Map by Author*)

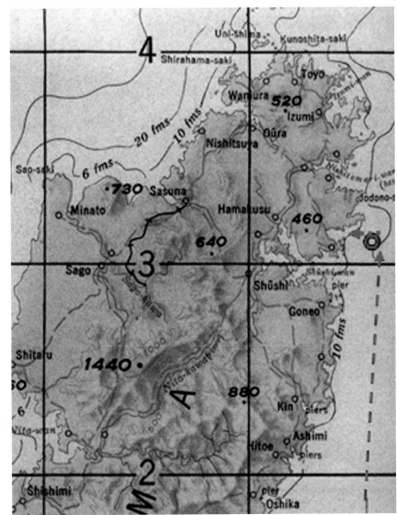

Map 128. The red circle indicates where we were forced to put the aircraft down on the sea. The inlet into which we taxied is on the east coast of Tsushima Island, just north of the inlet to Shushi Wan.

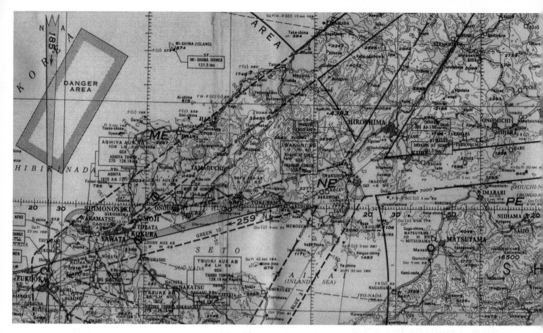

Map 227. This type of American-produced Airways map was very popular for planning purposes.

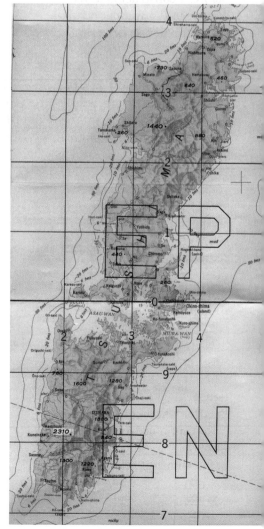

Map 228. Around Japan and Korea, this type of American-produced topographical map was favoured by RAF crews for map reading, including use with the ASV radar.

Once airborne, after more than a two-minute take-off run, Misty Donaldson
in the 1st pilot's seat made a slow climbing turn to starboard onto the course
I had given him. Our heavy aircraft, carrying a full fuel load, a crew of ten
and several passengers, began to claw its way laboriously towards our desired
cruising altitude of 5,000 feet. We were at first above the dense jungle of the
Malay Peninsula. With a steady drone from the engines, we slowly climbed
into a moonless, pitch-black but starry night sky. Looking upwards from my
navigation table, through the Perspex astrodome, I could see the canopy of
stars above us. I then stood for a few moments between the two pilots as we
crossed the northern coast of Malaya, waves at the shoreline glowing with
phosphorescence; below I could also see a few lights from fish traps off the
coastline. I noted down the time we crossed the coast and plotted a position-
line parallel to it on my chart. I then took a back bearing on Seletar MF radio
beacon, using the loop antenna I had painstakingly 'swung' three days
before. I constructed a 'fix' and made a small course alteration to bring the
aircraft back towards the intended track from which we had drifted slightly
during our post-take-off turn and the subsequent climb towards our
planned cruising altitude. We were heading towards my next turning point,
some five hundred miles away, which we should reach in about four hours. I
opened the Nautical Almanac and Astro-Tables and began to calculate my
first star sights to navigate us across the South China Sea, now unseen below
us. We were heading towards Triton Island, 48 nm^2 off the coast of French
Indo-China. Once there I planned to alter course towards the Paracel Islands
and thence to Hong Kong harbour. For the next four hours I was continually
calculating and taking star shots, constructing fixes, and between times
checking the accuracy of our compasses. Eventually, the radar operator,
sitting in his 'tent' behind me, pointed out on his radar screen a small island
ahead and slightly to port. 'That should be Triton Island', I said. I altered
course ten degrees or so to port to fly over it. When overhead, I logged the
time and the air position (from the air position indicator – API) and gave the
pilot a new course to steer towards the next turning point. I calculated the
wind velocity based on the Triton Island pin-point.[3] The ASV radar began
soon to show the coastline of French Indo-China, reducing in range to our
left, eventually closing to twenty miles. While I was writing in my log, I
became aware that someone had climbed the ladder from the lower deck and
was leaning on and looking over the main spar. It was AVM Mills. He gave
a broad smile and a 'thumbs up' – a comforting gesture that brought some
light relief to my night's work. Did he know how inexperienced I was?

After another three hours I saw for the first time the unforgettable,
iridescent blue, yellow and green hues of the coral and surrounding sea that
were the Paracels, a group of small islands and reefs. We over-flew them just
before sunrise. I detected the inviting smell of bacon, eggs, fried-bread and

tomatoes being cooked in the galley below. Sgt Vic Kapl, a former native of Yugoslavia now in the RAF, and one of our air gunners, doubled as crew 'chef'. During the night I had felt little need for food; occasional mugs of tea or water were sufficient. I had been too busy calculating, taking and plotting star sights, constructing 'fixes', calculating wind velocities and so on. Soon, a cheery Vic Kapl climbed the ladder from the galley and brought me a 'full English' breakfast and a mug of hot tea. Having just pin-pointed our position as we flew over the Paracel Reefs I knew the aircraft's position exactly. I felt I could relax for a few minutes and enjoy my breakfast – and the beauty of the sun rising over the South China Sea.

About an hour and a half later our ASV search radar began to detect islands that lie to the south and south-east of Hong Kong. At fifty miles' range from Waglan Island, which is a few miles outside the harbour and near my intended track into the alighting area, we began a slow descent. Now standing in the tent beside the radar operator, he and I looked intently at the screen, trying to locate the entrance to the harbour, which lay between rock-faced hills rising from the sea on either side. We had descended and were now only 500 feet above the waves. There was some mist but we soon saw and headed towards a gap now showing on the radar. F/O Donaldson called me forward and pointed through the windscreen in our one o'clock[4] towards a cliff, painted white, on the right-hand side of the gap that defined the track that led to the harbour. After passing through the gap, I could see Kai Tak airfield to the north, Kowloon to the west and Victoria Island to the south; these marked the outer limits of the harbour that now lay before us. Pre-landing checks already completed and our height now down to about three hundred feet, Misty Donaldson looked ahead for a stretch of water clear of junks and other shipping. Reducing speed and with flaps set for alighting, we eventually touched and settled smoothly on the water, Misty then gently throttling back first the inner and then the outer engines. We had been airborne for 9 hrs 40 min. It was the longest flight I had ever navigated. S/L Alec Barrell, my 'screen', who trustingly had rarely come to the flight deck, gave me a friendly, 'Well done, Derek'. I felt I'd reached some kind of milestone.

After being taken ashore by an RAF Marine Branch launch, a 3-ton truck drove us to the officers' mess. This was on rising ground a few hundred yards to the north and overlooking Kai Tak airfield and the harbour. It was early morning and my night's work was now catching up with me. It had been more than twenty-four hours since I had risen from my bed at Seletar the previous day. A young Chinese amah who looked after visiting officers, asked if she could do any washing for me. I gave her the clothes I'd been wearing, showered and then climbed thankfully onto my bed. Although early in the day, it was hot and humid; the electric ceiling fan in my ground-

The officers' mess at RAF Kai Tak. Older readers may recognise the rounded back of a Standard Vanguard parked in front of the mess. This may have been the Station Commander's official RAF car. A Morris Minor is easily recognisable. *Author*

floor bedroom turned slowly to give the air some movement – there was no air conditioning in 1952. I slept soundly for about five hours, woken by sunlight streaming through gaps in the almost closed shutters. The amah must have heard me get out of bed, and she appeared with a cup of tea. A few moments later she returned, carrying my uniform and other clothing, washed and ironed. The rest of the day was spent relaxing with the other officers in our crew.

I arranged a wake-up call for 05.00 hrs the following day. After a quick, light breakfast in the mess, we collected the route weather forecast and submitted an ATC flight plan, and I completed my flight planning. We boarded the aircraft and took off on the dot of 07.00 hrs for the return flight to Singapore. Unlike my first flight *to* Hong Kong the return southwards was completed in daylight. Cruising at around 6,000 feet, we were mostly above scattered, fair-weather cumulus clouds. This enabled me to plot our track with the aid of frequent sun sights taken with the sextant, together with drifts using the drift recorder. For the first time, while looking though the drift sight periscope – even from our cruising altitude of more than a mile above the sea – I clearly saw what I soon realized were flying fish, skimming over the sea surface. Occasionally I was able to make use of an ASV radar range off the coast of French Indo-China, and I obtained

A view of the eastern end of RAF Kai Tak in 1952, seen from the officers' mess and looking towards the south. A Handley-Page Hastings, then the backbone of RAF Transport Command, can be seen parked. Kai Tak runway ended just to the right of the picture. Our Sunderland is moored to a buoy off shore. An RAF Marine Craft Rescue and Target Towing Launch (RTTL) and other tenders, including a refuelling barge, can be seen on the slipway, close to the jetty or moored off shore. The take-off and alighting area for Sunderlands was in the harbour area in the left half of the picture and extending farther to the east. Kowloon is in the distance on the peninsula to the right, while the city of Hong Kong is on Victoria Island in the background. A ferry service linked Kowloon with Victoria. *Author*

welcome pin-points when we over-flew first the Parcels and, later, Triton Island. After about eight hours' flying I began to pick up signals and bearings ahead of us from Seletar MF beacon. Eventually, having experienced average headwinds of around 10 kts, we arrived overhead our destination and touched down smoothly on the alighting area at Seletar after covering the 1,418 miles in 11 hrs 15 min – an even longer flight than that *to* Hong Kong, two days previously. That night I slept very soundly.

Return to Hong Kong
I next returned to Hong Kong on 16 July, where we were to assume responsibility for search and rescue for a month. We arrived via a roundabout route, first staging through the Philippines to Iwakuni, Japan, for a twelve-day detachment. It was then that I flew my first three Korean

sorties. I will be describing Korean War operations from Iwakuni in detail in Chapter 4.

Two days after our arrival at RAF Kai Tak, Misty Donaldson was concerned that the stalling speed of D-Dog appeared to be significantly higher that it ought to have been. A tail trolley was therefore attached to the aft end of the keel and the aircraft was hauled tail first out of the water and up the slipway on beaching legs for a rigging check. After that had been satisfactorily completed, Dog was put back into the water. Unfortunately, one of the engines then refused to start. After fruitless investigations by engine fitters, Dog was once again towed to the slipway, and pulled up-slip. It was decided to fit a replacement engine. For reasons I cannot now recall, it was thirteen days before we could return PP155 to the water and fly it on an air test. Even then, further rectification was necessary. We flew the aircraft for a second time, and as it was satisfactory we flew for 2 hrs 40 min, training in the local area. The next fourteen days saw a big improvement in the serviceability of D-Dog, and we resumed our SAR duties. We flew several times, mainly practising approaches, landings and take-offs. These were mainly for the benefit of F/O Len Stapleton, our co-pilot, who was relatively new to the geography of Hong Kong and the hazards of taking off and landing in a harbour at times littered with junks, sampans or merchant ships. During this detachment, two other 88 Squadron aircraft, F-Fox and A-Able, staged through on their way to Seletar from Iwakuni. We took the

Sunderland F-Fox, PP148, on its way to Kai Tak, seen from D-Dog (PP155). *Author*

Sunderland A-Able, PP144.

opportunity to intercept them before their arrival, and flew in loose formation with them for a while.

While at RAF Kai Tak we got to know the station signals officer, F/L Eric Madger. His tour ended during our stay, and he and his wife were to travel to the UK in the troopship HMT *Cameronia*, leaving Hong Kong at 09.00 hrs on 10 August. Misty decided we would give Eric, his wife and his fellow passengers a farewell send-off, combining it with a short navigation exercise we had planned. On the day of his departure we took off from the harbour at 14.00 hrs and headed south from Hong Kong at 500 feet. We had been airborne a little under twenty minutes when our ASV radar operator reported a ship contact beginning to show at twenty-five miles and 20° to port. We altered course towards the contact and slowly descended to a hundred feet. Ten or so minutes later, now approaching what was definitely the *Cameronia*, we banked right and then left to fly in an arc around the ship's bow about quarter of a mile ahead, to let the crew on the bridge know we were there. We circled, flashing a short message to the bridge using our Aldis signalling lamp to give the ship's crew time to alert the passengers of our presence in the area. Misty then lined up on a heading parallel to the ship's course. As we passed the *Cameronia* he came down to fifty feet at a stand-off of about hundred yards. We flew twice past each side of the ship as members of our crew waved to ship's passengers from the open gun

PP155 (D) had required an engine change in late July and was brought up the slipway at Kai Tak. F/O Misty Donaldson (right), the captain, and F/O Len Stapleton, co-pilot, watch while the new engine is lifted into position (left picture). *Author*

hatches. After our final run we made a climbing turn around the ship, signalling 'bon voyage' to the bridge by Aldis lamp. We then resumed our navigation exercise, descending once more to a hundred feet, the blue–green sea sparkling beneath us in the strong afternoon sunlight. Taking drifts and observing the wind-lanes, I tracked along our planned route. Eventually this took us past Waglan Island and thence to Hong Hong harbour, where Len Stapleton selected a stretch of clear water, avoiding junks going about their daily business, and landed smoothly on the flat-calm sea.

Four days later we were ordered to return to Seletar. Despite the period of unserviceability that had prevented us from flying for two weeks in July, by the end of my first seven weeks on 88 Squadron I had flown 145 hours – mostly in fine weather – and I had been based at or staged through the Philippines, Japan and Hong Kong! What more interesting a life could there be?

New captain, new aircraft – same crew

We now move forward in time to October 1952. In September I had been promoted to flying officer, having completed twelve months as a pilot officer. My first captain, 'Misty' Donaldson, had ended his tour, and he with his wife had left us for England. Our aircraft, PP155 (D-Dog) was now flying on its way back to Wig Bay in Scotland for a major overhaul by Short Bros & Harland, the manufacturer. It was being flown there by a different crew. Our last sortie in D-Dog was on 24 September when we returned to Seletar from another detachment to Iwakuni and Kai Tak. Actually, we weren't sorry to lose PP155. She was five knots slower than any other aircraft in the fleet. We believed her fuselage and empennage were twisted; if you stood directly in front of the aircraft when it was on its beaching legs, you could see that the tip of the tailplane on one side was higher above the wing than on the other. We now flew PP148 (Foxtrot), and F/L Malcolm Laidlay was our crew's new captain. Malcolm was one of life's gentlemen – and a fine pilot and captain, too. Otherwise, our crew, now all unmarried, was unchanged.

On 30 October, with Malcolm Laidlay as captain, we flew to Kai Tak for search and rescue standby for a two-week period. Our SAR duty officially covered daylight hours only, and we never flew from Hong Kong at night.[5] Except on Sunday (when the airfield closed to most traffic) we were on standby throughout daylight hours, but were allowed to fly locally if we stayed within an hour's flying time of the Island. On 3 November, we were scrambled to look for two sailors missing in a small boat. After four hours of searching, the sailors were reported safe. On 5 November, we were ordered to fly as SAR escort to an RAF York carrying HRH the Duke of Kent from Kai Tak to Changi, as far south as 13° N. However, after 2 hr 40 min the York had to shut down an engine and return to Kai Tak; the York on three engines flew about 20 kts faster that we did on four. We tried to keep the aircraft in sight by flying in a slow descent – the York captain wasn't going to wait for us! On the 7th we provided SAR cover to 13° N when the York was serviceable and flew HRH to Singapore. During our fourteen-day detachment, we practised bombing in the open sea, air-to-air gunnery on a target towed by a Beaufighter and numerous circuits and landings. At times we had to weave around junks while travelling at 50–60 kts on the 'step' of the hull. We flew low-level DR navigation training flights to Pratus, a small island surrounded by shallow water and reefs a hundred miles or so to the south-east of Hong Kong. We flew there close to the sea, relying on drifts for navigation. On arrival we passed low over the island and waved to the Chinese fishermen, some wading waist deep in shallow water off the shoreline while casting their nets. On the return leg while I was momentarily standing between the two pilots, we suddenly saw a large shoal of flying fish, ahead, leaping from the sea and accelerating to fly anything from twenty to fifty yards well clear of the sea surface before re-entering the water – only to re-emerge a few seconds later. Until then I had seen these wonderful creatures as mere specks flying across the sea when looking through my drift sight from several thousand feet above them; I had never before seen them at close quarters.

A Bristol Beaufighter lands on Kai Tak's westerly runway. This was a target-towing aircraft that supported the Hornets of No. 80 Squadron based at Kai Tak and Vampires of No. 28 Squadron at Sekong in the New Territories. Sunderlands used to take advantage of the local presence of two fighter squadrons to carry out 'fighter affiliation' training with them. This offered good practice for the fighters in attacking large aircraft, and equally good training for us in evading fighters if attacked. *Author*

D-Dog being prepared for flight. One crewman is in the bow making preparations to put the aircraft on short-slip, while another is on the aircraft's upper surface, about to take down the mooring mast. *Author*

Two Hornet fighters of No. 80 Squadron, RAF Kai Tak, carrying out fighter affiliation training with D-Dog on 8 August 1952 east of Hong Kong. *Author*

The Nissen huts which made up much of RAF Kai Tak. One such hut served as the duty SAR Sunderland crew room in the early 1950s. The runway and the flying boat alighting area are to the left, out of the picture. 'Lion Rock' can clearly be seen dominating the airfield. *Courtesy RAFSA*

On 16 November we flew again to Singapore, and after an engine change and air test, returned to Hong Kong, where we remained for a further eight days. By the end of November, since joining the squadron on 24 June, in addition to our SAR standby duties at Kai Tak, I had completed two detachments to Iwakuni, flying seven Korean missions. I'd also visited the French Naval base at Cat Lai near Saigon in French Indo-China, and had flown three Firedog operations over the Malay Peninsula in support of our troops fighting in the jungle: more about those later. I next want to describe a very different type of operation.

Notes

1. S/L is short for Squadron Leader (the Glossary shows today's abbreviations). Throughout this account I intend using rank abbreviations commonly in use in the 1950s (F/L for Flight Lieutenant, F/O for Flying Officer, P/O for Pilot Officer, etc.). They are shorter and I don't think anyone will be misled by them.
2. nm is nautical miles. A nautical mile or sea mile is a unit of length corresponding to one minute of latitude along any meridian. It is also 1 minute of longitude at the equator. It is 1,852 metres in length or approximately 1.15 statute miles. One nautical mile per hour equals one knot (kt), or one nautical mph.
3. A pin-point is the latitude and longitude of a known geographical feature exactly beneath the aircraft.
4. 30° in azimuth on the starboard bow to the right of the aircraft's nose.
5. I know of only one exception to this in the period 1952–4. Stuart Holmes, a friend who served with me on 88 Squadron, recently told me that in June 1954, while at Kai Tak on SAR standby, his crew were asked, thirty minutes before nightfall, if they would search for a man who had fallen overboard from the troopship *Empire Fowey* as it sailed out of the south-east entrance to Victoria harbour. The officers of the crew were in the mess and the SNCOs were all about to enter the cinema on the base. They all ran to the pier-head, as did several off-duty ground-crew personnel. Amazingly, the aircraft took off only seventeen minutes after the crew had been alerted. As darkness fell, the search around the *Empire Fowey* was abandoned, and after being informed that a flare-path was being laid in the harbour by the RAF Marine Craft Unit, the Sunderland returned to Kai Tak (rather than flying 600 miles to Sangley Point in the Philippines). Stuart Holmes recalls that by using the lights of Victoria Island and Nathan Road (the main shopping street in Kowloon), to orientate themselves, they lined up with the flare-path and made an uneventful night landing.

Chapter Two

Ferry Flight to and from the UK

A bolt from the blue

I flew to Seletar from Hong Kong on 3 December, with Malcolm Laidlay as captain. The following morning our flight commander, F/L Nobby Hall, told us our crew was to ferry another of the squadron's aircraft, RN303 ('C') to the UK and deliver it to Short Brothers & Harland at Wig Bay on Loch Ryan near Stranraer in Scotland. We should plan to leave Singapore on 12 December. On arrival in Scotland we were to take two weeks' leave, then collect a replacement aircraft and fly it back to Singapore. We were expected to return to Seletar on about 10 January 1953, after an absence of twenty-five days.

After my initial elation at the prospect of this adventure it dawned on me that I had only eight days in which to collect all the necessary information and plan fifteen – perhaps sixteen – flight stages covering a distance of fifteen thousand, five hundred nautical miles – a daunting task!

The crew

Wing Headquarters had appointed F/O G.A. Chesworth to captain the crew for the ferry flight in place of Malcolm Laidlay. I think this was because Malcolm was about two months from the end of his tour. Although serving on a different squadron (No. 205), George Chesworth was already well known to most of us, as he lived in the officers' mess. George was an experienced pilot and aircraft captain. While we were sad to lose Malcolm Laidlay, we couldn't have wished for a better substitute as captain.

F/O Neil (Sandy) Innes-Smith, a former RAF Cranwell College graduate who had arrived in Singapore to join 88 Squadron on 1 November, was to join the crew as George's co-pilot. P/O David Germain was also to fly with us as 2nd navigator. David was one of fifteen navigators posted to Singapore immediately after graduating from basic navigation training and being awarded his navigator's brevet without then going through the Advanced Flying School, the School of Maritime Reconnaissance and the Sunderland Operational Conversion Unit. He and his compatriots had therefore missed seven months of instruction and some two hundred and fifty flying hours of training. After arriving in Singapore, David had first been put to work as an assistant in the Far East Flying Boat Wing operations room and then as a watch officer at FEAF Headquarters, Changi. He had received some instruction in maritime operations under the tutelage of various Flying Boat Wing staff, and flew several sorties with one or other of the three Sunderland squadrons. A flight to the UK and back would help to build up his experience. The Air Ministry had apparently posted the fifteen navigators direct to Seletar immediately after graduating from Navigation School, in response to a call from Far East Flying Boat Wing for urgent navigator reinforcements.

Others in our already constituted crew were Master Engineer Jock ('Haggis') Davidson and flight engineer Sgt John (Lofty) Land; air signallers F/Sgt Filby and Sgts Brearley and Nairn; and air gunners, Sgts Whiskie and Kapl (whom I mentioned was the 'chef' in our crew). Also with us as far as the UK was F/L Paddy Hatton, an FEFBW staff officer and navigator, whose overseas tour had just ended. Paddy told me he would like to take a turn at the navigation table for a few hours on one or two homeward-bound legs; I said I would be glad to calculate and take sun sights for him. We were also to fly a Mr S. Cope, the Air Ministry's chief moorings officer, as far as China Bay, Ceylon. Additionally accompanying us were a fitter and a rigger, Cpl Dick Bowden and LAC Dick Kerry, who would stay with us for the entire round trip. They would certainly earn their passage!

Flight planning

Planning a ferry flight to and from the UK was time consuming. Taking into account whatever else might intervene to distract my attention before our departure, eight days seemed a very short time in which to complete all the necessary flight planning and other preparations. I was relatively 'green' and had never before navigated through any of the geographical areas between Singapore and the UK, a distance of 7,750 nautical miles in each direction. As 1st navigator I had to make sure I had prepared and had with me all the necessary information before we left Singapore. Though we had been told which main bases to stage through, I had to select the routes, draw up all my charts and prepare navigation flight plans between the destinations on each of the eight stages, out and return. I first had to identify and obtain all the appropriate charts and topographical maps, then choose, draw and measure the tracks and distances for each leg, avoiding prohibited areas, find suitable diversion alighting areas, calculate and mark the safety heights, note and plot potentially useful radio beacons and DF stations. I would have to calculate the final courses, estimated times of arrival (ETAs) and fuel requirements, and provide the pilot with timing information for each air traffic control flight plan just before our departure on each leg after we had received the forecast wind velocities and temperatures from the Met office. I would also then calculate the critical point (CP) and point of no return (PNR) in case of unsuitable weather or sea state at the destination, or some other serious unserviceability *en route*.

I had to obtain RAFAC[1] and 'planning' documents for the Middle East, Africa, the Mediterranean and mainland Europe, as well as the United Kingdom. RAFACs contained essential information on the latitude and longitude positions, radio frequencies and call signs of air traffic control centres, airfields, alighting areas and navigation aids such as MF beacons, VHF DF stations and communication frequencies and call signs for weather broadcasts. I ordered Admiralty charts for our planned and diversion alighting areas (showing water depths, anchorages, reefs, etc.), and Terminal Approach charts for all airfields that might be usable as letdown aids at staging bases and diversion alighting areas where we might have to land in case of major unserviceability, bad weather or high sea state at our planned destination. Sea state was an important consideration for flying boat crews. Notices to Airmen (NOTAMs), showing the location and current status of Danger and Prohibited Areas, Heads of State Flights, temporarily prohibited live-firing areas and other warnings, had to be read daily and relevant details noted.

Only two of the eight remaining days had passed when my preparations were interrupted, firstly by the need to fly on an air test on 6 December, and secondly by the need to plan and then fly as navigator on an overnight flight that would run into a two-day detachment away from Singapore. This was for a flying exercise with the French Navy off French Indo-China. We took off from Seletar in the middle of the night, at 01.40 hrs on 7 December, and flew to Cat Lai, landing at 07.05 hrs. Cat Lai is on the fast-flowing Dong Nai river a few miles from Saigon (now called Ho Chi Minh City). The river was notorious for its sometimes fast current and floating debris and logs; these could do a lot of damage to the hull if you hit them. We landed safely, refuelled the aircraft and went ashore for briefing. We took off again the same morning at 10.50 hrs. The French included several litres of red wine in our flying rations – we left these unopened until our return! We flew for 5 hrs 10 min, co-operating with French naval forces in the South China Sea. After returning to Cat Lai at 16.00 hrs and refuelling the aircraft, we went ashore (with our bottles of wine) to our overnight accommodation at the base. By then we had been working – and I hadn't slept – for almost a day and a half.

That evening the officers in our crew dined with the French naval officers in their mess. Much of the conversation at dinner was about the deteriorating political and security situation in French Indo-China. By then,

Communist-led Vietminh insurgents were launching hit-and-run attacks against French forces around Saigon. As we found out on a future occasion, it was advisable to have an armed escort when travelling by road between Cat Lai and the city. After dinner, the assembled officers entered the garden, continuing our conversations with our French hosts on that hot and humid evening. There was an ornamental pond on the mess lawn. I soon noticed that several French officers, while continuing to converse with Gallic nonchalance, relieved themselves in the pond – no doubt to the dismay of the carp and much to our surprise! It appeared to be a local custom. The following morning, we took off at 09.20 hrs, arriving at Seletar in time for lunch.

It was now 8 December, and we were due to depart for the UK in only five days – our departure had been slipped to 13 December. I restarted my flight planning, but was soon called to fly on an air test, this time on another 88 Squadron aircraft, PP144 ('A'). I was making good progress, but needed to complete all my planning within the next four days. Except for those needed on the first stage, I packed the remaining topographical maps, Admiralty charts and already-completed flight plans and Mercator plotting charts into a separate large green canvas navigation bag of the type we then used. On 12 December, I stowed it aboard the aircraft ready for departure the following day.

F/O George Chesworth. *Air Mail, December 2000, courtesy AVM G.A. Chesworth*

We planned to stage through China Bay (near Trincomalee in Ceylon), Korangi Creek (just south of Karachi in Pakistan), Bahrain (in the Persian Gulf), Fanara (on Great Bitter Lake, Suez, in Egypt), Marsaxlokk (Kalafrana Bay near Birzebbuga in Malta), if necessary RAF North Front, Gibraltar, or Marseilles Marignane in France – depending on route weather and sea conditions; thence to RAF Pembroke Dock (south-west Wales), where we would clear HM Customs, and finally to Short Bros & Harland maintenance base at Wig Bay on Loch Ryan, near Stranraer in south-west Scotland. I now have no record of the exact stage distances, but as near as I can calculate, the return route will have been about 15,500 nautical miles.[2]

On the morning of 12 December, while RN303 C-Charlie was still 'up slip' and positioned on the compass base, I completed a full 'swing' to correct and calibrate the aircraft's DRC, P10 and standby compasses. Later the same day the aircraft was towed to and lowered down the slipway into the water, and the beaching legs and tail trolley were then removed. We started the engines, taxied to the buoy, refuelled the aircraft, and at 15.00 hrs, with our new captain, F/O George Chesworth, 'at the helm', we took off for a two-and-a-half-hour air test. F/O Sandy Innes-Smith, co-pilot, and P/O David Germain, 2nd 'nav', flew with the crew for the first time. Early in the air test I directed the aircraft to a small island off the north coast of Malaya; when overhead I completed a loop swing to calibrate errors in the MF DF antenna and draw up a correction card. Unfortunately, the aircraft had a number of technical faults that would have to be rectified and another satisfactory air test completed before we could set off for Scotland. Our departure was now certain to be delayed beyond 13 December; however, our clear goal was still to spend Christmas in the UK!

On the morning of the 14th we completed a second and more satisfactory, though not fault-free, air test. We decided to depart for the UK early the next day, 15 December, and completed our final preparations. I again checked that the canvas 'navbag' containing all my completed route planning and other documents for the outbound and return stages was complete and safely aboard. Our diplomatic clearance was confirmed, we ordered route Met forecasts and in-flight rations, and booked transport (MT) to collect us from the officers' and sergeants' messes at 04.45, in time for an 06.15 hrs take-off.

After the delays we had experienced in clearing technical faults on the aircraft, our revised plan was to arrive at Wig Bay on or about 22 December, take fourteen days' leave over Christmas and the New Year, and return by train to Stranraer on 5 January. We would then carry out an air test on the replacement aircraft on 5 or 6 January and depart Wig Bay the same afternoon, to reach Singapore a week or so later. This would mean we would be away from Singapore about four weeks.

Seletar to China Bay, Ceylon

A wake-up call at around 04.00 hrs on 15 December allowed time to climb aboard an aircrew coach waiting for us at the front of the officers' mess at 04.45 hrs. We loaded our suitcases containing clothes for all climates that would have to sustain us in the coming weeks. We were driven to the airmen's mess, where we collected our in-flight rations before proceeding to the slipway. The co-pilot, 2nd nav, two flight engineers, three signallers, two air gunners and four passengers were then ferried to the aircraft by an RAF marine craft tender, and we began the necessary pre-flight checks and preparations for flight.

This routine was followed before every sortie. George Chesworth and I usually went together to collect the *en route* and terminal weather forecasts. In the flight planning office I would then apply the forecast winds and temperatures to the navigation flight plan and calculate the leg timings and total flight time. I would give these to George who would complete and submit the ATC flight plan. I would also calculate and plot the Point of No Return (PNR) and Critical Point (CP) on my chart. On the first stage these were between our nominated diversion, Glugor (Penang), and our destination, China Bay. I was ready. There was little or no wind for take-off at Seletar and the temperature was close on 80°F. Under these conditions, our heavily laden aircraft would take quite a while to 'get onto the step' and might take close on three minutes to reach flying speed for our take-off just before dawn.

Once on board RN303, I entered the post-take-off course, speed and height into my navigation log, while completing my equipment checks. Log entries included the DRC compass and repeater readings. I set the correct magnetic variation on the variation setting control (VSC), tested and set the air position indicator to the latitude and longitude of the take-off area, tuned the R1155 radio receiver and checked the loop antenna in the visual and aural modes. I also cleaned the drift recorder lens, checked the wind-finding attachment (WFA) and generally organized myself for the flight. When at Iwakuni, I would switch on the Loran and begin to set it up. Before I came on board the co-pilot would have checked that there was no sea water in the bilges; the flight engineers would stand on the wings to turn-over the engines, using a long starter handle, and complete other external and internal checks. An air gunner or signaller would have retracted the nose gun turret and prepared the mooring gear ready for slipping the buoy. The wireless operator would begin tuning his transmitter and receiver. When the captain was ready, he would first start the two outboard engines, and the flight engineer would then shut down and close up the auxiliary power unit (APU) in the starboard wing root inboard of No. 3 engine;[3] on re-entering the aircraft he would put the astrodome into the upper hatch and lock it in position. When the two outboard engines were warm, the crewman in the nose on intercom would be told to release the mooring buoy. He would stow the bollard and wind forward and lock the nose turret. Other crew members would close the bulkhead doors. Once clear of the buoy, the pilots would start the two inboard engines. The radar operator would then switch on and check the serviceability of the ASV radar and the IFF. When clear of other moored aircraft and the cylinder heads and engine oil were at the right temperature, the pilots would turn downwind. After a precautionary test of each magneto, they would run up the two inner and then the two outer engines. During the run-ups they would first exercise the constant-speed propellers and then open the throttles to the take-off position and check the boost; they would then throttle back to zero lb/sq. in. boost and test each magneto in turn to ensure the drop in engine revolutions did not exceed 100 rpm.[4] Finally, they would switch off the fuel booster pumps and check that the engine-driven pumps were operating satisfactorily.

On approaching the take-off point, the navigator – who usually acted as look-out – would stand on the folding platform next to his navigation table, his head in the astrodome. On this particular day I looked in all directions around the alighting and take-off area – and on the downwind and approach flight paths – to make sure that all was clear for take-off. Satisfied, and when the pilots were ready and had been given a green Aldis light or radio call from the RAF safety launch that would have swept and checked that the take-off area was clear, the first pilot would sound 'T' in Morse on the warning horn – heard throughout the aircraft – and announce, 'Stand by for take-off.' On this occasion, seeing that all was clear, I replied, 'Clear above and astern – standing by booster pumps' (these were fuel booster pumps and switches on the engine starting control panel just aft of the astrodome hatchway). Illumination of any of the four fuel pressure warning lights during the take-off run would necessitate warning the pilots and pressing the appropriate fuel booster pump switch (see Appendix 4).

For take-off, the pilot would at first hold the control column hard back and gradually increase power on the two outer engines to take-off boost. He would try to keep the wings as level as possible by using the ailerons. The nose would at first rise steeply, but after a short while would gradually lower as the aircraft slowly gathered speed through the water. When the pilot saw that spray was clear of the inner engine propellers, he would open the throttles of the two inboard engines to take-off boost and gradually ease the control column forward to a position slightly aft of neutral. He would aim to maintain the aircraft directionally parallel to the flare-path dinghies that marked the take-off run, keeping an eye open for any obstructions ahead. Any tendency to swing was checked initially by throttling back the appropriate outer engine until rudder control was gained. After what often seemed a very long time the speed would gradually build and it would be possible to feel the nose slowly lowering as the hull of the aircraft lifted higher and higher in the water until it was on the 'step' of the hull and skimming smoothly and lightly on the sea surface. Once on the 'step', the sea offered less and less drag, directional control became very responsive to the rudder, and speed through the water built more rapidly. As take-off speed was approached at 80–85 kts (depending on the aircraft's weight), the pilot would ease the control column steadily backwards until the aircraft left the water. The take-off run could be anything from 1½ to 3 minutes.

Throughout the take-off run, I would remain in the astrodome at the engine starting control panel, hands poised over the fuel booster pump switches, watching for any red light indication. We followed this same start-up, taxiing and take-off procedure on every sortie. Sometimes, when an aircraft was very heavy with a full fuel load and weapons, and when the ambient temperature was high and the sea calm with little or no headwind, take-off runs might have to be abandoned after three minutes or so. After a pause to allow the engine temperatures to cool, the pilots would try a further take-off, perhaps in the reverse direction. They might also ask the safety launch to run at speed down the take-off run to disturb the surface of the sea. Eventually, a take-off would be achieved.

After a long take-off run to the north-west, we became airborne at our first attempt at 06.10 hrs shortly before first light on 15 December, with about 1,450 nm to fly before we reached China Bay. For the next ten hours of so I would mostly be at work at the navigation table. The aircraft at first climbed very slowly – perhaps 100–200 feet a minute – one-third flap initially still extended while speed built up to 110 and then 115 kts. We gently turned to port, onto 240°T,[5] flaps now fully up. We headed towards Kuk Up Island in the Strait of Malacca. At the coast I altered course to the north-west, my track then roughly parallel to the west coast of Malaya.

In the good weather we experienced that early morning, navigation through the Malacca Strait was straightforward; pin-points and radar fixes on the coastline for the first two hours, followed by MF Loop bearings on Butterworth beacon. When the sun was sufficiently above the horizon, I supplemented these with an occasional sun sight. By 09.30 hrs we had the northern tip of Sumatra on our ASV radar. Once off Diamuntpunt, as I show on Map 45, I altered course to make good a track of 281°T to take just us north of Pulau We and directly towards China Bay. On reaching We Island I had an 850 nm[6] leg ahead to cross the Bay of Bengal. When the north-west tip of Sumatra was well behind us and beyond ASV radar range, I took a series of loop bearings on the MF beacon on Car Nicobar – like Pulau We, badly hit by the Boxing Day 2004 Tsunami. Transferring the first two bearings forwards in time, to the last, this gave me a fix. For the next five hours I would be reliant on dead-reckoning (DR) navigation using drifts, sextant sights on the sun and a few long-range MF loop bearings.[7]

During our crossing of the Bay of Bengal at the northern end of the Indian Ocean, the weather remained fair. The sea, 6,500 feet below, was calm or 'slight', making it difficult to be sure that my drift measurements, taken using the drift recorder, were exact. If we had chosen to fly at 1,000 feet above the sea, to obtain more reliable drifts, and taking into account the forecast winds and temperatures, it would probably have extended our flight time by about fifty minutes due to the 11 kts lower true airspeed and no wind advantage. I hoped that the forecast wind velocities and temperatures at our flight level, shown in the route forecast, would be reasonably accurate. This was not always the case. In the 1950s there were no weather satellites and forecasting was based on much more sparse information; it lacked the benefit of the decades of data gathering and computer-based analyses that have led to the infinitely more reliable flight forecasts available today.

During the first half of the Ocean crossing I had intended to obtain loop bearings on Car Nicobar MF beacon and two sun shots hourly, although an intermittently overcast sky sometimes prevented this. During periodic breaks in the thin cloud above us I checked the accuracy of our main compass (the DRC) and the pilots' P10 compass. I compared these with our heading according to the sun's azimuth, as measured by me using the astro-compass (see Appendix 3). Although, as I have mentioned, drift-taking was difficult, I was able to obtain aural loop bearings on Car Nicobar MF beacon to a distance of about 300 miles, which was exceptionally good. At around midday, local time, a most probable position (MPP) put us about five miles south of our intended track. I had constructed the MPP by comparing my DR position – derived from the air position indicator reading and a wind velocity based on drifts and the fix on Car Nicobar MF beacon – with position lines from sextant measurements of the sun's altitude (now due south of the aircraft) and long-range loop bearings on Car Nicobar. I altered course to starboard to arrest any further drift south, and aimed to converge onto my intended track.

Just past the midway point, I could see through the drift recorder that the wind on the sea surface had strengthened a little, making it easier to track the waves across the glass screen of the recorder. By using my stopwatch to time the movement of waves across the drift recorder screen, I was able to obtain a groundspeed estimate of 146 kts; this gave a tailwind component of 8 kts. I applied the resultant wind vectors to the air position indicator (API) latitude and longitude, recalculated my DR position and revised our ETA based on the wind velocity alone. An hour later, an MPP I constructed from sun position lines and a loop bearing when the sun's azimuth was parallel to our track now put us two to three miles north of my intended track. I made a small alteration of course to port. Using the most recent wind plus the latest sun and MF loop position lines, I revised our ETA at China Bay which did not greatly change from my earlier estimation. We still appeared to be close to the intended track. It is sobering to consider that, today, most aircraft crossing the Indian Ocean would probably have a triple inertial navigation system and a global positioning system, providing readouts of latitude and longitude accurate to within a few tens of metres. There would be no need for a navigator. This is what fifty years of advances in technology have achieved.

I continued to take pairs of sun shots every 30 minutes, plus frequent drifts. An hour and twenty minutes before our ETA, I tuned into Trincomalee MF beacon (TM) which the loop indicated was on a relative bearing of 002°. Allowing for drift, this indicated that we were still close to our desired track. About 10 hrs 5 min after take-off, the ASV radar operator reported a coastline ahead, and soon afterwards, the entrance to China Bay. We altered course slightly to position the aircraft correctly and flew past the town of Trincomalee. We contacted the Tower and then the Marine Craft safety launch, entered the circuit and landed in China Bay. The flight had taken us 10 hrs 30 minutes. The total distance was 1,448 nm, giving an average groundspeed of 138 kts.

Sunderland 'C' of No. 88 Squadron, believed to be moored in Malay Cove, China Bay. In the background may be the aircraft flown from Seletar by S/L Harold Francis that arrived on 18 December with the spare parts required for RN303. *Courtesy Tony Burt*

While navigation during the sortie had been uneventful and more or less as I expected, by the time we arrived at China Bay the aircraft had a series of significant unserviceabilities. According to George Chesworth's recollection (which I learned from Tony Burt), faulty equipment included 'a carburettor, a magneto, an artificial horizon, a fuel booster pump, a fuel pump and a propeller constant-speed unit': not a good start. The likelihood of spending Christmas at our homes in the UK had all but vanished by the end of the first stage. As we guessed, none of the required spare parts was held at China Bay. We sent an AOG ('aircraft on ground') signal (telegraph message) to Seletar requesting spare parts.

During the Second World War, China Bay (which also had an airfield) had been a Fleet Air Arm (FAA) and RAF base. However, since 1946 it had mainly been used by flying boats as a staging and deployment base; the now less frequently used airfield was sometimes invaded by wandering cattle, and to scare them off pilots often considered it prudent to perform a low pass over the runway before landing. The station CO was F/L 'Happy' Day. He had only a small staff and few facilities, the kind of position that demanded someone with a good sense of humour. 'Happy' was just such a man.

According to recent recollections by David Germain,[8] the officers' mess – once a fine building – had been unoccupied since the Second World War. Neglected by the Air Ministry, it had become so dilapidated that there were now cracks in the walls and floor. Indeed, I also remember that many of the buildings were being encroached upon by an advancing jungle. I recall, too, being scrutinized by some disturbingly curious and none-too-friendly-

Members of the crew of Charlie keep cool in the sea off the same beach while waiting for the arrival of replacement parts for the aircraft. *Author*

looking monkeys about four feet tall crouching menacingly in the branches of trees close to a track along which I was walking. David Germain believes that at the time we were there, aircrew were accommodated in what was probably the former sick quarters, next to the food hall, where there 'was also an ample supply of beer'. We made the best of our unwanted stay at China Bay, visiting the coast not far away, where a glistening and amazingly transparent aquamarine sea contrasted with the whitest of sandy beaches I have ever seen. We saw small-holdings nearby being farmed by locals driving bullocks which pulled farm carts and ploughs.

After a couple of days, our squadron CO, S/L Harold Francis, reacting in his usual 'press on' manner, flew with an 88 Squadron crew overnight from Seletar to deliver our spares. This was on the morning of 18 December. Our flight engineers and airmen fitted the replacement spare parts between the 18th and 20th, making us ready to leave early on 21 December.

China Bay to Korangi Creek

That morning, after a very early get-up – this was the way of life on 'boats', and something you simply had to get used to – we slipped the buoy, taxied and took off from China Bay at 06.05 hrs. My initial track was to the west across Ceylon to just beyond the south-western tip of India. As soon as India was behind our starboard quarter at 75° 55' E, I altered course to make good a track of 331°T towards our next destination, Korangi Creek, still nine hours away; it is located a few miles south-east of the city of Karachi.

Flying over the Arabian Sea and after some seven hours of DR navigation – mainly sun sights, three-drift winds and occasional MF loop bearings – we passed abeam Bombay (Mumbai) about 120 miles to the east of us. Two and a half hours later the coastline came within range of our ASV radar and we eventually crossed into Pakistani air space near the mouth of the River Indus. We then flew direct to Korangi Creek, our alighting area on the inland sea area to the south-east of the city of Karachi.

A Sunderland 'on the step' and probably at about 70 knots, with a few more knots' speed to gain before a slight backward on the control column by the pilot will lift the aircraft clear of the water. *Courtesy RAFSA*

Following our landing after a 9 hr 55 min flight, and while the pilots, flight engineers and our fitter and rigger were completing their post-flight inspections and refuelling the aircraft, an engineer noticed a leaking exhaust elbow in one of the engines. This was potentially a 'flight stopper'. After six days in Ceylon the thought of a further delay was most unwelcome. Too late to rectify the problem that afternoon, we would try to find out if a spare was available locally or whether we would have to inform Seletar. On the way by RAF coach from Korangi Creek to our accommodation at Mauripur, we were driven past the Maintenance Unit, Pakistan Air Force Base, Drigh Road, where we could see what appeared to be Pratt and Whitney Twin Wasp R1830D engines lying in a 'dump'. These were probably from DC-3 Dakotas, but were the very same engine as was fitted to the Sunderland Mk V. Our flight engineers must have taken note of this. We continued our drive into and through Karachi. In some areas I was appalled at the squalor, the corrugated-iron shacks, beggars, ragged street sellers, children playing in the dirt road with no shoes on their feet; a body covered by a white sheet, bouncing on a stretcher as it was held high on the shoulders of its two bearers hurrying with it along the road towards a burial ground. It was a different world from anything I had experienced before. (See map 25)

Korangi Creek to Bahrain
When, the following morning, the coach came to collect us from the officers' mess, our signaller and air gunner crew members told us that the flight engineers and two tradesmen had much earlier gone by taxi to Korangi Creek. On arrival at our aircraft, we found them at work replacing the defective exhaust elbow. They said the aircraft would be ready for take-off in half-an-hour. Apparently they had 'rescued' a spare exhaust elbow from

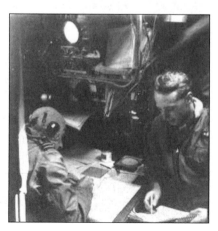

The author pre-calculating sun sights for F/L Paddy Hatton, at the 'nav' table. *David Germain*

the engine dump we had passed the previous evening. We asked no further questions and duly took off at 07.45 hrs!

The flight to Bahrain was relatively short – only 6 hrs 35 min – and an easy day for the navigator as our track was always within radar range of, and sometimes across, land. The barren nature of much of the coastline and that of the Oman Peninsula which we crossed was astonishing to someone unfamiliar, as I was, with this part of the world. We unfortunately struck further technical problems during the latter part of the flight, and shut down one engine, landing at Bahrain on three. The problem was another defective carburettor. It was now 22 December. It was unlikely we would receive a new carburettor from the UK and be able to fit it before Christmas. We resigned ourselves to spending Christmas at Bahrain and making the best of it!

Christmas at Bahrain

We spent five days at Bahrain where we were exceptionally well received. Everyone at the RAF station could not have been more welcoming. As a way of expressing our thanks, we held a so-called 'cocktail party' on board our Sunderland over the holiday period. Although Sunderlands passed through Bahrain quite often, they were still a relative novelty – certainly as a venue for a party. As Bahrain airport was then a major staging post for BOAC, we naturally invited BOAC personnel – including any air hostesses who happened to be available. I don't remember much about the party except that it was very crowded; guests were standing or sitting on the lower and upper decks, and some on the top of the fuselage and wings. I'm told about eighty people came aboard. The pity is that I have not been able to unearth a single photograph taken at the time.

L to R, front: Sandy Innes-Smith, Paddy Hatton, Derek Empson. 2nd row: Cpl Dick Bowden, LAC Dick Kerry, Master Engineer Davidson. *David Germain*

L to R, at the RAF Bahrain officers' mess, Christmas 1952: standing at the back, George Chesworth, 4th from the left, Paddy Hatton, then Derek Empson. Others now unknown. *David Germain*

We were invited to join in Station activities on Christmas and Boxing Day, including Christmas Day lunch in the airmens' mess, the officers serving the airmen in the traditional manner. The Resident, the official British government representative in Bahrain, kindly invited our crew to a reception held at the Residence.

In addition to BOAC, many airlines staged through Bahrain; charter companies, such as Dan Air (Dan Dare, as we called it) also refuelled there. Aircraft most commonly seen were DC-3s, DC-4s and DC-6s, Argonauts, Tudors, Hermes and an occasional Constellation – hardly a Boeing aircraft in sight as far as I can recall. All bar one were piston and propeller-driven aircraft, but on Christmas Eve, a BOAC Comet was due to land from London at midnight to refuel and slip crews before continuing eastwards. The Comet was 150 mph faster than any propeller-driven airliner then in service. Approaching midnight, many of our crew waited at the airport for the Comet to arrive. When it did so, we and others from the RAF station were there to greet the passengers, joining them in the airport bar. Security wasn't then what it is today! We chatted and drank with the passengers until the aircraft was ready to depart. Then, led by an RAF airman playing the bagpipes, we accompanied them to the bottom of the steps leading up to the Comet, bade them farewell and wished them a Happy Christmas.

Bahrain to Fanara

We received a replacement carburettor on 27 December. Our ground crew and flight engineers quickly fitted it. George Chesworth decided to air test the aircraft *en route* – we had delayed long enough and New Year was looming! Having said our farewells, we took off from Bahrain on 28 December at 07.50 hrs. Our route took us to the northern end of the Persian Gulf and thence over Iraq. We passed RAF Shaibah. Older, former RAF members may recall the song, 'Shaibah Blues'; I remember singing it at Dining-In Nights at RAF Jurby ITS.[9] As I looked down at the shimmering, barren, sandy waste below, it brought the lyrics to life. We next passed RAF Basra, in 2009 once again all too familiar to many in our armed forces. The next turning point was a few miles east of Baghdad, where I altered course initially west, across several hundred more miles of desert. Later, we turned west–south–west to follow the route of an oil pipeline. Trying to map-read over the mostly featureless desert was difficult; David Germain recalls trying to identify which section of the pipeline or which particular track we were passing over when these could just be seen below through the shimmering heat haze. Radio beacons were scarce, so the bubble sextant, astro-compass and drift sight were again put to good use. I think we were flying at about six thousand feet.

Continuing westwards into Jordan and then to the northern end of the Gulf of Aqaba, I finally headed west towards the Suez Canal. We landed on Great Bitter Lake after a flight of exactly eight hours. The crew refuelled the aircraft and were ferried ashore by the Fanara-based RAF Marine Craft Unit. We were taken to nearby RAF El Hamra, a tented RAF Regiment base and transit camp on the western side of the Treaty Road. It was opposite

F/O Sandy Innes-Smith and the author determined to enjoy camping at RAF El Hamra. *David Germain*

Kasfareet, a wartime RAF airfield, and in 1952 a maintenance unit and storage depot.

The crew were allocated two- or four-man tents that we tried our best to 'enjoy'. Nevertheless, it spurred us on to an early and certain departure for Malta the following morning. That evening, I went with George Chesworth by MT[10] to the Met office at RAF Fayid, several miles to the north. The weather forecast for the route was good, but there had been strong southerly winds around Malta for several days. Only now were they beginning to subside. Since sea swell heights and lengths always reflect past winds, this might prove problematic on arrival at Marsaxlokk. Malta's alighting area was well known for its difficult sea state conditions due to the swell that often entered the bay from the Mediterranean Sea.

Fanara towards Malta

Not enamoured of our accommodation, we were up in good time to take off at 7.55 hrs on 29 December. Even so, the possibility of reaching the UK by New Year's Eve was remote. We took off, our route soon taking us across the amazingly fertile Nile Delta – surprisingly green after seeing little but barren rock and sand for the past week. Pyramids could be seen to the south. Some time later, the Mediterranean Sea coastline to starboard, we passed close to El Alamein and Mersa Matruh, names familiar to me from wartime days when, as a schoolboy, I had followed the mixed fortunes of the Eighth Army on a map of North Africa. The aircraft track I had now drawn passed over the desert where the British and Commonwealth Divisions had fought their way back and forth during successive battles against the Afrika Korps and the Italian Army in the early 1940s. My interest in this glimpse into recent history was interrupted when about three hours after take-off the wireless operator received, by HF W/T (wireless telegraphy), a signal from Malta ordering us to return to Fanara; the combination of swell and wind conditions in Marsaxlokk were judged unsuitable for landing. Reluctantly, therefore, we set a reciprocal course for Great Bitter Lake, where we touched down 6 hrs 35 min after take-off. Disappointed, we refuelled the aircraft, were taken ashore with all our baggage, and disconsolately returned to our encampment at RAF El Hamra.

Sandstorm at El Hamra

Another thirteen days passed before the next entry in my flying logbook. We must have been prevented from departing the Canal Zone by continuing adverse sea state forecasts at Marsaxlokk. We remained there until 11 January 1953. It was almost four weeks since we had taken off from Seletar, and we had completed only four of the eight stages of our outward journey.

On 29 December we were hit by a sand storm. Warned that it was coming, my fellow crew-members and I commandeered additional sandbags from some of the unoccupied tents and stacked them around our own to try to stop the driving sand from getting into our luggage, clothing and everywhere else. The storm, which blew for much of the night, was a new experience – one of many – and the additional sandbags were only partially successful in limiting the ingress of sand into our suitcases.

The following morning we went by RAF motor launch to board C-Charlie, now bathed in sunshine on Great Bitter Lake. Sergeant Vic Kapl, our excellent on-board 'chef', rustled up something from the aircraft's larder to raise our spirits.

New Year at Kasfareet

On returning ashore, a squadron leader pilot whom we had not seen before was waiting on the jetty to greet us. I can't recall his name but he was from RAF Kasfareet, the RAF base where, in words of the wartime song, *Shaibah Blues*, the lyric says '…we passed Kasfareet where there's ****-all to eat, they've thrown all our rations away!' Our newly found friend said he himself had been a Sunderland pilot several years before, and was curious when he saw ours sitting on Great Bitter Lake, apparently going nowhere. He'd decided to investigate – for which we were to become grateful. We explained that we were likely to be at Fanara over the New Year. He said we must therefore come to RAF Kasfareet to 'see in' the New Year. He was the president of the mess committee (PMC) and would arrange everything. He straight away took some of us to the officers' mess, where he proudly

L to R: the author, F/O Sandy Innes-Smith and F/L Paddy Hatton after an overnight sandstorm. *David Germain*

showed us the public rooms, most of which had been transformed using wood and hessian, artistically painted to look like the inside of a Norman castle. The officers had made pikes and heraldic shields, and built and painted false walls and ceilings. They were even constructing a stream with a footbridge in the mess hallway. The PMC himself was the instigator, organizer and principal artist. New Year's Eve promised to be something special, and it was. We saw 1953 'in', in style.

Our crew, which had temporarily moved from tents at RAF El Hamra, to RAF Kasfareet, moved again, this time to RAF Fanara, where the officers were accommodated in a houseboat moored alongside Great Bitter Lake. I remember very little about how we occupied the remainder of our stay in the Canal Zone. I know we periodically travelled by road to RAF Fayid for Met briefings on the weather and sea state in Malta.

On 6 January, we were briefly joined by F/L Mel Bennett and F/O Stuart Holmes flying Sunderland EJ155 *en route* from Wig Bay to Singapore. They had been delayed in Malta for a month while a new exhaust collector ring was manufactured. On 7 January EJ155 took off from Great Bitter Lake heading for Bahrain, but had to return to Fanara with technical problems. She left again for Bahrain on 9 January, this time successfully.

Fanara to Malta

On 10 January, we decided on a further attempt to reach Malta the following day. The *en route* weather to Malta was expected to be good, and although a slight swell entering Marsaxlokk from the south-east was again forecast; we decided to go anyway. By coincidence, on 10 January, a UK-based Sunderland crew, captained by F/L Mitchell, arrived from Malta in RN302, 'C', bound for Seletar. This aircraft was the nominated replacement for our own, RN303, 'C'. So for a day, there were two 'Charlies' with consecutive registration numbers on the water, side by side. On 11 January 1953, both were to depart – RN302 to Bahrain, RN303 to Malta. We will meet up again with RN302 later in this account after our return to Seletar. (See map 34)

On 11 January at 07.05 hrs we took off for Malta for the second time. We flew at only a few thousand feet as I at least was keen to try to identify wrecks of former 8th Army and Afrika Korps equipment occasionally seen scattered close to the desert tracks below. We eventually crossed the Libyan coast about 15 nm north-east of Benghazi. Two hours forty minutes later, in the mid-afternoon, we arrived overhead Marsaxlokk on the south-eastern tip of Malta. There was little wind on the sea surface, but you could see a low swell rolling through the entrance into Birzebbuga Bay (Marsaxlokk) from the south-east. In the colour map section you can see a view looking approximately in the direction in which we made our approach to land in the bay (see map 35). This Google Earth image, taken by satellite in 2008, shows that the bay is now more industrially developed that it was in 1952. Then, the docks on the far shoreline had not been constructed. The shore in the foreground, too, was less developed in the 1950s.

F/O George Chesworth, in the first pilot's seat, approached to land towards the south-west with Birzebbuga headland to our right. Unavoidably, with little or no headwind our speed over the water for landing would be about the same as our airspeed, around 75–80 kts. George descended into the bay over relatively high ground to the north-east of the alighting area until we were just above the water. After a short pause we touched the swell for the first time, then, several seconds later, for a second time and then a third and perhaps a fourth; we were still becoming airborne following each contact with the sea. The danger when landing or taking off in swell conditions was that 'porpoising' could set in, the nose of the aircraft dropping and perhaps burying itself into a rising swell crest. In the worst circumstances this could break the aircraft's back. Although a great many open-sea landings and take-offs by Sunderlands were successfully completed, pilots had to judge such operations with great care. It was not so much the height of breaking waves that was the problem but the length and height of swell crests and the direction of the aircraft relative to them that were most significant.

I turned in my seat to watch through the aircraft's windscreen and could see the shoreline approaching ever closer; George suddenly said, 'Over-shooting', and he accelerated all four engines smoothly to full power. A 'go-around' is always a critical time in any aircraft as the pilots make the transition from an intended landing to an enforced overshoot. The signaller and I decided that discretion was better than valour, and quickly took up our crash positions behind the main spar, facing aft. We glanced to our left through a glass porthole in the starboard side of the aircraft and soon saw the shoreline whip past, followed by Maltese sandstone buildings perhaps a few tens of feet below, the engines still at full power. For some time not a word was spoken as the two pilots focused on establishing and maintaining a climb gradient greater than that of the rising ground ahead!

We passed safely over the crest of the hillside and continued to climb back to circuit height. George Chesworth then gently eased back the throttles and turned left, to the north-east, onto a 'downwind' leg before turning to port again and preparing to line up for a second approach and attempted landing. I wondered whether we might eventually have to fly to Bizerte, our diversion alighting area near Tunis.

We began another approach, this time on a slightly different track, and I think we crossed the north-east shoreline at a lower height than before. We touched the sea, and after little more than a slight lift off the first swell crest, the aircraft began to settle smoothly, as George progressively throttled back the engines and the aircraft slowed, the hull finally settling deep into the water. It was a textbook landing in the kind of tricky conditions for which Marsaxlokk was renowned.

There was a sequel to our first aborted landing. Many years later, George Chesworth recalled he met a Royal Navy commander who was stationed at RNAS Halfar in 1953 and lived in a large three-storey house on the hill overlooking Marsaxlokk. Late one January afternoon he was with his son, in the boy's top-floor bedroom, when the lad, who was looking out of the window, extremely excitedly shouted, 'Look Daddy, there's an aeroplane coming up the hill!' The commander joined his son at the window and confirmed there was indeed an aeroplane – a Sunderland flying boat – coming up the hill and passing by, slightly below window level!

We were accommodated in Nissen huts near the transit mess at RAF Luqa. I was not to know that twenty-one years later, by then a wing commander, I would be posted to RAF Luqa to command Operations Wing. In addition to responsibilities at the airfield, No. 1151 Marine Craft Unit (MCU) at Kalafrana, which in 1953 looked after the needs of flying boats in Marsaxlokk, was one of several units around the island that came under my command; among others were the air defence radar station at Madalena, and Maltese Fire Service units at Mtarfa Royal Naval Hospital and at the former Royal Naval Air Station at Hal-Far. By 1974, the role of the 1151 MCU had become search and rescue, sea survival training and operating Air Commander Malta's pinnace, the RAF having ceased operating flying boats in 1959.

I recall little about our short stay in Malta in 1953 except a journey by Maltese bus – a St Christopher medallion dangling in front of the driver – who drove at break-neck speed over potholed, dusty roads to the ancient city of Valletta. We remained in Malta for two full days, until 14 January. We decided to route to the UK via Gibraltar.

Malta to Gibraltar

Our decision to stage via Gibraltar to RAF Pembroke Dock, rather than fly direct to the UK, was due, I think, to strong headwinds, heavy cloud and a high icing risk in the vicinity of Carcassonne in southern France. On 14 January, at 07.05 hrs, we took off without difficulty from Marsaxlokk. We had an uneventful 7 hrs 25 min flight along half the length of the Mediterranean. It was the first time I had seen 'The Rock': who could fail to be impressed by its sheer size and defiant appearance? We completed a normal circuit and landed on the sea off North Front airfield into a stiff breeze on a choppy sea. With a light fuel load and no significant swell, this was not a problem. The Sunderland could cope well with a choppy water if landing into a strong wind because speed across the water at touch-down, when the aircraft was also light, was then relatively slow. We remained at Gibraltar for a week, a period of gales and rough seas preventing us from continuing our journey. Apart from the evident 'Britishness' of the town and the somewhat tense relationship with the Spanish at the border crossing, I remember little about our stay at Gibraltar.

An impressive sight while we were at 'Gib' was HMS *Newfoundland*, a Colony-class cruiser, commanded by Captain M.G. Goodenough RN, moored to the outer breakwater. She had recommissioned at Devonport in November 1952, and when we saw her, she was on her way to join the Far East Fleet. In April 1954, HMS *Newfoundland* escorted HM the Queen, sailing in SS *Gothic*, from the vicinity of Cocos Island, following her tour of Australia. Coincidentally, No. 88 Squadron Sunderland aircraft later also escorted the Queen and SS *Gothic*, when we flew from China Bay while the ship passed to the south of Ceylon. Interestingly, in June 1954, HMS *Newfoundland* bombarded Communist terrorists (CTs) in the jungle

HMS *Newfoundland* moored to the outer breakwater at Gibraltar. *David Germain*

north of Penang. Later in this book I shall be describing our own involvement in Firedog sorties against the CTs in approximately the same area of jungle.

Gibraltar to Wig Bay

It was not until 09.55 hrs on 21 January that we took off from Gibraltar for Pembroke Dock ('PD'), the long-established RAF flying boat base in Pembrokeshire. Heading initially west until clear of the south-western tip of Portugal (we didn't have diplomatic clearance to over-fly Portugal or Spain), we then altered course to the north, keeping the coast of Portugal, and later Spain, twenty miles or so to starboard. Around midday we left Cape Finisterre on our starboard quarter and headed towards the Isles of Scilly. After 7 hrs 30 min we alighted in Angle Bay, Milford Haven, and taxied the long distance to the trots at PD to moor among Sunderlands of Nos 201 and 230 Squadrons. Here we cleared customs, stayed overnight and on 22 January took off for a 1 hr 25 min flight to Short's maintenance base at Wig Bay, Scotland. After signing over RN303 for its major overhaul we set off for Stranraer railway station and the journey to our respective homes for two weeks' leave. Our intended one-week journey from Singapore had taken thirty-nine days to complete.

On leave during the 'Great Storm'

The date of 31 January 1953 was remembered in the UK for a number of reasons, the foremost of which was the so-called 'Great Storm'. A Met Office report of the time stated, 'An unremarkable depression, 996 millibars (mb) at 18.00 hrs on 30 January, centred just to the south of Iceland, deepened unexpectedly to 969 mb by 13.45 hrs on 31 January.' Tragically, it led to the loss of the Irish Sea ferry, BR/S *Princess Victoria* and 133 of its 172 passengers and crew. Winds reaching over 100 miles an hour swept through the area. These and abnormally high tides battered the coastal defences of Scotland and Northern Ireland. The depression also caused a storm surge in the North Sea, with consequent widespread flooding along the east coast. No fewer than 300 people lost their lives around the British Isles. However, the greatest single tragedy was that of the Stranraer–Larne ferry, which sank off the coast near Belfast.

While on leave I had read and seen on TV news broadcasts the sinking of BR/S *Princess Victoria*. What none of our crew knew was that a number of Short Bros & Harland workers from the Wig Bay maintenance base were on board and were among those who lost their lives. We learned this when we returned there on 5 February. Shorts also told us the aircraft we were to collect and fly to Singapore (SZ599) had been moored in Wig Bay throughout the storm. Hurricane Force 12 winds, sometimes exceeding

100 mph, had battered the aircraft. At times its propellers had been windmilling, such was the strength of the wind, the aircraft weathercocking with each change in wind direction, but through it all remained securely tethered to its buoy. Had it broken free it would surely have been wrecked. This would have been a special tragedy because, as I found out only recently, SZ599 was the last Sunderland Mk V to come off the production line, and that was on 14 June 1946 – coincidentally my fifteenth birthday!

We went aboard SZ599, swept rainwater off the flight deck, inspected the aircraft and took off on an air test. With us were several clergy and dignitaries. We flew to the location where the BR/S *Princess Victoria* had foundered and circled while a short service took place; we also dropped a wreath into the sea. On landing back at Wig Bay, one of the floats appeared to have taken in seawater, but in view of the tragic manpower losses suffered by Shorts, we decided to accept SZ599 without a float change. We stayed overnight and took off the following afternoon for RAF Pembroke Dock, where we planned to change the leaking float.

Wig Bay to Pembroke Dock – Day 54

On 6 February 1953, fifty-four days after we had left Seletar, at 15.35 hrs we took off from Wig Bay and began our return journey to Singapore. We landed at PD after a 1 hr 20 min flight. We reported the damaged float and a few other minor 'snags' that had come to light while flying from Wig Bay. We were told the aircraft could be made serviceable in time to depart for Malta on 8 or 9 February 1953. We made plans accordingly.

Further Delays at Pembroke Dock

The next entry in my logbook is 14 February (Day 62), a gap of eight days during which one of the floats was changed, but apart from that I don't know for certain what delayed our departure; most likely it was fog. When we eventually took off for an air test and loop swing on the 14th, our run of bad luck continued. One of the engines failed immediately after take-off. We circled and landed fifteen minutes later. After four days we completed a post-engine-change air test and what must have been a very quick loop swing, because the total flight time was only sixty minutes – signs of desperation were creeping in!

There followed another eighteen days without any entry in my logbook. Our departure to Singapore was this time definitely thwarted by bad weather. There was a long spell when it was extremely cold, at times with snow, and at others, widespread dense fog. This affected not only the UK but the European mainland. Consequently no diversion bases were available. I recall that one evening during this period, a crew colleague and I crossed in a little ferry boat from PD to Milford Haven to meet a couple of WRNS

RAF Pembroke Dock viewed from the south. Sunderlands can be seen moored on the water. *David Germain*

on a date (I can't remember how we came to arrange this). After a pleasant evening, on return to Milford Haven we found that the last ferry boat to PD had been cancelled because the fog was so thick. We decided to make our way to the railway sidings at Milford Haven, where we found an empty carriage, climbed aboard and spent a very cold night before catching the first ferry back to PD in the morning. This foggy and freezing weather must have persisted for well over a week. We just had to sit it out.

Pembroke Dock to Bizerte
After thirty days at Pembroke Dock, at 06.30 hrs on 8 March we at last took off for Malta. I had selected the shortest and quickest practical route, taking us just to the west of Brest and thence across France close to Bordeaux, Toulouse and through the Carcassonne 'gap' to cross into the Golfe de Lyon and the Mediterranean Sea. Two hours before we were due to arrive in Malta we received an adverse landing forecast by HF W/T radio from Malta. The message told us not to continue to Malta but to divert to Bizerte near Tunis. This was one of the possible diversion alighting areas for which

Bizerte, near Tunis. The old ATC tower of what is now Sidi Ahmad airfield SW of Bizerte town, seen from Sunderland SZ599 after alighting there on 8 March 1953. We were diverted to Bizerte because of bad weather in Malta. *David Germain*

I had prepared and gathered information while flight-planning the journey before leaving Singapore.

Only a small alteration of course was necessary to reach our destination, where we landed after an eight-hour flight. As we came in to land I saw a Dornier Do-24 flying boat moored in the trots. This was a type used by the Luftwaffe during the Second World War to rescue downed aircrew, and was now rarely seen. Our crew were required to refuel SZ599 in what for us was an unusual way, with the refuelling bowser anchored behind the aircraft and the hoses passed over the tail and along the top of the fuselage. We went ashore to eat and were accommodated in the French messes. That evening while sitting on my bed I amended my chart and prepared a new navigation flight plan for the following day's flight to RAF Fanara on Great Bitter Lake beside the Suez Canal. (See maps 41 & 42)

Bizerte to Fanara

The next morning, 9 March, we were up by 05.00 hrs. After visiting the Met office for route and landing forecasts and filing our flight plan, we went aboard SZ599 and took off at 06.20 hrs. Former Sgt John Land (Lofty), one of the two flight engineers in our crew, recently reminded me that flying rations issued to us at Bizerte that day included long French loaves, garlic sardines and – in the French tradition – red wine. The route I had planned took us eastwards to intercept my original track from Marsaxlokk to Fanara (see the yellow dashed track from Bizerte on the map). We took off at 06.20 hrs, soon passed Malta to port and continued towards Libya. Not long after crossing the coastline north of Benghazi, the visibility ahead worsened dramatically. We entered a bank of dark cloud that turned out to be a sandstorm. We climbed to try to get above it but could find no upper limit. We finally levelled out at around 7,500 feet. All the while sand was working its way through every hole in the far-from-airtight fuselage – through gaps around the pilots' windows, through the nose turret and where my drift sight periscope went through the fuselage wall. The landing forecast we received by W/T for Great Bitter Lake remained reassuringly good. Eventually we emerged from the eastern limits of the worst of the storm, and later the sunlit fertile Nile Delta came into view. After circling ships transiting the Suez Canal we completed our landing checks, received a 'Green' from the RAF launch and touched down on Great Bitter Lake at the end of a nine-hour flight.

Having completed the first two legs of our return journey since at last departing the UK, still on schedule – despite the weather diversion to Bizerte – our bad luck returned and we remained at Fanara for eight days. Yet again we had suffered an unserviceable carburettor – perhaps due to the sand storm, who knows? A spare was flown to us from the UK. We spent a leisurely week awaiting its arrival.

Fanara to Bahrain

Serviceable on 17 March, and after an exceptionally early get-up, we took off at 06.15 hrs for Bahrain. I at first followed the reciprocal of my outward track, over the oil pipeline, as on 28 December; but over central Iraq I chose to over-fly the airfield at Habbaniya, an RAF station to the west of Baghdad. I had landed there in an RAF Hastings transport on 15 June 1952 when *en route* to Singapore on posting to 88 Squadron. I remember being impressed by the attractiveness of the base, and I was keen to see what this historically interesting RAF station, originally named RAF Dhibban after the nearby village, looked like from the air. According to the RAF Habbaniya Association website,[11] the name in Arabic means 'of the oleander', and was a place of great beauty with eucalyptus trees, hibiscus and oleander shrubs, roses, ornamental gardens and green lawns. Some 10,000 civilian staff of many different nationalities serviced the base. They lived in the civil cantonment, a separate 'town' within the base area. The last officer i/c the cantonment was S/L F.N. Morris, who handed over to an Iraqi Army officer in October 1955. The station commander of RAF Habbaniya, a group captain, traditionally reviewed station parades on horseback. The station also had the Royal Exodus Hunt with kennels and a full pack of foxhounds. Control of Habbaniya passed to the Iraqis in May 1955, and the RAF ensign was finally lowered on 31 May 1959. After passing overhead in our Sunderland on 17 March 1954, we continued to Bahrain, landing after 7 hrs 40 min.

Bahrain to Korangi Creek
We spent the following day at RAF Bahrain and took off bound for Korangi Creek, Karachi, on 19 March at 06.00 hrs. This was a straightforward flight within radar range or sight of land, and a relatively relaxing day navigationally. We alighted after a short flight of 5 hrs 45 min. The aircraft was serviceable – or serviceable enough – and our crew immediately refuelled it and were driven by coach to RAF Mauripur, where we stayed the night.

Korangi Creek to China Bay
Up very early at 04.45 hrs on 20 March, we collected the route weather forecast, completed and filed our flight plan and rattled our way in a green-painted RAF bus to Korangi Creek. Engines were started, the buoy was slipped and we took off at 06.20 hrs and set course to back-track the route I had chosen from China Bay to Korangi Creek on 21 December. After an hour or so, for the next several hours we were too far from the coast to obtain any fixes using the ASV radar. My DR navigation became a mixture of drifts and 'astro' shots on the sun, crossed by loop bearings on the relatively few MF beacons then sited along the west coast of India – Bombay was one. About nine hours after take-off I altered course around the southern tip of India towards Ceylon and gave George Chesworth my ETA at China Bay. He jokingly bet me I would be at least two minutes in error! It was then that I decided to tot up how many days it had been since we departed Singapore, and was horrified to find it was not far short of a hundred. I concluded that if my ETA at China Bay *was* a minute or two in error, it would be a drop in the ocean compared with the three months we had so far been on this journey! After a flight of 10 hrs 10 min we landed at China Bay, refuelled, and finding no significant snags, went ashore for a cold beer and something to eat. After a short night's sleep we hoped we would at last be able to set course across the Bay of Bengal for the final leg of our journey.

China Bay to Seletar
After a wake-up call at 04.30 hrs on 21 March, we prayed that everything would go as planned for our last leg. At 06.00 hrs we lifted off the calm waters of China Bay and set course, just south of east, to cross the Indian

Ocean. After a couple of back bearings on the Trincomalee MF beacon, for the next five hours it was a succession of 'astro' sights on the sun, drifts, astro-compass checks, and an occasional three-drift wind. The sun was initially in the east. This gave us regular checks on our distance flown and groundspeed, but once I could no longer obtain back bearings on Trincomalee MF beacon, I had less accurate information available on how well we were maintaining our intended track. This made it necessary to take very frequent drifts and check the accuracy of our compasses regularly with the astro-compass.

Towards the latter part of the morning, when the sun had crept towards a more southerly bearing, it became more useful for checking how well we were keeping to our intended track. I was eventually able to obtain a couple of loop bearings on our port bow from the MF beacon on Car Nicobar Island. An hour or so later the signaller operating the ASV radar detected first the Little Andaman Islands to port, and later the north-west tip of Sumatra and Pulau We to starboard at much greater distances. This information put us close enough to our intended track and effectively meant that the navigationally most testing part of the flight was behind me. It was time to eat lunch!

On passing Paulo We to starboard, I had another four hours to navigate the length of the Malacca Strait using mainly loop bearings and radar. I decided to track down the centre of the Malacca Strait, rather than closer to the coastline as we had done on the outward flight. This was because I anticipated we might have to manoeuvre the aircraft to left or right to skirt around heavy storm clouds that at this time of day would often be encountered along the length of the Strait. Cumulo-nimbus clouds tend to develop in that region in the afternoon. However, on that day the weather was kind to us and the time finally came for me to alter course to the east to cut across the southern tip of the Malay Peninsula. We would then pass RAF Tengah and Johor Baharu to port while heading straight for Seletar. We contacted Seletar Tower by VHF, the controller welcoming us on our return and passing us the necessary landing instructions. (See map 45)

Alighting at Seletar – Day 97

The air signaller, sitting on my right, wound in his trailing aerial as soon as the 1st pilot, positioning SZ599 on the downwind leg, sounded 'L' on the warning horn. I stood on the platform beneath the astrodome beside my navigation table, to act as look-out. No other aircraft were in the circuit. Several Sunderlands were at their moorings, gleaming white in the Singapore sunshine. Pre-landing checks were read out and responses made. At the end of the downwind leg we began a slow 180° descending turn, speed reducing to 115 kts and turning onto a north-westerly heading, two-thirds flap selected. The pilot lined up the aircraft for landing and we continued a steady engine-assisted approach, descending at 200 feet per minute, the speed slowly reducing to 95 kts. As we approached the water the rate of descent was reduced, the speed then falling back gradually towards 80 kts, the aircraft in a level attitude. Shortly after the slight cushioning 'surface effect' was felt just before touching down on a calm sea, our hull began planing smoothly on the calm waters of the Johore Strait. Still standing in the astrodome I looked aft and saw where the keel had first kissed the sea and then left a straight and gradually widening swath of white foam as it cut ever deeper into the water as our speed decreased. Our flight time was 10 hrs 30 min. It had been ninety-seven days – more than three months – since we had taken off from this same stretch of water on 15 December 1952.

We taxied towards our allotted buoy, shut down the inboard engines and streamed the drogues. After mooring, we went through the same routine as after every sortie. The two outer engines were shut down, and as soon as the propellers had stopped turning the pilots aligned all four engines so that one of the three blades on each engine was positioned and parked vertically. This gave maximum clearance for boats passing beneath the wings. The flight engineers climbed through the open hatch next to my table, onto the top of the fuselage and wings, to open and start the auxiliary power unit. The refuelling barge arrived and tied up along the starboard side of the aircraft's nose. Usually assisted by the co-pilot, the flight engineers began to refuel the aircraft after first receiving visual evidence from the refuelling barge coxswain that the fuel was free of water droplets.

At the same time, a post-flight inspection was completed by all the various crew specialists, who informed the captain, sitting in the wardroom with Form 700, about any equipment 'snags' they wanted to report. I closed and signed my navigation log, switched off my equipment, reset the API, packed my navigation instruments, flight plan, log sheets, Met forecast and Mercator charts into my navigation bag. I tidied and stowed away my topographical maps and the Nautical Almanac and Astro-Tables I'd been using. When all post-flight actions had been completed, members of the crew helped each other to load the crew's and passengers' suitcases through the port-side bomb door, which had been opened, onto a marine craft that had come alongside. Because of the large amount of luggage we had with us on this flight, another launch came to the port front door to take the crew ashore.

When we reached the pier there was a little leg-pulling as the CO, S/L Francis, and the flight commander of 88 Squadron, F/L Les Tester, were waiting – 'Where on earth have you been?' Although ours was the longest recorded Sunderland ferry flight to and from the UK, apparently a few others had taken even longer to transit in one direction than we had! Readers might think that frequent aircraft unserviceability and susceptibility to other delays – adverse sea states, for instance – which will often feature in this account – might have generated an aversion by crews to the aircraft. Not a bit of it! Everyone regarded the Sunderland with great affection; it had few vices and much to admire and enjoy, despite its age and lack of technical sophistication. Crews virtually looked on 'their' aircraft as 'home' and equipped it with many 'home' comforts. This almost always included a large, lockable box, stowed near the galley, into which we stored additional tinned food bought by the crew. It could even include the occasional 'private' modification to the aircraft. For example, I remember Sgt Vic Kapl, one of the two gunners in our crew, fitting his personally designed roller-bearing device to the lip of each 0.5 in. ammunition storage canister, so that the ammunition ran more smoothly into the two beam cannon while they were being fired, ridding them of annoying – if only occasional – stoppages.

UK ferry flight statistics

Our memorable ferry flight had ended. Though not as long as the ten-year voyage of Odysseus, it had nevertheless taken ninety-seven days to complete the round trip, including thirteen days' leave in the UK. For eighty-four days we had *tried* to make progress in one direction or the other, but had repeatedly been frustrated by bad weather, an unsuitable sea state, unserviceability, or simply waiting for the delivery of spare parts, which took a long time in the 1950s.

Discounting 2 hrs 35 min of air tests flown at Wig Bay and Pembroke Dock, and the 6 hrs 15 min we spent on an aborted flight towards Malta from the Canal Zone, when we had to turn back because of the sea state at Marsaxlokk, our flying time to Wig Bay (with eight stages) was 60 hrs 30 min, and the return flight with only seven stages was 52 hrs 30 min, a total of 113 hrs. This gives an average groundspeed of 137 kts, assuming the total distance was 15,500 nm, which is about what I would have expected.

Notes

1. RAFAC booklets, each edition covering a particular geographical area, listed the latitude/longitude positions of airfields and flying boat bases, their heights, runways, navigation and approach facilities and communications frequencies and call signs. Associated 'Planning' documents contained more detailed information on Air Traffic Control Areas, Airways, Danger Areas, etc.
2. 1 nautical mile equals 1.15 statute miles.
3. The engines were numbered 1 to 4, No. 1 being the port outer, No. 2 the port inner, and so on.

4. Revolutions per minute
5. True Course or True Heading; Magnetic Course after the application of Magnetic Variation
6. 850 nautical miles, equal to 920 statute miles
7. Readers who wish to gain a better understanding of DR navigation in the Far East in the 1950s, and the Sunderland's navigation equipment, can refer to my notes at Appendix 3.
8. *En Garde* magazine, journal of No. 88 Squadron Association, Issue 24, June 2006, p. 5.
9. Initial Training School, where aircrew cadets were given basic training; those who passed became officer cadets and trainee pilots or navigators.
10. MT – Mechanical Transport, an RAF truck or car
11. RAF Habbaniya Association website, administered by the son of S/L Morris: http://www.habbaniya.org/

Chapter Three

An Unwanted Dilemma

Return to reality

On 21 March 1953, the day of our return to Singapore, the CO told us SZ599 was allocated to another squadron and we were to fly the new C-Charlie, RN302, which we had briefly seen staging through Fanara on 10/11 January *en route* from the UK to Seletar. S/L Harold Francis also told us our new crew captain would be F/L David Cooke, just posted from RAF Kai Tak, where he was formerly CO of the Hong Kong Auxiliary Air Force, flying Spitfires and Harvards. However, David had for several years been a Sunderland pilot and captain, including during the Berlin Airlift in 1948 when he and his squadron had delivered coal and salt by Sunderland from Finkenwerder,[1] near Hamburg, to Lake Harval, Berlin.

Our three-month 'sabbatical' over, we returned to reality. On 23 March, with Dave Cooke as captain, we flew a 7 hrs 20 min Operation Firedog over the Malayan jungle. We dropped 240 bombs and fired many thousands of rounds of 0.5 in. cannon and 0.303 in. machine-gun ammunition over a five-hour period into an area of primary jungle about an hour's flying time north of Singapore. Two days later, we were summoned to fly to Iwakuni for a five-week detachment on Korean operations, departing on the evening of 25 March.

The Yoshimi incident

On the evening of our planned take-off, we learned, sadly, that Sunderland PP148 (F) had crashed while alighting in darkness at Iwakuni in strong, gusting winds and a rough sea; it was at the end of a transit flight from Hong Kong. PP148 was the aircraft our crew had flown from October to December 1952. According to the 88 Squadron diary,[2] PP148 had orbited Iwakuni for two hours waiting for a forecast abatement in the wind, but at about 21.15 hrs, in darkness, after one voluntary touch-and-overshoot, the aircraft attempted a landing apparently using the daylight-landing technique but with the landing-lights on, to illuminate the sea surface. Radio contact with the aircraft was lost immediately after touch-down, when the landing-lights were also seen to go out. Rescue craft were quickly on the scene but sadly F/L C.R. Mitchell (2nd pilot), M/Sig J. Scott (signaller), F/Sgt R.C. Haines (air gunner) and Sgt J.L. Millgate (flight engineer) were killed. The aircraft was being flown by F/L R.M. (Bob) Wilkinson, whose only injuries were to his hands. The remainder of the crew were rescued. When the aircraft was recovered from the seabed, it was evident that the nose section had caved in and the rear fuselage and tail section had broken off in the vicinity of the beam gun hatches, allowing the sea to rush into the fuselage.

Our crew, with myself as 1st navigator, were told we were now to take with us to Iwakuni two members of the court of inquiry that would try to establish the cause of the fatal accident. The president was to be G/C Kettlewell, the station commander of RAF Kai Tak, whom we would collect from Hong Kong. The second member was the Officer Commanding Far East Flying Boat Wing, W/C Donald McKenzie. He would fly with us from Seletar. Our departure was delayed until 02.00 hrs on 26 March.

I spent the four hours until dawn taking star sights while we crossed the southern part of the South China Sea in darkness. I had F/O David Germain as 2nd navigator, and he helped by doing the calculations while I took the sights and plotted the position lines and fixes. We landed at Kai Tak after midday after a flight of 10 hrs 50 min. I fell into bed, and early the following morning, 27 March, we took off from Kai Tak bound for Iwakuni, together with our two passengers. My planned route was to take us well to the south of mountainous Formosa, then north-east, eventually crossing Okinawa and thence north to Iwakuni, an expected flight time of just over ten hours according to forecast winds.

The *en route* and landing Met forecasts included increasing cloud amounts and strengthening winds as we approached Iwakuni. A deep depression over Japan was forecast gradually to fill or clear to the north. I think we initially transited at around 7,000 feet, later increasing to 9,000 feet to gain benefit from a southerly air stream from the east of Formosa. Winds at this level were forecast to increase to 35 or 40 kts. Once we had passed over Okinawa, cloud amounts increased significantly. I soon began to pick up southerly winds at our cruising altitude which, based on radar fixes on islands to the north of Okinawa, were unusually high – between 50 and 60 kts – giving us a groundspeed approaching 200 kts.

My planned track was parallel to and off-shore from the east coast of Kyushu (Japan's most southerly main island) and from there straight to Iwakuni. This lies about twelve miles to the south of Hiroshima on the east coast of Honshu in a triangle roughly bounded to the south-east by Shikoku and to the south-west by Kyushu. Iwakuni alighting area was usually approached by Sunderland flying boats via what we generally referred to as the Inland Sea, between Honshu and Kyushu Islands.

When we were abeam Yaku-Shima Island, some fifty miles south of Kyushu, we entered solid and turbulent cloud with heavy precipitation. In a short while we encountered carburettor icing, signified by one or more of our engines suddenly losing revolutions and then racing. This problem was quickly overcome by adjusting the engine anti-icing system. Soon after the radar operator had passed me a 'fix' abeam the south-east tip of Kyushu, about 190 miles from Iwakuni, the flight engineer reported a smell of burning, and the radar operator immediately jumped over the main spar beside my table and ran back to the equipment bay aft of the flight engineer's station. He then reported over the intercom that he had switched off the ASV radar because smoke was issuing from one of the radar modules. We were now without radar, my most important navigation aid.

At about this time, the pilots began to make calls on our VHF radio, which had only four, fixed, crystal-controlled channels. Over the intercom I could hear two-way conversations between other aircraft and USAF ground VHF DF stations in Japan on at least one of the channels, but no ground stations or other aircraft replied to any of our calls. The pilots persisted for some while, but we were soon forced to conclude that even though our VHF receiver was serviceable, the transmitter – which had been working earlier in the sortie – was now u/s. We had no spare aboard. The signaller was told to contact Iwakuni on HF W/T (using Morse code) and obtain the actual and forecast weather for our ETA. When we received a reply some minutes later I cannot now remember exactly what weather was reported to us, but believe it included a surface wind of 25 kts gusting to 35 kts, rain and a cloud base around 600 to 800 ft. The low cloud base was my main concern now that we lacked any ASV radar to assist us in our descent to Iwakuni.

In normal circumstances when we had radar and full communications, such cloud and surface conditions would not be of great concern especially for a pilot and captain as experienced as Dave Cooke. Both he and our co-pilot, Sandy Innes-Smith, were trained and qualified to cope with such weather, wind and sea conditions. However, on this occasion, with neither ASV radar nor two-way VHF communication, how could I best navigate and descend the aircraft from 9,000 feet through the deep layers of turbulent cloud within which we were now embedded, avoid high ground and position us safely below the cloud base, over Iwakuni alighting area?

When I tuned in to Iwakuni MF beacon on my R1155 receiver I could hear heavy static from electrical storms nearby. I could see that these were affecting the stability of DF bearings because the loop antenna direction needles were not holding steady. I continued to use the latitude and longitude positions of my air position indicator to enable me to plot DR ground positions based on the wind I had calculated from the last ASV fix before the radar caught fire and was switched off. Combining these DR positions with MF bearings from Iwakuni beacon – albeit of somewhat doubtful accuracy – I was sure we were still heading towards Iwakuni more on less on track. However, I had doubts about our groundspeed and ETA overhead Iwakuni because I had not yet found any means to obtain bearings across our track. As I could not see the sea surface through the thick cloud, I could not use the drift recorder to check the drift and ground speed.

While I continued to 'home' the aircraft towards Iwakuni by DR and the MF DF loop, for the first time in my relatively short flying career I remember experiencing several seconds of foreboding. I could see clearly that our situation was becoming more serious by the minute. I quelled my momentary fear and told myself to concentrate on making the best use of whatever information I could obtain and not to make any mistakes. I considered the possibility, once overhead Iwakuni, of carrying out a loop letdown on the Iwakuni MF beacon, following the flight pattern specified in the terminal approach chart. However, I could not ignore the fact that the loop needles remained steady for no more than at most a quarter of a minute before beginning to swing, first one way, then the other, like a drunken man. This was probably due to static electricity from nearby storm clouds, but it could possibly be the onset of night effect. This gave me serious doubts whether we could safely rely on these bearings for our descent; and once down to our safety height at 3,800 ft, we would then have to continue our descent below the height of hills as high as 2,300 ft not far from Iwakuni. Also, the expected cloud base at Iwakuni was lower than the designated 'break-off' safety height for the approved MF letdown pattern. HF W/T was our only communication link with Iwakuni, and I knew the ground operator's terminal was in the base operations communications centre, *not* in the Iwakuni air traffic control tower. Could and would Iwakuni ATC see us on their radar? How would we know? Would there be other aircraft descending or taking off in our vicinity? Would Iwakuni ATC, as a precaution, clear the air space for us? We had no reliable means of quickly finding answers to these questions. While we had three hours of fuel remaining, nightfall was only a little over an hour away and this was another factor to consider. For two or three minutes I studied my plotting chart and the topographical map that covered Iwakuni and southern Honshu to the south and west of Iwakuni. I could think of only one way we might, with at least some degree of confidence, be able to descend through this thick cloud and safely reach the cloud base – at whatever height that might be. I had to navigate the aircraft to some location, not too far away, where I could be fairly certain we were over the sea before descending to the cloud base. Once below cloud we could then assess whether we could reach Iwakuni before nightfall. If we couldn't – well that was a problem we would have to deal with later.

Dave Cooke was at that moment standing on the flight deck behind the central throttle pedestal – I think he was in the process of moving from the right-hand to the left-hand pilot's seat. I walked forward, tapped him on the shoulder and told him I had been thinking about how we might best descend safely to land at Iwakuni. I said I had considered a loop letdown, but demonstrated to him the way the loop needles were swinging to left and right every so often. Because of this, the high ground, the high break-off height of an MF letdown, the low cloud base and our lack of two-way VHF communication with Iwakuni tower, I said that I thought it would be unwise to follow that course. Dave Cooke agreed. The unexpectedly strong southerly winds we had experienced from Okinawa to the east of Kyushu had put us beyond the 'point of no return' to Buckner Bay, on the island of Okinawa, especially before nightfall; so that wasn't an option. We could try descending to the south of Iwakuni and east of Kyushu, but with such strong winds and high ground in that area, and without radar, I thought that too would be very risky.

I therefore suggested to David that we should fly just north of west from Iwakuni, aiming to cross the Japanese coastline twenty to twenty-five miles north of Shimonoseki, not descending below our safety height until, on the basis of DR and radio altimeter indications, we considered we were at or beyond the coastline.[3] It would take about thirty-five to forty minutes to fly there from overhead Iwakuni and would put us over the Sea of Japan between Honshu Island and South Korea. We should then descend using the radio altimeter to check our height above the sea (assuming we were over the sea) until we broke through the cloud base. Once below cloud – and safely over the Sea of Japan – we should turn to the south-east towards the coast of Honshu. Visibility permitting, once we reached the coast we should hopefully then be able to identify our position on the map. On the *Google* map I have prepared for this book (map 48), the continuous white line is my intended track from overhead Iwakuni, and the dashed white line is the approximate track we would take through the Inland Sea to Iwakuni to reach it before nightfall. If that could not be guaranteed, we would have to find somewhere to put the aircraft down. Without radar we might not be able to 'see' our way in the expected weather conditions through the Inland Sea, where there were few towns to use as landmarks at night. There was also high ground at and beyond either coastline, and on islands to the south that partially blocked the entrance to Iwakuni alighting area.

Dave Cooke agreed this plan. I used the loop antenna to position the aircraft as accurately as I could overhead Iwakuni and then set course along my intended track using back bearings on Iwakuni MF beacon when the needles were steady. Judging by the longer-than-expected time it had taken us to reach Iwakuni from the south, and from the API indication when the MF loop indicated we were 'overhead', it was evident that the wind over Iwakuni was nearer to an easterly direction than the earlier strong southerly of the previous hour when we were east of Kyushu. I decided initially not to lay off any drift on our new track to the west from Iwakuni, but to use MF back bearings and alter course on the basis of that information to try to keep as near as possible to the track shown on the map. Dave Cooke agreed that we should begin a descent, initially to no lower than our safety altitude, after we had flown along this track for about twenty minutes. If, on reaching our safety altitude, barometric and radio altimeter indications and comparisons were good, and when I felt reasonably certain we had reached the coastline, we would then cautiously resume our descent until we broke through the cloud base.

Twenty minutes after leaving the Iwakuni 'overhead', we began descending to our safety altitude. After a further fifteen to twenty minutes I reckoned we should be at the coastline bordering the Sea of Japan, still heading towards Korea. Dave Cooke recommenced our descent, radio altimeter by now switched on. As we descended lower and lower, eventually he selected the more accurate bottom scale as we approached the upper limit of its height range. He then instructed all crew members and passengers not working at crew stations to open the gun and galley hatches on the lower deck and position themselves in the hatchways, on intercom, and to look vertically downwards into the cloud in which we were still embedded. At the first sight of any ground or sea below the aircraft, they were *immediately* to report over the intercom what they saw. Meanwhile, in between taking back bearings on Iwakuni MF beacon, I was searching my RAFAC, unsuccessfully, for an MF beacon that might give me an across-track bearing to confirm where we now were in relation to the coastline.

We continued cautiously and steadily descending. According to the pilots' radio altimeter we were now below a thousand feet above the sea – or were we still above land? We could not yet be sure. We were still in cloud and it was snowing, hard. A few minutes later, the 2nd navigator, David Germain, recounts,[4] 'My head was out of the open galley hatch – boy, it was cold, wet and very draughty. Then I think three of us all shouted at once – "The SEA!" I am fairly sure we broke cloud at about 300 ft.' On hearing the shout 'Sea!' over the intercom, I moved forward from my 'nav' table to stand behind the pilots and look through their front windscreen. We were then in and out of the base of the cloud, very low. From my recollection of the scene, I agree with David Germain's estimate that the main cloud base *was* at around 300 feet. The sea below was extremely rough, a mass of white foam from breaking waves with flying spume. Comparing my recollection of its appearance with the Beaufort scale, the surface wind speed was probably between 45 and 48 kts. This is defined as a 'severe gale or storm'. Prominent wind-lanes indicated the wind's direction as north to north-easterly, almost the reciprocal of winds I had found to the south-east of Kyushu. It confirmed my impression that it must have backed towards an easterly direction overhead Iwakuni. This would indicate that the centre of a deep depression must have been to the east or south-east of where we had broken cloud over the sea, and to the west or south-west of Iwakuni, possibly in the Inland Sea or over northern Kyushu. Visibility was intermittently between half a mile and a mile and a half as we passed in and out of showers, sometimes of snow and at other times of sleet or rain.

Having at last safely broken through the cloud base over the Sea of Japan, I gave an alteration of course to the south-east to head obliquely towards where the Honshu coastline should be and in the general direction in which I hoped to find Shimonoseki. If we could reach Shimonoseki, we might be able to gain access at low altitude to the Inland Sea – depending on the visibility. It was doubtful whether we could now reach Iwakuni before nightfall. We would have no radar for navigation, or VHF communication.

It was after no more than three minutes that, slightly to our right, waves could be seen breaking on the shoreline of an island that began to emerge to starboard through the murk, its upper levels hidden in cloud. Looking at my map, I thought this could be Futaoi-Shima Island at 34° 06' N 130° 47' E; you can see it on the map near the arrowhead leading from 'B'. We flew past it, roughly maintaining our heading, when two to three minutes later another coastline began to appear through the gloom, to port and ahead of us. We were still flying in very turbulent conditions at about 250–300 feet, the same stormy sea below us, in and out of snow, sleet or rain showers. We were now heading towards a headland beyond which, as we approached it, we were amazed to see a large natural harbour, sheltered by the hilly land-mass from the worst of the northerly storm-force winds. It was devoid of shipping and there was a solitary ship's mooring buoy offshore. By comparison with the sea then below us, the sea within the harbour was at most choppy. After the succession of problems that had beset us over the past two hours, it appeared at last as if fate had taken pity and dealt us a winning hand.

David Cooke calmly said, 'OK chaps, we're going to land here', and sounded 'L' on the warning horn. The crew quickly closed all the hatches and watertight doors and put out the primus stoves, the signaller wound in the trailing aerial, and everyone took up their landing positions. The co-pilot read out the pre-landing checks as Dave Cooke completed a circuit and lined up on his chosen direction for landing. Within two to three minutes we had landed and were taxiing on choppy water in the harbour. I looked at my watch. We had been airborne for 10 hrs 15 min. I studied my topographical map but couldn't decide exactly where we had landed. I concluded it was probably too small a town or village to be identified by name on the map in front of me. We taxied around the harbour discussing whether to drop the anchor or secure the aircraft to the steel ship's buoy we had seen from the air. We then saw a lamp flashing Morse from a building ashore. It simply asked, 'What happened?' We flashed the agreed reply from the astrodome, using our own Aldis lamp to request a boat to come alongside. The crew improvised a means of securing the aircraft to the large metal buoy, using an inflatable mattress to protect the aircraft's bow. In due course, a motor boat chugged out to the aircraft. An officer of the Japanese Self-Defence Force (JSDF), Naval Section, was in the boat and greeted us in English. We thanked him and asked if he could find us somewhere to stay the night. He said he would find us accommodation and then send a boat to pick us up. We thanked him, and asked where we were. 'Yoshimi', he replied.

After we had landed, the wireless operator had immediately sent a message by HF W/T to Iwakuni Operations telling them we were safely down, and giving the rough latitude and longitude I had quickly passed to him. Apparently, this put us in the hills somewhere nearby, and Iwakuni queried it! After we had spoken to the Japanese officer, who had told us exactly where we were, we confirmed our position as Yoshimi. The latitude and longitude of Yoshimi harbour is 34° 04' N 130° 54' E. Judging from the 2008 *Google Earth* image and from Internet information, Yoshimi, which in 1953 was a small fishing village with a JSDF unit and an anchorage, is now a sizeable town.

The co-pilot, F/O Sandy Innes-Smith, the two flight engineers and two other crew members offered to stay behind overnight to maintain the boat guard. This was standard practice in case the mooring should become entangled, break loose, or any other kind of emergency should arise. The boat guard crew would have electrical power from the petrol-driven auxiliary power unit which had already been started. They had primus stoves for cooking, plenty of water on board and a toilet, flushed by sea water. Sgt John (Lofty) Land, one of the two flight engineers on board who volunteered to be on the boat guard, recently told me that some time after the rest of the crew had gone ashore, a local boat came alongside and offered them fish to eat.

Including the two members of the court of inquiry – whom, in the excitement, I had almost forgotten were on board – about eight of us went ashore, where we were met by the JSDF officer. He had already arranged overnight accommodation in what seemed to be the equivalent of a village inn. This was only a short walk from where we had come ashore. The inn staff welcomed us, bowing politely in the usual Japanese manner. There were about four Japanese women, dressed in kimonos, obviously pleased to have so many unexpected overnight guests on such a wet and stormy evening. They offered us Japanese beer as we removed our shoes and sat on the floor around low tables, and talked with pent-up excitement over the events of the last two hours. The room was heated by several large earthenware pots filled with burning charcoal.

Soon, a hot meal was being prepared. The first course was fish soup. I remember this because it was the first time I had tasted it, and I thought how pleasant it was. This was to be followed by a meat and vegetable dish, probably *sukiyaki* (though this is not what the Japanese normally call it) – thin slices of beef with mixed vegetables simmered in a little liquid and raw egg with soy sauce added. As we sat cross-legged on the raffia (*tatami*) floor, the meal slowly simmered in front of us in a large heavy metal pan placed over one of the charcoal burners and attended by one of the inn staff. When the meal was ready, we were helped to it, the food being placing in small dishes. We ate it somewhat inexpertly with the aid of the rather thin, pointed Japanese chop sticks. To drink, we were now offered *sake*; this is traditionally drunk from a very small porcelain bowl, which is what we were given. The staff, in kimonos, now squatted upright on their haunches and shins, behind us, waiting for any further instructions. As the meal and drinking drew to a close we raised our *sake* bowls to toast our hosts for their kindness – this was greeted by much bowing and discreet giggling behind the hand!

We were then invited to bathe. We were each provided with a bath-robe and shown somewhere to undress. We were then led to the bath; it was about one and a half metres square, very deep and hot, known as an *ofuro*. We were invited to bathe two at a time. Throughout this traditional Japanese 'ritual', fully immersed, we were attended by two – very properly behaved – lady members of the staff who assisted us with sponges and soap. There were no taps, and the water may have been from a hot spring, because it seemed to have a high soda content. It was very relaxing, especially after our hectic day, an excellent meal, a few beers and the *sake*. Baths over, we were shown to our bedrooms, each with a thin mattress on the floor and a very solid, sausage-like pillow placed on the *tatami* floor. The rooms had sliding, paper-covered partitions dividing one from another. As I lay down on my mattress I felt a twinge of guilt that our stalwart volunteer boat guards had not been able to indulge in all that we had enjoyed that evening; they could only be looking forward to a rather cold and possibly sleepless night on a choppy sea. Each would have to mount guard in two-hour spells. The day's excitement thankfully behind me, I soon fell asleep not waking till morning.

The following day, 28 March 1953, we were in no rush to get up. After a light breakfast, we paid the bill. We saw that the weather was much improved. The wind had dropped and backed towards the west–south-west, causing more waves in the harbour than on the previous evening. There was a slight cross-swell, and our take-off area was no longer sheltered by the high ground that had shielded it from the worst of the previous day's storm. We eventually went aboard RN302, C-Charlie, started the outboard engines, released the buoy and after all four engines had reached their proper temperatures and the other pre-take-off checks had been completed, Dave Cooke sounded 'T' on the warning horn. Late during our relatively short take-off run – the aircraft was now very light with only a few hundred gallons of fuel in the wings – we hit two or three wave crests solidly as our speed rose to about 75 kts, and these propelled us into the air.

We turned to port after take-off and I set course for Shimonoseki, the city I had been heading towards the previous afternoon. I could now see it six miles ahead of us, south-east of Yoshimi. We flew directly over it. Visibility was good as we continued eastwards along the length of the Inland Sea. Three-quarters of an hour later we turned northwards, weaving our way around some islands, and headed towards Iwakuni alighting area. Once overhead, we flashed the US Navy seaplane tender *Kenneth Whiting* using our Aldis lamp. We were given a 'Green', completed a circuit and landed after a 55-minute flight.

Members of the court of inquiry whom we had brought with us as passengers on our rather eventful flight were now able to begin their sad task of investigating the fatal crash of Sunderland PP148 at Iwakuni. They could have been forgiven for wondering, during the previous afternoon when they had looked downwards through open hatchways into dense, turbulent cloud and driving sleet, whether they would ever be in a position to begin their task.

Notes

1. During the Second World War, Finkenwerder was the Blohm & Voss aircraft factory where (*inter alia*), BV-222 flying boats were designed, manufactured and assembled. It is now a design, manufacturing and assembly centre for Airbus and Airbus-Military aircraft, with a runway extension for the A380.
2. Email from Tony Burt, 4 February 2008. Information assumed to be entered in the F540.
3. The radio altimeter measured height above the sea or land surface below the aircraft by transmitting a modulated radio signal vertically downwards and analysing the reflected signal.
4. Email dated 1 January 2008 from David Germain to Derek Empson.

Chapter Four

Korean War Operations from Japan

Patrols flown by Sunderlands

Sunderland flying boats on operations in support of the Korean War were based at Iwakuni. There were several different patrols, all pre-planned and tasked by the US Navy in the name of the United Nations. A control ship, the seaplane tender *Kenneth Whiting*, and a small tender, either *Floyds Bay* or *Gardiners Bay*, were anchored in the Iwakuni 'seaplane' alighting area. The day before each mission we were briefed at Base Operations, ashore. One of the two main types of air surveillance patrol (ASP) was called ASP Tsushima. The Tsushima Strait lies between the Sea of Japan at its eastern end and the Yellow Sea to the west. ASP Tsushima was flown daily along briefed tracks covering the busy east and west shipping lanes in the strait between the southern coast of Korea and Japan. I have drawn a representation of these tracks on the *Google Earth* map (map 50). The patrol duration was between 8 hrs 30 min and 12 hrs 30 min, depending on how many ships were in the shipping lanes that day; you had to report on and photograph them all.

The second main type of shipping surveillance patrol was the Fox family of patrols. These were the Fox Red, Fox Blue and Fox Green. All Fox-type patrols were flown over the Yellow Sea. I have drawn a representative amalgam of Fox Red, Fox Blue and Fox Green patrol tracks on the second *Google Earth* map (map 52). The patrol part of the mission was flown in daylight hours. These patrols, too, were on pre-planned routes, but – as for ASP Tsushima – you had to divert from them to survey each ship detected; you were briefed then to regain your pre-planned track so as not to miss any ships. The laid-down patrol tracks – depending on the Fox 'colour' – extended from about latitude 31° 30' N in the south, to around 38° 15' N in the north, throughout the Yellow Sea. In the west of the area we were briefed to keep more than twelve nautical miles from the coast of Communist China (i.e. outside their claimed territorial waters), and we flew as far north as perhaps 75 nm north-east of the Chantung (or Shantung) Peninsula. When close to Chinese territorial waters RAF Sunderlands generally flew at low altitude – typically 100 feet or less – so as not to advertise their presence too overtly. Elsewhere during the patrol we would fly at 700–1,200 feet, to increase our ASV radar detection range for shipping to between 30 and 40 miles. While Sunderland crews completed their patrols with meticulous care, for obvious reasons we tried not to provoke reaction from the Communist Chinese; my impression was that USN Mariner and Privateer maritime patrol (or 'VP') aircraft covering Fox patrols tended not to fly at such low altitudes, although I believe there were good reasons for this which shall touch on later. We also tried to avoid flying directly towards the coast of China at any great altitude – and certainly not infringing territorial waters – anywhere along the coastline between 31° 30' N (not far from the Yangtze-Kiang estuary and just east-north-east of Shanghai) and close to Qingdao and the Shantung Peninsula (37° 28' N 122° 35' E). This seemed to pay off, as will be seen later. When we arrived in a Fox patrol area and were sure there were no ships or small fishing boats in our immediate vicinity, the aircraft captain would give the air gunners permission to test their defensive armament; four 0.303 in. machine-guns in the tail turret, two in the nose, and two 0.5 in. cannon, one on each beam. The pilots might also test the fixed, forward-firing 0.303 in. machine-guns in the nose.

As illustrated on the map (map 52), Fox patrol tracks were orientated roughly north–north-west south–south-east, linked at the ends by short 25–35 mile tracks. The area extended westwards in some places to within 15–20 nm of the coastline of Red China. At that time Communist Chinese forces were actively engaged in support of North Korea. Sortie durations varied between 10 hrs 15 min and 13 hrs, depending on the Fox 'colour' and the number of ships encountered. We deviated as necessary from the ordered patrol tracks to intercept, reconnoitre and photograph all ships detected by radar, or visually by the pilots or nose, beam or tail gunners.

The third main Korean War mission was the West Coast Weather (WCW) patrol. I will describe the weather-data-gathering process in a few moments. The WCW tracks in the Yellow Sea were fewer than on a Fox patrol, and linked perhaps five weather-reporting datum positions. Some were quite close to the coast of Red China, and at night Sunderland crews again tried to fly in a way that did not provoke the Communist Chinese air defence forces on the mainland while fully completing our task. I remember on some of the WCW missions I flew, our air gunners reported lights from aircraft when we were not too distant from the Chinese coast, especially off Qingdao and Tsingtao. We would then dim all lights, take up 'action stations' and alert the whole crew. A look-out would be posted in the astrodome.

West Coast Weather patrols generally took between 9 hrs 30 min and 10 hrs 30 min to complete, depending on wind strengths. The shortest I flew was 8 hrs 30 min; that was on 6 July 1952, my second Korean sortie. On that occasion, by dawn we were flying close to the west coast of Korea at around 37° 30' N, and the weather was 'gin' clear. F/L Bert Houtheusen, my aircraft captain for that particular flight, suggested we fly diagonally south-east across the Korean Peninsula, over-flying Taegu, Pusan and thence direct to Iwakuni. That cut about an hour (140 nm) off our planned flight time. Usually, weather conditions were not so obviously favourable, and the generally adopted practice was to skirt around the Korean Peninsula, transiting via the Tsushima Strait, through the Shimonoseki gap and Inland Sea. Using that route, the crew had more navigation options if the weather deteriorated approaching Japan. On this particular day, however, we knew that fine weather extended all the way to Iwakuni. It was interesting to cross and see the southern part of Korea where in 1950/51 there had been fierce fighting before United Nations forces had driven the enemy north to the vicinity of the 38th Parallel.

The last type of Korean patrol, which I flew twice, was a Task Force Replenishment Group patrol. This was flown to the east or west of Korea, day or night. In the east the track was over the Sea of Japan to within 90 nm of Vladivostok and the Soviet border. Our role was to report the weather and warn of any threats we might detect approaching in the direction of the task force while aircraft carriers were refuelling and unable to fly-off or land aircraft. This patrol seemed to be tasked almost exclusively on USN aircraft and was rarely flown by the RAF

Attacks by Communist Chinese fighter aircraft
During the period when both RAF and USN aircraft were engaged in Fox or West Coast Weather patrols around Korea, there were many instances when USN Mariner and Privateer VP aircraft from Iwakuni were attacked by Chinese fighter aircraft over the Yellow Sea. A likely reason that USN aircraft bore the brunt of these attacks was that they were fitted with electronic surveillance measures (ESM) equipment. No such equipment was fitted in the Sunderland. USN aircrews were tasked to identify and fix the position of Chinese defence radars inland or near the coastline of China. However, the ESM equipment in these USN aircraft was basic by today's standard, and it required the aircraft to head directly towards the radar to obtain a bearing on it. To fix the radar's position accurately required two or three bearings, with a cut of 30–45°. Moreover, to detect ground-based radars at forty to fifty miles meant the aircraft had to fly at not less than 1,000 to 1,750 feet directly towards the Chinese coastline when obtaining a bearing. The Chinese defence system, detecting USN aircraft at such altitudes heading directly towards their coastline, must have considered this provocative; nevertheless, that was the task given to US Navy aircrews, and they did not flinch from it – but there was a price to be paid.

For example, on 31 July while patrolling over the Yellow Sea, a PBM-5S2 Mariner flying boat of VP-731 from Iwakuni was attacked by two MiG-15s. Two crew members were killed and two were seriously wounded. The Mariner was badly damaged but able to make a safe landing at Paengyong-Dao, Korea. On 20 September 1952 my crew were flying PP155 ('D') on a Tsushima patrol when a PB4Y Privateer of VP-28 from Iwakuni, seventy-five miles to the south-west of us, was attacked by two MiG-15s in position 31° 35' N 122° 23' E, off Shanghai in the southern extremity of the Fox patrol area. Five firing passes were made, but the PB4Y was not damaged and returned safely to base. A third instance was on 23 November 1952. Another Privateer of VP-28 was attacked by a Chinese MiG-15, again off Shanghai, but was undamaged. Six more attacks were to follow. On 23 April 1953, a US Navy P4M-1Q Mercator (similar to one I had seen at NAS Sangley Point on 6–9 September 1952) was attacked by two MiG-15s while flying off the Yangtze estuary. The MiGs made several runs and the Mercator crew returned fire, but it was not hit, and neither were the MiGs.

An Armistice in Korea was signed on 27 July 1953, but patrols by USN and RAF aircraft continued, and the Communist Chinese fighters ignored the cease-fire over the Yellow Sea. On 2 October 1953, a PBM-5 of VP-50 from Iwakuni was intercepted by two MiG-15s, thirty miles east of Tsingtao (also called Qingdao, as on the map). This was a sensitive area of coastline for the Chinese; our crew were always on the look-out for trouble along this stretch of coast, whether flying a Fox or a night-time West Coast Weather patrol. The two MiG-15s made no fewer than twelve firing passes, hitting the VP-50 Mariner, flying at 1,000 feet, twice in the tail with 37 mm cannon shells. The crew, commanded by Lt Hanson, fortunately received no injuries and returned safely to Iwakuni.

Plane commander Lt Richard Erb of VP-50 flew a Fox Blue on 6 November. When east of the Shantung Peninsula they detected a Soviet V-band radar and manoeuvred to fix its position which was on Lingshan Dao Island near Qingdao. As the PBM-5 was exiting the area a crewman saw aircraft approaching, and after tracer ammunition was seen passing over and under the Mariner's wing, a MiG-15 flashed past so close that Lt Erb could clearly see the pilot's head in the cockpit. Meanwhile, the PBM was descending rapidly towards 100 feet over the sea. Just before the next MIG-15 pass, Lt Erb pulled his aircraft into a steep 60° port turn. After three more attacks and evasive manoeuvres by the Mariner, the MiG pilot gave up. The PBM-5 was undamaged. A more serious incident, the sixth, occurred on 10 November 1953. A PBM-5 Mariner flying boat of VP-50 from Iwakuni was lost over the Yellow Sea. This may have been due to a technical fault in the aircraft. SS *Swordknot*, a merchant ship, recovered debris, including two BPM-5 floats, from the sea near Cheju Do. Fourteen men were tragically lost. A People's Republic of China PLAAF pilot claimed to have shot down this aircraft off Qianlidao, much farther to the north-west, but this claim is usually discounted. Another attack definitely took place on 18 November 1953, again off Shanghai, when a PBM-5 of VP-50 based at Iwakuni 'picked up an unexpected tail wind while approaching Shanghai and got close to the coast of China before the crew determined their position.'[1] The crew had been flying at low level and only switched on their radar occasionally, to avoid warning the Chinese of their approach. After the Mariner turned away from the coast it was quickly jumped by two MiG-15s. Three firing passes were made but the aircraft wasn't hit. The next attack was on 4 January 1954. A US Navy P2V-5 Neptune of VP-2 from Iwakuni flew north across the DMZ (Korean Demilitarized Zone),[2] then along the North Korean coast to the coast of China before turning south. The USA reported as likely that this aircraft had suffered an attack by Chinese fighters. The crew reported engine difficulties and headed for the K-13 airbase at Suwan in South Korea. However, the P2V crashed not far from K-13 airfield, although, mysteriously, the US report states this 'may have resulted from an additional attack by a US Navy AD-4B Skyraider on night patrol'. The ninth encounter with Chinese fighters took place on 9 April 1954 when a US Navy P2V Neptune was attacked during a Fox patrol over the Yellow Sea. The exact location was not stated. Three firing passes were made and the Neptune returned fire, but neither aircraft was apparently damaged.

While it has often been written that weather was the main hazard around Korea, in practice there was clearly the additional threat of attack by Chinese PLAAF MiG-15 fighters, something that we were always aware of. While the RAF had at most four Sunderlands at Iwakuni at any one time, the US Navy had two squadrons deployed for Fox, West Coast Weather, Tsushima Strait and Japan Sea patrols. The two USN squadrons flew three to four times the number of patrols flown by four RAF Sunderlands rotating through Iwakuni, although these completed about thirty sorties a month. Nevertheless, we can think ourselves fortunate that an RAF Sunderland was never attacked by fighters. By contrast, the US Navy experienced at least nine direct attacks, resulting in more than twenty airmen being killed, two injured, one (possibly two) USN patrol aircraft destroyed and a further two damaged, one seriously. I believe the difference between the USN and RAF loss rates was due to the additional ESM role played by USN aircraft, which forced them to fly at higher altitudes and more provocatively. RAF Sunderland crews were nevertheless skilful in fulfilling their shipping surveillance efficiently while maintaining a 'low profile'. On weather data-gathering missions at night, both the USN and RAF had to fly at the same, sometimes high, sometimes low, altitudes off the Chinese coastline, but thankfully we avoided any aircraft losses. Although losses suffered by the USN were serious, the fact that there were not more was entirely due to the skill and alertness of USN PBM-5, PB4Y, P2V-5 and P4M-1Q Mercator airplane crews. It also doesn't speak highly of the skill of the People's Republic of China PLAAF fighter pilots at that time.

At Iwakuni, we received some rather unconvincing guidance on how to evade capture in North Korea should we be forced to land in North Korean waters or north of the DMZ. We were issued with a *Pointie-Talkie* sheet and were told that if we were able to strike up a conversation with a North Korean, we should 'hold our left ear-lobe between the thumb and forefinger of our right hand'. This would be recognized by members of the 'resistance'. What our confidant would do in return wasn't stated. The *Pointie-Talkie* sheet had thirty-five 'useful phrases', such as 'NAH-noon YUNG-gook GOON-in IMNEE-dah', meaning, 'I am a British soldier', and 'TAWN too-ree-gess-SOOM-nee-dah', meaning, 'I will pay you'. There were tips on pronunciation – pretty important, having looked at some of the phrases! Each phrase was written in phonetic English in addition to Korean script.

Korean patrols flown in March and April 1953

Over the three years of the Korean War and the one-year post-Armistice period, I estimate Sunderlands of the FEFBW must have flown about a thousand sorties and over 10,000 flight hours. From my own observation between mid-1952 and August 1954, and from pre- and post-flight briefings given by US Navy officers, it was evident that RAF Sunderland crews carrying out patrols under US Navy orders throughout the Korean conflict were highly regarded by the US Navy. This was despite the fact that there was comparatively little contact between our crews and those of US Navy Mariners and Privateers who were flying almost identical sorties to the RAF. Nevertheless, we seemed to have a very good relationship with the USN Operations Centre, and the operation ran very smoothly. In retrospect, I feel benefit might have been gained from more contact between crews of the two nations.

To provide a snapshot of what it was like to fly on Korean patrols, I am going to touch on some of the sorties our crew flew in March and April 1953. After rectifying the ASV radar and VHF transmitter faults that could so easily have ended in disaster on 27 March 1953, our crew was briefed at Base Operations to fly a night-time West Coast Weather mission on 31 March. We were ordered to collect and report meteorological data in the Yellow Sea. We took off in darkness at 22.10 hrs. After transiting the Inland Sea and then the Tsushima Strait, which took us almost three hours, we finally arrived over the Yellow Sea. I navigated the aircraft successively between various specific pre-planned datums within the general patrol area shown on the map for Fox patrols. At each datum we were ordered to record visibility and cloud amounts, and at specified altitudes, the outside air temperature and wind velocity. We also descended to 100 feet above the sea, using our trusted radio altimeter to measure our actual height over the water. We would then reset the 2nd pilot's barometric altimeter to read 100 feet and note the resultant barometric pressure on the altimeter's Millibar scale. Having navigated the aircraft to each of the designated reporting points, each time repeating the data-gathering process, we then flew to a pre-briefed location to rendezvous with the US Navy Task Force 77 (CTF77). We then passed our weather data to them by VHF communications in a set format. Throughout the three to four hours we had been gathering data over the Yellow Sea, sometimes not many miles from the coast of China, the pilots, gunners and signallers on look-out had kept a sharp eye open for any possible Chinese fighter aircraft in the area. On at least one such sortie – though not on this one – an air gunner had reported seeing aircraft lights when we were east of Qingdao, one of the 'hot spot' areas. We took up 'action stations' as a precaution, mounted an additional look-out in the astrodome, dimmed the aircraft lights and kept a close watch on the intruders. After a while, they vanished in the darkness of the night.

On two occasions on a West Coast Weather patrol, a Chinese or North Korean, speaking English with an American accent, called us on the designated VHF channel three-quarters of the way through our patrol, asking us to pass our weather information, presumably hoping we would not then communicate it to Task Force 77. We were wise to this ruse, and, as briefed, asked the caller to 'authenticate' (i.e. respond to a code that changed every few minutes every day); we required a correct response to our challenge before we would transmit our data to anyone. The caller could never give a correct reply. On the night of 31 March/1 April, after completing our patrol we transited back to Iwakuni and landed after 9 hrs 45 min.

During March 1953 my crew flew eighty-nine hours, of which thirteen were at night. In the following month, still at Iwakuni, we flew five ASP Tsushima patrols, one Fox Blue and two Fox Reds, and another West Coast Weather patrol at night, a total of nine sorties and ninety-five hours' flying. The weather was especially poor on 15 April while we were on a Tsushima patrol. We flew at about 500 feet, just below the cloud base, with the visibility down to a mile or so. On the return transit from Shimonoseki to Iwakuni, along the length of the Inland Sea, the radar operator and I, using the ASV and a topographical map, jointly navigated our way from Shimonoseki, along the Inland Sea, eventually turning north and 'feeling' our way into the Iwakuni alighting area. My next detachment to Iwakuni

The Russian cargo ship *Minusinsk*, north-east of Shantung or Tsingtao Peninsula on 21 June 1954, MLA 210/9 knots (RIG-1 HKHBHKHF).

was in September 1953. During that month, three 88 Squadron aircraft ('A', 'B' and 'C') flew almost a sortie a day or night; my crew clocked up more than ninety-eight patrol hours. (See map 54)

Shipping surveillance

The purpose of Fox Blue, Fox Red, Fox Green and ASP Tsushima patrols was shipping surveillance. We flew in radio silence except for short, hourly position reports sent to Iwakuni in Morse on HF. On each ship sighting we would fly at a hundred feet or so at a distance of about 100 to 300 yards (depending on the size of ship) past the length of the vessel, usually at least twice. We would note its type (freighter, tanker), class if known (e.g. Liberty, Victory), its name and nationality. We would take oblique photographs using a hand-held F24, or the better US-made K20 camera, to record the deck and superstructure profile. The crewman with the camera would stand in the open beam gun hatch. We would record the ship's course and speed and if necessary make a very low pass at close range across the stern, to read and note the port of registration. We would observe and record whether the ship was 'in ballast' or 'laden', and note and photograph any visible deck cargo. We were required to estimate the ship's tonnage and report its RIG-1 configuration; this abbreviated the arrangement of hatches (H), masts (M), kingposts (K), the bridge (B) and funnel (F), from bow to stern (e.g. HKHBHKHF).

Having noted all the required data, the navigator would plot the ship's position, time, course and speed on his navigation chart to avoid accidentally visiting the same ship twice. During the seven sorties our crew flew in April, we photographed and recorded details of sixty-seven merchant vessels. Typically, we would reconnoitre ten to sixteen ships within the ASP Tsushima area, but usually only two to four ships in the Yellow Sea during a Fox patrol.

Compared with Fox and West Coast Weather patrols, navigating ASP Tsushima sorties was not too demanding, providing the ASV was serviceable. We were often within radar range of Tsushima, Cheju or other islands close to the shipping routes south of Korea. This was where our pre-designated ASP Tsushima patrol tracks were laid out by the US Navy planners, as roughly indicated on the map seen earlier. Although we suffered ASV radar failure on 27 March, in my experience, complete radar failure was rare – which was fortunate. Our air signallers on board were very skilled and often able to recover radar unserviceabilities during a sortie by changing the modulator or some other unit. Experience taught us to carry certain spare units that most often failed. Radar, so essential for our main patrol

A former volcano on a peninsula off the south coast of Korea – a familiar landmark for Sunderland crews patrolling the Tsushima Strait. *Author*

task, was therefore usually available for navigation whenever we were flying within range of some navigationally useful land or island. While the technical characteristics of the ASV Mark 6C were optimized for submarine and ship detection rather than navigation, we were nevertheless thankful when it worked – and it usually did.

The daily shipping surveillance missions flown in the Yellow Sea and Tsushima Strait were in support of United Nations sanctions and embargoes against North Korea, following their invasion of South Korea in June 1950. These were kept up without interuption until the autumn of 1954. It was challenging flying and good training, and much more interesting than practising a 'creeping line ahead' patrol in front of an RAF Marine Craft. Of course there were potential dangers, as shown by the high number of attacks against USN aircraft flying similar patrols to ours, but that was not in the forefront of our minds. Some of the island scenery we flew past, especially on Tsushima patrols, was fascinating; a common landmark and one that always intrigued me was what appeared to be a long-extinct volcano. What I found especially interesting was the fact that the 'basin' was so fertile; it was clearly being farmed but we could see no obvious means of access from the land, below.

Navigating Korean War patrols

Between Iwakuni and the Fox Blue, Red and Green and night-time West coast weather patrol areas in the Yellow Sea, we transited over the Inland Sea and Tsushima Strait. Once to the west of Cheju Do we were mostly beyond radar range of Korea. On the most westerly leg of the Fox patrols we came within radar range of the Chinese coast – depending on our height – but not necessarily within range of a piece of coastline that was navigationally helpful for a fix (e.g. a headland). However, a range position line could be useful, if only to ensure that we were not encroaching into Chinese territorial waters. Hence, navigating Fox and West Coast Weather patrols required more intensive work by the navigator than the ASP Tsushima. Fox patrols also required constant drift taking, two-drift winds at the ends of legs and occasional sun shots. We were also dodging about investigating possible or actual ship contacts, which made navigation more difficult and the air position indicator more important. Night-time West Coast Weather patrols required a mixture of drifts and two- or three-drift winds obtained by back bearings from the tail gunner, or using the astro-compass, on flame floats while at low altitude. I rarely used the wind-finding attachment on a west coast weather patrol. Loran position lines were also helpful. There was tendency not to use Loran because coverage wasn't as good in the Yellow Sea as it was farther to the east; also, the Loran set in the Sunderland required a lot of manipulation to set it up properly. However, I felt the setting-up time

Shipping surveillance. Typical first camera shot, in this case of the *Marshfield Victory*, taken at a distance to capture the full length of the vessel. Further close-ups might be taken of any deck cargo and the port of registration on the stern. *Author*

was time well spent. While it wasn't a quick-fixing aid and you couldn't use it as a letdown aid in bad weather (as you could use Gee Mk 3 in the UK), two or three Loran position lines per hour were at times very helpful when combined with conscientious drift taking.

Although Korean patrol patterns were based on pre-planned tracks decided by the USN, to intercept and reconnoitre all vessels visually you constantly had to divert from these tracks. This could require deviations of perhaps ten to twenty-five miles. After flying around each ship at between fifty and two hundred feet for five to ten minutes, photographing and recording all the required information, the navigator would then give the pilot a course to regain the specified track at a convenient position. He would make sure, by reference to the ASV radar, that no other ships had been missed. In practice, therefore, the duration of any of the patrols could vary by as much as two hours. More information on DR navigation and the equipment we used is at Appendix 2.

Contribution made by Sunderland crews during the Korean War
As I have already mentioned, the various different types of daily and nightly operational missions flown by RAF Sunderland crews from Japan were

Liberty ship *Audrey II*, 7,000 tonnes, in the Shimonoseki Strait.

A rare sighting of a surfaced transiting USN submarine.

Photographs believed taken by crew members of RN302 C-Charlie during the April 1953 detachment to Iwakuni

Checking out a USN corvette in the Yellow Sea.

Photographs believed taken by crew members of RN302 C-Charlie during the April 1953 detachment to Iwakuni

A Japanese ferry on its way from Pusan in South Korea to Shimonoseki.

shared with our US Navy VP colleagues throughout the Korean War from June 1950 until August 1954. The RAF contribution initially came only from detachments of Sunderlands of No. 88 Squadron from Kai Tak. The squadron, renamed from No. 1430 Flight on 1 September 1946, had until mid-1950 been engaged mainly on courier services, carrying supplies and mail for allied occupation forces in Japan. The squadron never missed a mail delivery because of bad weather. They also flew Japanese war criminals to Japan guarded by Gurkas armed with Kukris![3] A few weeks after the outbreak of the Korean War, No. 88 Squadron was redeployed from its Kai Tak base to Seletar, where it joined Nos 205 and 209 Squadrons to form the Far East Flying Boat Wing. After that, the Korean War task was shared equally between Nos 88, 205 and 209 Squadrons in rotation every four to six weeks.

For navigators, most sorties required constant attention to DR navigation to maintain an accurate plot of the aircraft's position. The weather could at times be testing, with turbulence, poor visibility, low cloud, rain, snow and icing. Hence, all crew members needed to keep their wits about them; there was no place for complacency. In winter, the icing risk often forced us to transit to and from our patrol area via the Inland Sea below the cloud base, which could be as low as 500 feet; the Sunderland's de-icing equipment was not very effective in conditions when the icing risk was high.

Because of icing – combined with a lack of modern navigation aids – we sometimes had difficulty persuading the US Military air traffic control

The Australian officers' mess waitresses in their traditional kimonos rather than their white mess uniforms. Shukosan (Sukisan), daughter of Mrs 'Mumma-san' Ohara, is second from the left. *Author*

authorities at Iwakuni to agree to our filing a visual meteorological conditions (VMC) flight plan when they knew the cloud base was perhaps 600 feet and the visibility no more than a mile or two. However, there was no way we were going to climb into thick cloud when the icing risk was moderate to high in order to transit via airways under IFR across Honshu to the Tsushima Strait; nor, similarly, would we do so on the return flight. Eventually, they seemed to accept our situation and point of view.

On rare occasions when they insisted we file an instrument meteorological conditions (IMC) flight plan, we would cancel and refile 'VMC' as soon as we became airborne. This might on the face of it seem somewhat irresponsible, but it was the lesser of two evils when there was a significant risk of airframe icing which the aircraft simply couldn't reliably cope with, and we didn't want to cancel a mission because of weather conditions. I never heard of an RAF Sunderland crew cancelling a mission due to bad weather – certainly, *we* never did. Nevertheless, weather, sometimes combined with poor equipment serviceability, tested the professional skill, airmanship and seamanship of Sunderland crews.

Off duty in Japan

Whenever we landed at Iwakuni or were about to fly on a mission, a rather unhappy-looking, sixty-something-year-old Japanese gentleman would coxswain the large open launch ferrying us between the slipway and the

One of the bungalows where RAF officers were accommodated on the base at Iwakuni. *Author*

aircraft. We addressed him as 'Pappasan'. Everyone said he was a former Japanese admiral – but no one really believed it!

Although we worked hard and flew every third or fourth day, whenever we were not being briefed, flight planning, flying or debriefing, our time was more or less our own. This usually meant we had one, sometimes two, full days between missions. Officers were automatically members of the Royal Australian Air Force officers' mess, where bar prices were ridiculously low (a brandy was a few old pence) – even a dog with a taste for beer, which was owned by one of the Australian officers living in the mess, could sometimes be seen leaning on a wall for support! We were well looked after in the mess dining-room by attentive and polite Japanese waitresses. RAF officers weren't accommodated in the mess, but in bungalows on the base. Each had a Japanese lady to look after it and its occupants. I usually managed to stay in 'Mummasan's' bungalow. She was Mrs Ohara, a charming lady. Her husband died in 1945 at Hiroshima railway station, where he had just arrived by train from Iwakuni on his way to work, when the atomic bomb exploded overhead. Her daughter Shuko (known as 'Sukisan') was a waitress in the officers' mess. She and the other waitresses can be seen in the photograph on the previous page. Mrs Ohara kept the bungalow clean and did our washing and ironing. Occasionally, she would invite one or two of us to her home for an evening meal. Together with her daughter, we would sit on the matted floor, in winter around a large earthenware charcoal-filled burner on which Mummasan or Sukisan would prepare a Japanese dish; while the meal cooked in front of us we would chat about all sorts of things, warmed by the heat of the burning charcoal. Both spoke quite good English and had been well educated, although, since the war, without a male bread-winner, they were no longer as well off as when Mrs Ohara's husband had been alive.

There was an RAF Base Unit at Iwakuni with a small staff to service the needs of RAF personnel – mainly the flying boat detachments and those few RAF fighter pilots who were on exchange postings with No. 77 (RAAF) Squadron, for most of the time based in Korea. They initially flew Meteor 8s, but later, F-86s. The RAF Base Unit issued us with 'Scrip' currency for use in the officers' mess. They also provided each Sunderland crew with a jeep; when we needed transport for the whole crew we telephoned Transportation to provide a bus. The main base was a mile from the slipway, which was to the east of the airfield runway and reached via a stony track, dusty in summer and full of rain-filled potholes in winter.

It is almost unbelievable, today, that in 1953, RAF aircrew at Iwakuni received a free issue of two hundred cigarettes a week. We called these 'Bushfires' – they were awful. How attitudes towards smoking have changed. We were permitted to make use of the US officers' club, where we paid in US dollars. Club food was typically American and good value, especially salads, steak and burgers. We soon came to know the meaning of 'sunny-side-up' and 'over-easy' – and acquired a taste for iced tea, as well as 'Bud' and Schlitz. The club put on film shows and regular half-price 'happy hours'. The resident US Navy VP squadrons had a small club room on the base, on one wall of which was displayed a life-size poster of Norma Jean Mortensen – better known as Marilyn Monroe, the number one pin-up girl of that era. In December 1953, 88 Squadron threw a drinks party in House S-511. Guests were invited from all the units on the base, USN, USAF and RAAF. Cocktails were 'strong and generous'. A visiting RAAN pilot from the Australian aircraft carrier HMAS *Sydney* (formerly HMS *Terrible*) subsequently claimed that he had extreme difficulty in identifying the correct flight deck the next morning, and completed fourteen circuits before putting down! The remains of the enormous punch-bowl were bottled and shared among squadron members.

The airfield was on the outskirts of the town which gave the base its name. West Iwakuni was a couple of miles to the west, beside the Nishiki River, where there is the historic Kintai Bridge. Arched and of interlocking wooden construction, the spans are mounted on stone plinths. In springtime, trees in blossom, lining the river promenade, were beautiful. In a tradition stretching back three hundred and fifty years, fishermen could sometimes be seen using tethered cormorants to catch fish in the river. A Kintai Bridge Festival is held on 29 April each year, in Kikkoh Park, led by a 'Young Warriors' procession. The Kintai was originally a bridge to the main gate of a castle until it was dismantled by order of the Shogun in 1615. A replica of the castle tower stands high on a hill above the river. Iwakuni is also known for its rare breed of albino snakes, which, unlike most albinos, breed other albinos. These are kept in a small sanctuary in Kikkoh Park.

In 1952–4, Iwakuni was just a small town. There were some shops, several traditional pachinko (slot machine) parlours, much used by Japanese men on their way home from work. There was a night club, but there must have been at least fifty bars or other drinking 'dens'. Most bars played popular American music, especially Country and Western. Japanese beer – Kirin and Asahi – was 100 yen a litre bottle; 1,000 yen was worth a pound sterling. When we had a free day, we often walked into Iwakuni in the afternoon or evening. One of several popular bars not far from the base entrance was the Shangri La, where we would buy Asahi or Kirin beer, listen to the music and chat with the bar owner's attractive daughter. Today, Iwakuni is a city, unrecognizable as the small town we knew with its wooden shacks intermingled with smallholdings. A potholed road from the base to the town was flanked by paddy fields fertilized by human sewage, often seen being carried in 'honey-buckets' on a trailer being towed along the road by a tractor.

Kintai Bridge, 1953. *Author*

Sometimes we would take a motorized trishaw to West Iwakuni. Exceptionally we might travel to Hiroshima or Miyajima – on the island of Itsukushima – where Japan's most sacred Shinto shrine is sited. This is now a UNESCO World Heritage site. Most famous was, and still is, the torii, or 'gate', to the shrine. I visited both Hiroshima and Miyajima only once. I think my trip to Hiroshima was in September 1953. Rebuilding the city was well under way, but most buildings were still wooden and single storeyed. We saw the skeletal steel frame and dome of the former Prefectural Industrial Promotion Hall that was within 150 metres of ground zero. This has been left untouched as a memorial to the 140,000 people who are said to have died on the day the atom bomb was dropped. While there, I went to a Japanese cinema with very little leg-room and sat through a Swedish film with Japanese subtitles in order to see a Pathé Newsreel which included both the first conquest of Mt Everest (29 May 1953) by Sherpa Tensing and Sir Edmund Hillary (who passed away in 2008), and Queen Elizabeth II's Coronation on 2 June.

I have mentioned motorized trishaws; these were a popular mode of travel in Iwakuni. The tricycle usually had the driver at the front and the passengers at the back. Over the front wheel was a small petrol engine with a friction drive onto the tyre. Although pedal assisted, the friction wheel was inclined to slip when it rained. At the back there was a platform and a seat

An afternoon beer at the Shangri-La bar in Iwakuni. L to R: Navigators David Germain, Keith Readyhoof and the author. The young lady is the bar owner's daughter. *Author's camera*

wide enough for two people side-by-side. It was covered by a metal frame bearing a canvas hood with a cellophane window looking forward. In winter a charcoal burner provided a modicum of warmth for the passengers' legs and hands. These were very basic 'taxis', charging low fares.

Post-war Japanese cars were then only just beginning to appear. I distinctly remember one that was similar in appearance to a post-war Hillman Minx except that it was bigger. It looked as if the designer had copied the engineering drawings of the Hillman Minx but misinterpreted the scale! I have only recently been told that this car was most probably the Isuzu PH10, which was, indeed, based on Minx technology purchased from the British car manufacturer Rootes in 1953. Its lineage was unmistakable.

Outdoors, men and women wore wooden-soled sandals, raised on two lateral bars to keep their feet out of the worst of the puddles. In winter these were worn with padded linen socks. Shoes or sandals are always removed indoors.

In term-time, children at all schools were immaculately dressed in a common uniform. Girls wore a kind of 'sailor suit', white and navy blue. Boys wore a black (or possibly dark blue) unique design of uniform with a high buttoned collar and shiny metal buttons down the front. I believe this tradition continues today, though in a slightly more relaxed form.

Japan is renowned for its large number of public holidays, most of them on Mondays, to make a long weekend. These include Coming-of-age Day on 2 January, Showa Day on 29 April (celebrating Emperor Hirohito, emperor from 1926 to 1989); Constitution Memorial Day on 3 May, celebrating the 1947 Constitution of Japan; this is the only day in the year that the Diet (the Parliament) of Japan is open to the public. Children's Day comes on 5 May, Health Sports Day on the second Monday in September, and Respect for the Aged Day on the third Monday in September, to mention but six. There are fourteen public holidays annually. On such holidays, special Japanese-style flags are widely flown. Many depict fish of various kinds and in various numbers. On a public holiday you will see many such flags flown outside shops, restaurants and so on.

SAY IF THATS WHAT YUH HAD IN 1937
WHAT HAVE YOU GOT TODAY

(Cartoon by Kane)

What little I saw of Japan was fascinating. My main regret is that because we were briefing and flight planning one day, and flying for the whole of the next day or night, followed usually by only one day off duty, this left too little time to travel and investigate Japan more widely. Few RAF personnel took leave in Japan, though this would have been possible. Of course, in the early 1950s tourism hadn't yet developed; the poor state of most roads was

The wreckage of PP148 (F) recovered from Iwakuni alighting area following the fatal accident on the night of 25 March 1953. Our crew had flown this aircraft, captained by F/L Malcolm Laidlay, from October to December 1952. Following the accident, our crew, captained by F/L David Cooke, had flown the President of the Court of Inquiry from Kai Tak to Iwakuni, in an eventful flight, finally arriving on 28 March, as described in Chapter 3. *Unknown origin but kindly provided by Tony Burt via RAFSA*

another consideration. We were there to perform an operational task, and that clearly had priority. If for some reason while sight-seeing we had been unable to return to Iwakuni on time, we would have been in trouble! Japan is certainly one of several countries in the Far East that I was fortunate to visit between 1952 and 1954 that I would like the opportunity to visit again. However, if I *were* to visit Iwakuni I doubt that any part of it – except the Kintai Bridge – would be recognizable to me; it now has six railway stations rather than one!

Notes

1. It is believed that USN VP aircraft did not carry a specialist navigator. The task was carried out by a third pilot; he was often the most junior and therefore the most inexperienced.
2. According to Wikipedia, 'The Korean Demilitarized Zone is a strip of land running across the Korean Peninsula and serves as a buffer zone between North and South Korea. It cuts the Korean Peninsula roughly in half, crossing the 38th parallel of latitude on an angle, with the west end of the DMZ lying south of the parallel and the east end lying north of it. It is 155 miles (248 km) long and approximately 2.5 miles (4 km) wide, and is the most heavily armed border in the world.
3. *The Royal Air Force – The Past 30 Years*, by A.G. Treuenen James.

Chapter Five

Operations from Hong Kong

SAR and training flying

Having completed just over five weeks at Iwakuni, on 1 May F/L Dave Cooke and our crew of C-Charlie flew to Kai Tak for a one-month search and rescue (SAR) detachment. While there I carried out my first practice Lindholme gear drop. This was actually Air Sea Rescue Apparatus Mk 4, and was a survival system that we could release from the

A photograph, by John Land, flight engineer of SZ578, 'B' Baker of 88 Squadron, taken while moored. RAF Kai Tak is in the background. Kai Tak runway is to the left of the picture. The range of hills to the north of Kowloon and the Sunderland alighting area was about a mile away.
John Land

RAF Hornets formating on our aircraft before 'fighter affiliation'. *Author*

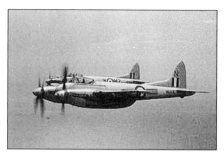

aircraft's bomb racks to any aircrew or ship's lifeboat or survivors in the water. It consisted of three cylindrical, buoyant containers linked in series by buoyant orange rope. The centre container carried a ten-man dinghy that inflated on hitting the sea. The end containers carried emergency rations and water and other survival equipment.

When released from the Sunderland's bomb racks, they deployed one by one at short intervals so that they stretched in a straight line over 450 metres. The stores floated on the sea surface. The aim was to drop them a few yards downwind of, and straddling, the survivors, who, blown by the wind, would drift onto the inflated dinghy and floating orange rope linking the survival packs. The survivors could then recover them, climb into the dinghy and extract food, water, etc. from the survival containers.

While at Kai Tak we flew numerous circuits, landings and take-offs. In suitable conditions, Dave Cooke would occasionally allow – indeed encourage – other crew members to pilot and even to land the aircraft; we all had a go at one time or another. David always sat in the other pilot's seat to guide us and make sure we didn't put the aircraft or crew at risk. We also practised air-to-sea gunnery, shooting at buoyant markers that we dropped into the sea. Another exercise was anchoring in deep water – truthfully, this was actually to provide an opportunity to swim from the aircraft in the warm waters of the South China Sea to the south of Victoria Island! We greatly enjoyed 'fighter affiliation' with de Havilland Hornets from Kai Tak or Vampires from Sek-Kong. We would arrange to rendezvous over the sea some distance from Hong Kong, usually at two to three thousand feet. After we met up with them, the fighters would fly off in a different direction. I would then stand in the astrodome as look-out. Our gunners, now manning all the turrets and guns (without ammunition) – and I in the astrodome – would keep a sharp look-out for the return of the fighters. As soon as we spotted them we reported their position over the intercom to the pilots and rest of the crew – saying, for example, 'Two Hornets, four o'clock high, about two miles and closing,' Then, at what I hoped was the critical moment when they were about to get us in their sights and 'open fire', I would call to the pilots to 'corkscrew starboard' or 'corkscrew port', depending from which direction the fighters were approaching. Our aim was to try to prevent the fighters from acquiring a steady 'bead' on us through their gunsights. A cine-camera in each fighter's gunsight would record how successful – or otherwise – we were in evading them. On the order 'corkscrew starboard' (or port) our pilot would push the control column forward to dive, while at the same time turning to starboard or port. After descending several hundred feet and gathering speed he would then pull out of the dive and immediately climb and turn in the opposite direction, following the corkscrew manoeuvre. We would repeat this on each 'attack'. After the exercise was over, we would be invited to go to the fighter squadron to look at the cine-film from their gunsight cameras to see how well we had evaded them. The corkscrew manoeuvre and our small-radius turns were actually quite effective. Remembering that Chinese fighter aircraft had already attacked US Navy patrol planes several times in the Yellow Sea, where Sunderlands were also on patrol every day or night of every week, our air gunners felt they too could benefit from camera guns in our turrets so that we could see how skilled our crews were at defending themselves against the kinds of MiG-15 attack that US Navy Mariner and Privateer VP aircraft had sustained.

The much-preferred and most often used take-off run direction at Kai Tak was between east and south-east, but on occasions, the wind in the

'Charlie' undergoing servicing while on beaching legs on the slipway at RAF Kai Tak. The officers' mess can just be seen beyond the starboard wingtip. *Author*

flying boat alighting and take-off area could blow quite strongly from a northerly quarter. A range of hills stretching from the north-west to the south-east was less than a mile away; hence a strong or fresh breeze from the north presented some difficulty, mainly for take-off. To overcome this, the aircraft was taxied downwind towards Victoria Island, and the take-off run was commenced heading north towards the Lion Rock range of hills. Once the aircraft was firmly on 'the step' – probably around 50–55 kts – the pilot could throttle back the starboard outer engine a little and then, using rudder while making sure the wings were kept level (to prevent a float from digging into the sea), turn the aircraft slowly through perhaps 45° or even 90°, like a speed boat. Once pointing in the right direction, full power could be restored to all engines. Using mainly rudder to maintain direction despite the cross-wind, the aircraft would accelerate and eventually reach flying speed, having completed its take-off run in a cross-wind direction. The same technique – speed-boating while 'on the step' – was also sometimes necessary if there were sampans, junks or larger ships to avoid during the take-off run.

While at Kai Tak on 8 May 1953 – the third anniversary of my joining the Royal Air Force – we took off and dropped about ten bales of hay through the starboard rear door of the aircraft, to Army mules in the hills in the New

An RAF Valetta transport aircraft based at Changi lands at RAF Kai Tak. On more than one occasion while on SAR standby at Kai Tak we were alerted when a Valetta suffered engine failure. *Author*

Territories north of Kai Tak. One bale broke as it left the aircraft, and much of it blew back into the tail section: hay was everywhere! We then flew east of Hong Kong, found a sea area where there were no sampans, dropped two or three marine markers into the sea (these emitted a flame and some smoke), and first the gunners, firing the 0.303 in. machine-guns in the nose and tail turrets and the 0.5 in. cannon in the beam positions, tried to hit the markers. After the gunners had finished, other crew members had a go; it was great sport! The pilots also fired the four fixed forward-firing guns, 'attacking' the markers while in a shallow dive towards the sea from a couple of hundred feet. We then spent another three hours on a low-level DR navigation exercise, remaining within an hour's flying time of Kai Tak because of our search and rescue commitment.

On 9 May, Kai Tak Air Traffic Control asked if we would act as a target for a new radar that had just been installed; we readily agreed, and our two pilots at the same time carried out instrument flying practice, thereby 'ticking a few boxes' of their monthly pilot training schedule. On 12 May, while we were sitting in the sweltering heat of the Nissen hut which was our flight-office-cum-crewroom – the electric fan at maximum rpm – we had a phone call ordering us to get airborne as soon as possible for an 80 Squadron Hornet that had shut down and feathered an engine *en route* from the Philippines to Kai Tak. We were airborne in about twenty minutes and met the Hornet approaching Waglan Island, a few miles south-east of Hong Kong. The pilot landed the aircraft safely. We decided to continue our sortie; we reconnoitred islands to the south of Victoria Island at low level – typically around 200 feet – taking photographs and observing fishermen going about their daily tasks. We also used our ASV radar to locate, home onto and then visually inspect and log details of merchant ships and junks passing through sea areas to the south and east of Hong Kong.

On 15 May, we carried out a navigation exercise with the aim of intercepting the Royal Navy aircraft carrier HMS *Ocean* on her way north to begin her third Korean War tour. *Ocean* had been visiting Hong Kong, and I went aboard to meet a former school friend who was a Fairy Firefly observer. We located her and, using our Aldis lamp, bade her '*bon voyage*'. While at Kai Tak we twice flew low-level DR navigation exercises to Pratus Island, south-east of Hong Kong; it was a bit of a game to try to surprise the Chinese inhabitants on the Island by our sudden appearance overhead at low altitude. We would then circle and wave to the fishermen tending their nets while wading waist deep in the sea. On 25 May we identified a Russian freighter in the area; this must have been a rarity for me to have noted it in my logbook. Three air tests brought the total number of sorties flown from Kai Tak in May 1953 to fifteen, amounting to sixty hours' flying.

From May – the month of this detachment – through to October, the weather in Hong Kong is hot and humid. Air conditioning was very rare in the 1950s – it was electric fans or nothing. The RAF flying boat offices at Kai Tak near the slipway had corrugated-iron roofs and were extremely hot inside. When we were at Kai Tak on SAR duty we had to be on the base, and were on immediate call throughout daylight hours. We were responsible for SAR on behalf of civilian airliners as well as RAF and Royal Navy aircraft. Practically the only way to keep cool during the day was to fly. Once in the air we often wore just a pair of shorts, with or without a vest. We would also open the aircraft's beam gun hatches to create a draught throughout the aircraft; so at least every other day we would fly both to carry out some useful airborne training – and to keep cool!

We thoroughly enjoyed our Kai Tak detachments. On one we even sent a private telegram to the Flight Commander at Seletar to persuade him to extend our stay by another seven days. Kai Tak officers' mess overlooked the airfield, which was also Hong Kong's international airport. The head office of Cathay Pacific Airways (CPA) was there even in 1953. Then, CPA had only three DC-3s and one DC-4. These flew six days a week. CPA now has 111 wide-bodied aircraft. BOAC flew daily from London to Hong Kong

The view looking north-west from RAF Kai Tak officers' mess towards Lion Rock. Kowloon is to the left of the picture and the New Territories were beyond the range of hills as far as the border with China. *Author*

using Canadair Argonauts. The runway at Kai Tak was only 7,200 feet long. In 1959 it was first replaced by two parallel 12,000 feet runways built on reclaimed land across what was the original flying boat alighting and take-off area. In 1998 a new Hong Kong International airport was built 12 miles to the west on reclaimed land north of Lantau Island, and is linked to Hong Kong and the mainland by road and rail.

In the previous chapter, I described how People's Republic of China (PRC) fighter aircraft had on nine occasions attacked US Navy VP aircraft flying over the Yellow Sea. It is appropriate to recall that on 23 July 1954, a DC-4 (VR-HEU) of Cathay Pacific Airways, on a flight from Bangkok to Hong Kong, was shot down by Chinese air force LA-9 'Fritz' fighters. It ditched off Hainan Island. Ten of the eighteen people on board were killed and eight survived. Aircraft from the USS aircraft carrier *Philippine Sea* (CVA-47), while locating some of the survivors, were attacked by two Chinese LA-7 fighters. These were promptly shot down by USN airmen of VA-55. Peking Radio announced that one Sunderland would be allowed into the area. F/O Sandy Innes-Smith with Sunderland SZ572 (C) at Kai Tak was alerted and took off within twenty minutes and flew to position 19° 15' N 111° 10' E east of Hainan.[1] An RAF Valetta already in the area reported seeing three survivors in a dinghy five miles south of Takhou Island. The Sunderland found the dinghy and dropped a marine marker, but a 6–8 ft sea swell precluded a landing. Shortly afterwards, a smaller, more open sea-capable US Rescue Grumman Goose arrived from Sangley Point, landed and picked up the survivors. As all had now been accounted for, the Sunderland, in company with the Goose, flew to Hong Kong.

Off duty in Hong Kong

Most of our off-duty time was during the hours of darkness after the airfield was closed. At other times (except Sundays), if we were the only SAR crew there – which was usual – we would be on immediate standby.

When off duty we might sometimes take a taxi to Kowloon and begin the evening with a beer or two at the famous Peninsular Hotel, one of the swankiest in Kowloon. This was where Sir Mark Young, Governor of Hong Kong, had formally surrendered the Crown colony to the Japanese on Christmas Day, 1941. However, this was not a shameful surrender. As graphically recounted by author Tim Carew.

For almost 18 days, a mere six battalions of inadequately equipped British, Indian and Canadian, troops – some newly recruited – had fought off 61,000 Japanese, killing an estimated 4,000 and wounding 9,000. British and Commonwealth losses were 1,045 killed, 1,068 missing and 2,300 wounded. Thousands spent four years of varying degrees of horror in Japanese prisoner-of-war camps.[2]

Chinese junks, a frequent hazard in the Kai Tak alighting area. *Author*

After leaving the Peninsular, we would often stroll around the shops in Nathan Road, bargaining good humouredly with Chinese shopkeepers, perhaps pricing carved ivory cigarette holders or figurines, imitation Rolex watches and 35 mm cameras, all at bargain prices. Later we might spend time in one of many bars, some with dancing – such bars were excellent places for 'people watching' and striking up interesting conversations with strangers.

One evening at around midnight, a few of us were sitting around a table on the pavement of a quiet Kowloon side-street off Nathan Road, drinking beer, when suddenly there was a commotion with many people shouting in Mandarin. Those serving us suddenly whipped our beer glasses away and vanished as police vans swept around the corner and stopped almost in front of us. The policemen ignored us and other European-looking people nearby who were now also sitting around empty tables. After much shouting, the police gave up looking for whatever or whomever they were seeking and drove off as suddenly as they had arrived. Our waiter immediately reappeared, apologized and asked if we would like another beer. We could hardly refuse!

Occasionally we would eat at Tckencho's, a well-known Kowloon restaurant famous for T-bone steak. And there was Harilela, a Kowloon tailor who became one of Hong Kong's richest Indians; after haggling over the price for a suit he would measure you, give you a fitting the next day and invite you to collect it the day after – you could have it a day earlier if you were in a hurry!

An RAF high-speed RTTL at Kai Tak. *Author*

A view of RAF Kai Tak flying boat alighting area. Low cloud and fog are creeping in through the south-east gap. This was the usual route taken by Sunderland aircraft when arriving or departing Kai Tak. *Courtesy RAFSA*

A Sunderland of No. 88 Squadron, on the slipway at Kai Tak, pre-1950. The aircraft, RN297, was then given the letter 'H'. Post-summer 1950, 88 Sqn a/c were A, B, C, D and F. *Courtesy RAFSA*

A Lincoln bomber taking off from Kai Tak's south-easterly runway. The well-known landmark, Lion Rock, can be seen in the background. *Courtesy RAFSA*

A view of RAF Kai Tak from the flying boat alighting area. The range of hills rises steeply to the north of RAF Kai Tak seen on the shoreline. *Author*

View from Hong Kong of the harbour and Kowloon city beyond.

Susie, the cheerful and attractive *amah* who often looked after us at the RAF Kai Tak officers' mess. *Author*

In May 1953, David Cooke, then our captain and recently posted from Kai Tak to 88 Squadron, still had access to a car at Kai Tak. One Sunday he drove Sandy Innes-Smith, David Germain and me on a tour of Victoria, visiting the Peak, Aberdeen – with its famous floating fish restaurants – and other landmarks. Hence, not only did Kai Tak offer a variety of flying but Kowloon and Victoria had a strong Colonial feel, along with Chinese, Indian, Eurasian, European and many other races, all living and working in close proximity. It was crowded, bustling, noisy and alive; usually hot and sticky, and always smelly – above all, unmistakably oriental.

Notes

1. Information kindly provided by Tony Burt on 23 January 2009.
2. Readers are recommended to seek out a copy of *The Fall of Hong Kong* by Tim Carew, Pan Books.

Chapter Six

What was Special about Flying Boats?

The Sunderland was an icon as well as being a joy to operate. I seldom heard any crew member criticize the aircraft or bemoan the additional chores that air crews had to undertake because they were operating a flying boat. They recognized the Sunderland's few shortcomings and acted accordingly. In this chapter I hope to convey what was different about flying boats – compared with their landplane counterparts – and what in particular made the Sunderland so special.

Before beginning the Sunderland conversion course at historic Calshot, I had completed eighty hours' flying in Lancaster GR3s at St Mawgan. No one who had flown in 'Lancs' could deny that it was an unforgettable experience; I can still hear the crackle from the exhausts of the Rolls-Royce Merlins as the pilot throttled them up and down while manoeuvring towards the runway. Who could forget the distinctive sound of four Merlins at full power on take-off? Once in the air the Lancaster engendered a wonderful feeling of dependability. Big and heavy though it was, it could display the manoeuvrability of a much smaller aircraft while circling above the sea at one to two hundred feet when the need arose. Those were fond memories and 'plus' points for the Lancaster.

On the other hand the cabin heating system, controlled by the pilot and flight engineer, could be stiflingly hot. Like every other aircraft type I flew in, the Lanc had a distinctive smell: it was of petrol. It was the first thing that struck me whenever I clambered up the metal ladder to enter the narrow fuselage with its relatively low roof. The navigator's station was almost in line with the four propellers, which made the engine noise very intrusive after several hours in the air. After night flying, the noise of the four Merlins would still be ringing in my ears as my head hit the pillow and I tried to fall asleep. However, even the Sunderland wasn't as quiet *inside* the fuselage as you might imagine if you had only ever heard one flying overhead when it emitted a wonderfully distinctive purr. Nevertheless, the Pratt and Whitney Twin Wasps were still quieter than the more powerful Merlins of a Lancaster. The biggest contrast with the Sunderland was how confined the Lancaster fuselage was. When moving forward from the navigator's crew station I had to squeeze past or underneath the flight engineer's seat to reach the bomb-aiming compartment in the nose, or to climb across the main spar to make my way rearwards towards the flame-float launching chute in the aft fuselage. I might occasionally have to find my way to the pee-tube or the even ghastlier Elsan toilet at the rear of the narrow fuselage. You couldn't comfortably walk around to stretch your legs, and there were no sizeable windows to take in the view; nor was there a galley in which to relax with a mug of tea and have a chat with other crew members for a few minutes. It was a strictly functional fuselage, no bigger then absolutely necessary for its designed purpose, a Second World War long-range bomber. Conversation off intercom had to be conducted by shouting. The Shackleton was an improvement – a little more space and a few more crew comforts, but the even more powerful Rolls-Royce Griffin engines drove inherently noisier contra-rotating propellers. The greater fuel capacity of the Shackleton gave a patrol endurance of between fourteen and eighteen hours; this meant that the quantum increase in decibels from the engines had to be endured for even longer than in the Lancaster.

Although both the Lancaster GR3 and the various marks of Shackleton were much admired and loved by many, the Sunderland was for me and for those who were 'boatmen', in a different league. The Nimrod is the landplane that for me comes closest to the Sunderland for crew comfort. In saying this I am in no sense equating the operational capabilities of these two aircraft which are poles apart thanks to thirty years of technology development. It was the fact that the Sunderland had to display good seaborne characteristics that greatly influenced the width, roominess and length of the fuselage; this led to a spacious crew area and introduced many other facets associated with waterborne operation that set it apart from its landplane counterparts. Together, these made a flying boat a more challenging, yet more satisfying, relaxing and interesting place in which to work. Let me try to explain why.

On Sunderland squadrons in the Far East, each constituted crew[1] had 'its own' aircraft. This engendered pride of ownership and increased a healthy sense of competition between crews. If another crew had to fly *your* aircraft – because theirs had become unserviceable at the last minute – you would very soon let them know if you felt they hadn't taken good care of it – but that rarely happened! From a personal standpoint, because I knew most of my flying would be in a particular aircraft, as its navigator I took extra-special care when swinging the compasses and calibrating the loop antenna. Similarly, air gunners took pride in the condition of their 0.303 and 0.5 in. guns, and the smooth running of the ammunition feeds. Indeed, every crew member tried to ensure that his 'part of ship' was not going to let the crew down. Quite apart from wanting to work in a clean, tidy and serviceable aircraft, we never knew who might be our next passengers! So great was the number of VIPs we carried, it was obvious that most senior officers – and their wives, if they were accompanying their husbands on official visits – preferred to travel by Sunderland flying boat than in a Hastings transport.

Major differences between flying landplanes and flying boats of course stemmed from their operating medium. This came into play during mission planning, sortie execution and aircraft maintenance. For take-off and landing, knowledge of the sea state and the alighting area were vital, as they were ever changing – unlike a runway, the condition of which remained essentially constant. Consideration of sea conditions included wave height, the length, height and direction of any swell, the associated wind strength and direction, and the speed and direction of any tidal flow. Elsewhere I describe the sometimes trying effects of awkward combinations of wind and tidal flow, especially when mooring. I read recently that at RAF Pembroke Dock flying boat base the record for missed approaches to the buoy for mooring stood at thirty-six! Knowledge of the whereabouts of any shallows was important, as were the location and identity of navigation buoys outside the trots and the alighting area; the likelihood of flotsam or jetsam and arrangements to have the area swept; the presence of shipping and other craft; and the direction of dinghies that formed a flare-path for night take-offs and landings. We also needed to know what RAF marine craft would be deployed and the radio calls or the lamp signals we could expect from them, and they from us.

Just as landplane crews had to choose suitable alternative airfields to which to divert in the event of serious technical problems or bad weather, so we as flying boat operators needed similar diversions, only these had to be water based. Unfortunately, there were few active and manned alighting areas and flying boat bases in the Far East compared with airfields – typically those that there were could be five hundred or more miles apart. Points of no Return (PNR) and Critical Points were therefore even more 'critical'. Indeed, we had to keep in mind potentially suitable rivers, estuaries, harbours and other sheltered sea areas where, in an extreme emergency, we might put the aircraft down safely – at least as a temporary measure. For mainly oversea patrolling – our main operational role – a flying boat was nevertheless inherently better placed than a landplane; a flying boat was at least designed to land on water – although in so far as open-sea landings were concerned, there were some significant limitations – as events described in this book show. Hence, while I don't claim that their affinity with the sea somehow made flying boats *better* than landplanes, it introduced a range of new skills and operational aspects that had to be taken into consideration. This further knowledge and these additional considerations brought with them an undeniable sense of achievement and enjoyment to flying boat crews that were denied to their land-based counterparts.

The close relationship of a flying boat crew with the sea began the moment we headed for the aircraft. We didn't walk to it across a tarmac apron, nor were we driven there in an aircrew coach; instead we stepped from a jetty into a motor launch, and when all were aboard and the painter 'let go', the RAF coxswain would open the throttle and the powerful engine would lift the bow as the craft accelerated and headed towards our moored aircraft. The crew, some seated, others standing or sitting on the engine cover amidships, would enjoy the rush of sea air as we sped across the water. If it was choppy, spray would periodically sweep across us, perhaps causing the coxswain to moderate his speed a little. Weaving past other moored aircraft tethered to their orange-coloured buoys, and passing other marine craft – pinnaces, high-speed target-towing launches, bomb scows and 'refuellers' – we would sweep past them towards our aircraft, slowing as we approached it to minimize the wash from the launch's wake. Already, therefore, we had made a connection with the element – the sea – which was so much part of 'being on boats'. Soon, the power of four Pratt & Whitney R-1830 engines and the Sunderland's 157 square metres of wing would lift us majestically into the air, always watched admiringly from ashore by whoever was in sight of the take-off run. Approaching the aircraft from the port quarter, now slowing to walking pace, the crew would scan the airframe for any obvious irregularities, and as we passed beneath the port wing, the pilots and flight engineers would look up at the port engine cowlings for any obvious leaks. We would arrive at the front door of the aircraft, just beneath the first pilot's port window. One of the crew would turn the release handle, allowing the door to open inwards. The captain and crew of ten or eleven, and any passengers, would climb aboard; it was like entering the front door of one's home, glad to be back in familiar surroundings. No other aircraft that I flew in, before or since, had that same welcoming feeling.

Pre-take-off checks would begin straight away, all crew members undertaking various standard or mutually agreed tasks. Some were similar to those on any landplane, but others were not. One, for example, was to raise the aluminium floor boards one by one throughout the length of the aircraft to check that no sea water had leaked into the bilges. Another was to pump sea water into the reservoir of the toilet (or 'heads'), situated in the nose section of the lower deck in a small cabin on the starboard side of the fuselage, opposite the front door.

An important pre-flight task for flying boats was preparation of the aircraft to slip the mooring. This was usually carried out by one (sometimes two) of the air gunners or air signallers. It entailed retracting the nose-gun turret, raising the mooring bollard and locking it into position. What followed was a somewhat complicated process so I shall simplify it in order not to confuse – or bore – the reader. In the bow section of the aircraft, opposite the front door on the lower deck, was a winch which housed the anchor chain. The aircraft's anchor was used only when no mooring buoys were available. At other times the anchor chain was secured to a mooring buoy. This was achieved by attaching the chain by a shackle to two mooring pendants that were connected to another chain that hung vertically beneath the buoy, and securing it to the sea bed. Also separately attached to the two pendants by a shackle was the aircraft's 'stowed' bridle. Shackled to the other end of the stowed bridle was a 'fixed' bridle, which in turn was permanently shackled to a bracket bolted to the aircraft's hull below the waterline. Hence, when moored, the aircraft was secured to the buoy both by the aircraft's anchor chain and by linked bridles. The visible part of a mooring buoy was an orange-coloured rubber sphere contained within a steel hawser harness. This included a hawser loop across the top of the buoy. This hawser loop, which stood about thirty-five centimetres above the buoy, had an important role to play, both when first mooring the aircraft to and just before 'slipping' from the buoy. On the type of buoys laid in the Far East, there was a short steel spike or bracket on top of the buoy. Looped grommets attached to the end of each anchor pendant were hung onto the spike when the buoy was unoccupied. This enabled them to be recovered easily by the bowman, using a boat hook, during the post-flight mooring process.

The process of disconnecting an aircraft from a buoy was complicated; I shall therefore not attempt to describe it in detail. Suffice it to say that the crewmen unmooring the aircraft had to go through some 'gymnastics'. This included opening the navigator's bomb-aiming window in the nose and easing his arms and the top half of his body through the aperture to reach into the sea and manipulate the shackles that linked the fixed and stowed bridles; it was most important to avoiding dropping these into the sea! This operation would take about five minutes to complete and would end with the aircraft being secured to the loop atop the buoy by a length of rope called the 'short slip', now attached to the aircraft's bollard. The stowed bridle would have been disconnected both from the buoy pendants and from the fixed bridle. The free end of the fixed bridle would have been secured by a shackle to a bracket fixed to the aircraft's hull. The aircraft's anchor chain would have been retrieved and wound into the winch housing. The crewman, his hands and arms wet (and in winter, cold) from immersion in the sea, would inform the captain when everything in the nose was ready for slipping the buoy.

The pilots meanwhile continued their internal and external inspections, removing the control lock fork, pitot and static vent covers, and inspecting the control surfaces by climbing onto and walking the length of the upper wing, the fuselage and the tail surfaces – all of which needed care, especially if it was raining. The flight engineers started the auxiliary power unit (APU) in the starboard wing root by first lowering a small platform in the leading edge. They checked that all access doors on the four engine cowlings were properly fastened, that there were no obvious fluid leaks and that the fuel tank caps were secure. Using a long handle they turned over each engine, to lubricate the cylinders before start-up, and completed other pre-flight checks. Similarly, the wireless and radar operators, the air gunners and the navigator(s) would be checking their equipment and completing various other internal fuselage and equipment checks in preparation for engine start and subsequent take-off. All this would probably take fifteen to twenty minutes. Everything now ready, the pilots and one of the flight engineers would start the No. 1 (port) outer engine. The pilots would switch on the ignition and press the pushbutton starter while the flight engineer operated the ignition booster coil and fuel priming pump. Once running, the propeller thrust would cause the aircraft to begin slowly rotating clockwise around the buoy; a flying boat had no hydraulic brakes or chocked wheels to hold it steady – another difference from landplanes. Once No. 1 engine was running smoothly, No. 4 (starboard outer) would be started. When this too was running smoothly, the thrust from its propeller would check the aircraft's rotation around the buoy. One of the flight engineers would then climb through the astrodome hatch to the upper surface of the wing to shut down the APU, closing the leading-edge access platform. Engine rpm were slowly increased to one thousand until the oil temperature reached 40°C. The aircraft was now ready to slip the buoy.

The pilot in the left-hand seat, acting as first pilot (both were first pilot qualified, and normally took it in turns) would use the aircraft's rudder and varying power on the port and starboard engines to manoeuvre the aircraft until it was pointing in a favourable direction to leave the buoy. The first pilot would then order the crewman standing in the nose by the bollard, and usually looking aft towards the pilots' windshield, by intercom and a 'thumbs up' to release the buoy. The bowman would acknowledge and quickly unwind the short slip from the bollard, letting go the buoy and reporting to the captain. The aircraft would begin to move forward under its own power, the buoy passing astern down one side or the other of the hull. The flying boat was now a vessel on the move.

The reader will appreciate that the direction in which the aircraft was pointing when the pilot decided to slip the buoy could be influenced by many considerations. A flying boat pilot couldn't just follow a briefed taxiway, as in a landplane. A flying boat could be moored in trots (an anchorage) among perhaps three to ten other moored aircraft. These would probably have no more than a hundred metres (about three wingspans) between them. The pilot had to consider the effects of wind direction, wind speed, and in some trots the speed and direction of the current. A flying boat always tended to weathercock into the direction from which the wind was blowing (like a wind-vane), and this could not be counteracted by brake application, as on a landplane. Depending on the direction of the wind relative to the aircraft, the rudder, too, might be of limited help. Sea current also could be very tricky to counteract. When moving with the current, aircraft speed relative to other moored aircraft is increased; but if a turn across current is then necessary, the turn radius will be much greater than if no current were present. Much, therefore, depended on the choice of direction in which to manoeuvre and the skilful use of the engines for steering; too much engine power could build up too much speed, again increasing the turning circle and reducing manoeuvrability. Remember, also, that when the aircraft slips the buoy and begins to manoeuvre its way through and out of the trots and into clearer water, it initially has only has two of the four engines running. Hence, throughout the manoeuvring process, simultaneously, the pilots and an engineer will be starting and warming up the two inboard engines. Another consideration is that this process – and that of manoeuvring safely in order to moor to a buoy – had frequently to be undertaken in darkness; these were no floodlights to illuminate the trots.

Whether at anchor or moving across the water a flying boat was a 'vessel' and had to abide by all the rules and practices of sea. Crews had to learn and practise seamanship as well as airmanship. At anchor, flying boats had to display a white mooring light – the crew erected a light-equipped mast on the top of the fuselage before leaving the aircraft after every sortie. Once an aircraft slipped its moorings and began to manoeuvre on the water as I have just described, the crew had to abide by the rules of the sea; fortunately, many were similar to rules of the air, which themselves had, in the early days of aviation, been derived from those of the sea.

In unfamiliar alighting areas or in emergency situations – one of which I shall describe later – we carried a lead-line, marked in fathoms, to measure the sea depth. If, also, we wished to anchor in unfamiliar waters we would need to know whether anchoring was feasible with the amount of chain we had on the aircraft's winch. The aircraft also carried a fog bell; this was stowed in the nose compartment. In some circumstances it could be necessary for the aircraft's crew to mount a boat guard if the weather was very foggy and shipping was nearby. The fog bell would then have to be rung at set intervals as a warning. Crews had to be able to find and manoeuvre their way around alighting areas safely by day and at night, identifying the significance of different buoy types and flashing lights that marked channels or underwater obstructions. In addition, at some of the bases from which we operated – Seletar, for example – merchant ships, aircraft carriers and other warships at times passed up or down the Johore Strait. Similarly, junks, sampans, tankers, freighters, passenger liners and warships were an ever-present danger in Hong Kong harbour, our alighting area when flying from Kai Tak. Flying boat crews had to be sailors as well as airmen.

A Sunderland's engines were never started by servicing personnel alone. It was always necessary to have a skeleton aircraft crew of at least a pilot and three others, including one flight engineer and an air signaller. As soon as an engine was started, the aircraft would not only rotate around the buoy but, though unlikely, it could break away from the mooring. It was essential, therefore, to have a crew on board capable of manoeuvring the aircraft safely on the water. If, as was usual, it was required to run-up the engine to maximum power, this could only be done after slipping the buoy and manoeuvring to the alighting area. Hence, another major difference between landplanes and flying boats was the extent to which the aircraft's aircrew became involved with the serviceability state of the aircraft. Consequently, they came to know many of the fitters and riggers very well.

Once the Sunderland was boarded, its spaciousness and the large numbers of portholes and hatches throughout the length of the aircraft were obvious. In most parts of the aircraft, you could walk upright on metal decking. There were two decks in the Sunderland. The lower started in the nose compartment. This section included the nose-gun turret with its two 0.303 in. Browning machine-guns, the navigator's bomb-aiming window, the Mk 3 low-level bombsight and four forward-firing, fixed 0.303 in. machine-guns that fired through small ports in the side on the fuselage near the nose; finally an anchor and a winch. On the starboard side just aft of the winch was the lavatory, or heads; this had a flushing toilet and washbasin – much more civilized than the chemical Elsan toilet fitted in the Lancaster and Shackleton. The aircraft's main entrance and exit door was at the aft end of the nose section. Walking aft through a small vestibule you then entered the wardroom – sometimes referred to as the officers' wardroom. If it ever was intended only for officers it was never to my knowledge used other than by the whole crew. It was also usually where any passengers normally sat for take-off and landing and ate their meals, prepared in the galley. The wardroom was about 6 ft 6 in. (2.0 m) long by 9 ft 6 in. (2.9 m) wide, with a central gate-legged table and two canvas bunks, one on either side on the table; for most of the time the bunks were used as seats; inflatable mattresses were laid on them for greater comfort and for sleeping. The wardroom had about five portholes on both port and starboard, and so was light and airy.

Passing through a door on the aft wall of the wardroom on the port side, you entered the galley. This also extended across the 10 ft (3.0 m) width of the aircraft, and was equipped with primus stoves and ovens. It was here that, using much imagination and not a little self-taught culinary skill, one or two crew members acting as 'chef' managed to produce many wholesome and appetizing meals and drinks. In the winter, when flying around Korea and Japan, sometimes in sub-zero temperatures in an unheated aircraft, bowls of hot vegetable or meat-flavoured soup and 'ten-tin' stew were life-savers. At other times, a mixed grill or a 'full English' breakfast served at dawn towards the end of a ten- or eleven-hour patrol or transit flight was heaven. In the summer months in Japan or Hong Kong, or at any time of the year in lower latitudes towards and around the Philippines, North Borneo, Singapore, Malaya and Ceylon, fresh salads with cold ham and chicken, followed by fresh or tinned fruit and cream, together with a continual supply of cold water or fruit drinks, made hard work and long working hours a pleasure. Also in the galley, in the port and starboard fuselage walls, were two 3 ft square hatches, hinged at their top edge so that they could be fully opened and latched to the underside of the upper deck, which formed the ceiling of the galley. Below these hatches, inside the fuselage, were semicircular bins, in each of which were stowed a strong canvas drogue, connected by a quarter-inch and immensely strong hawser that was shackled to a strongpoint on the fuselage. These drogues could individually or together be put into the sea through the open hatch. They were frequently, but not always, deployed when entering the trots during the mooring process to slow down or add directional control to the aircraft in the final stages of the approach to the buoy. This will be described later. There was an aural and light signalling system, initiated from the pilots' flight deck, which was used to tell crewmen in the galley when and which drogue(s) should be deployed, and for the galley crewmen to acknowledge.

Continuing aft through a door, you entered the bomb-room. This was where 250 lb depth charges, 20 lb fragmentation or 25 lb practice bombs were suspended on carriers that, for release, ran out to port and starboard on electrically driven trolleys through 7 ft wide apertures left in the fuselage walls when two large bomb-doors were dropped on guidance rails under their own weight. Opening of the bomb-doors was initiated electrically from the pilots' flight deck. Still walking aft, you passed more bunks, to port and starboard. Mounting some steps you were next beside the port and starboard 0.5 in. cannon stations. Hatches, about 3 ft 3 in. (1 m) square, hinged at the top, were opened in flight and latched to the roof of the fuselage. This allowed each of the cannon to be swung out through the apertures, one on each side of the aircraft. The cannon barrels protruded into the slipstream to provide about a 60° arc of fire in azimuth and 120° in elevation. Spent cartridge cases fell at the gunner's feet into a well. Large-capacity ammunition stowage drums were attached to the fuselage walls forward of the guns. Moving aft from these gun stations you could walk all the way to the tail turret, only having to stoop for the last fifteen feet or so. The rotating turret, with its four 0.303 in. Browning machine-guns, had about a 210° field of fire in azimuth and 150° in the vertical plane. Now moving forwards, on the starboard wall you passed the direct reading compass (DRC) master unit and reached a rear access door, infrequently used. Almost opposite it was a small workshop bench, vice and cupboard; the whole of the lower deck was spacious and one could wander around it more of less without getting in anyone's way. If you were not required at your work station or as a look-out, or to assist in the galley, you could rest on one of the bunks. What an enormous contrast to a Lancaster or a Shackleton.

Although there were two further routes from the lower to the upper deck, the most usual was to climb the stairway ladder from the galley to beside the flight engineer's station. Aft from there, through a low door, was an equipment deck on which were mounted various radar and radio equipments and the flap motors. Air-droppable stores could also be placed there in racks. Forward of the flight engineer's station was the main spar. Crossing this was the only mild gymnastics you had to perform to move around the entire aircraft. This brought you forward to the (upper) flight deck. The navigator's station, facing aft, was immediately to starboard. Attached to and forward of the main spar in a central position was a platform (that could be folded away) on which one stood to look out of the astrodome; this could be removed to provide a 1 m square exit from the aircraft to the upper fuselage and upper surfaces of the wings. It was through this hatch that the crew climbed to access the auxiliary power unit (mounted in the starboard wing root). It was used by the pilot to inspect the aircraft control surfaces before flight, and where the air crew gained access to petrol tanks in the wings, for post-flight refuelling from a barge that would come alongside the aircraft.

Inside the fuselage, on the flight deck, the wireless operator's station was on the port side. To starboard, forward of the navigator and facing forwards in a canvas tent, was the ASV Mk VIC search radar station. This was operated by any of the air signallers and by the navigator, to whom it was easily accessible. The central flight deck walkway measured about 2.4 m (8 ft) in length from the main spar to the central throttle pedestal and 0.9 m (3 ft) wide when standing between the wireless operator's and navigator's stations. Either side of the central pedestal were the two pilots' seats, the first pilot to port and the second to starboard. The autopilot was mounted behind the first pilot's seat. Further descriptions, photographs and more detail about the aircraft's equipment are given in the Appendices.

Compared with any other RAF aircraft fulfilling a maritime patrol role in the 1950s, the Sunderland – though not the most modern – was certainly the most spacious and comfortable. It was also almost certainly the best platform for visual search and photography. However, one undoubted drawback in cold climates was the absence of any cabin heating; instead, Sunderland crew members were given electrically heated inner suits. However, as I describe in Chapter 14, due to the inadequacy of the aircraft's electrical system it was inadvisable to use more than four or five suits simultaneously. Instead, when flying from Japan in winter most crewmen wore multiple layers of clothing. In the coldest weather, under my inner flying suit I wore Long Johns and sometimes pyjama trousers as well as uniform trousers. As the navigator, my main problem was cold hands, which I needed for writing and manipulating the sextant and Loran set. I found the best solution was to wear lightweight Cape leather gloves with silk inners. We were also issued with a heavy-duty anorak with a hood, together with white Mukluk flying-boots that had special thermal inner soles.

Following from the internal spaciousness of the aircraft was the sheer pleasure to be gained from the surroundings in which we worked; and for many of our sorties and much of the time, crew members manning active positions (e.g. the wireless operator) were constantly busy. Naturally I am most familiar with the role of the navigator, and for most sorties navigators had relatively few moments of idleness. There were some pilot training sorties, and when, for instance, we were flying around familiar islands, along a coastline, or orbiting and inspecting vessels in the vicinity of Hong Kong or off British North Borneo, during which the navigator's constant presence at the navigation table was unnecessary. On many occasions I had another navigator with me who was 'at the table'. It was then that I could sometimes move around the aircraft, or take a turn as look-out and take photographs from the beam gun hatches, sit in the nose turret, stand behind the pilots looking though the cockpit windows, or chat to other crew members or passengers in the wardroom or galley for a few minutes. It was the wonderful ambience of the Sunderland, together with the added challenges – of which there were many – resulting from operating from the sea or a river, that helped to make being a 'boatman' such a pleasure and such a memorable experience.

Another aspect that gave great pleasure during my two and a half years on Far East Flying Boat Wing was the variety of different types of sorties we were called on the fly. Some, like those around Korea and the Yellow Sea, and Firedog operations over the Malayan jungle, or searching for smugglers and pirates between the Philippines and Sabah, were serious affairs; others were not so serious, such as arranging our own training flying when based on SAR standby at Hong Kong, when we might land on the sea in a sheltered area near islands south of Victoria, drop the anchor and go for a swim. But on all types of sorties, it was the sheer pleasure of flying them in such a pleasant and prestigious aircraft that was a constant source of joy. The weather in the Far East over the sea in the daytime was very often sunny with fair-weather cumulus to fly under or around. When flying beneath it, the radar might detect light rain falling from an isolated, distant cloud – or was it a shoal of fish? Either could momentarily fool the operator into wondering whether he had detected a small vessel on the sea surface. At higher altitudes, when cruising at five or even nine thousand feet, the visibility was often almost unlimited.

By contrast, you could suddenly come across a really severe thunderstorm or – more often at night when flying from Singapore to Hong Kong – a line of turbulent, cumulonimbus clouds barring your way. You would look on the ASV radar for gaps or passages of less dense cloud; whether or not you were successful in this you had to pick a course and 'bite the bullet'. The pilot would enter the densely black cloud at the aircraft's best speed and prepare to be tossed around. Sometimes, amid flashes of lightning, a glance at the altimeter at my navigation station would confirm the feeling in my stomach that we were suddenly descending rapidly, while the pilot, flying on his primary instruments, maintained the aircraft's attitude relative to the artificial horizon. A few minutes later we might enter a strong updraft and regain all the height we had lost a few minutes earlier. Despite this, I always felt extremely confident in the capabilities of the Sunderland to withstand whatever was thrown at it by way of bad weather. Many of our pilots were young and on their first squadron tour; nearly all were on their first Sunderland tour. Few had hundreds or thousands of Sunderland hours' experience to fall back on. Nevertheless, I thought the standard of piloting and airmanship throughout my tour was very high. While not unknown, it was very rare for a non-pilot to express concern about a pilot's skill or airmanship performance. But whether flying conditions were good or poor, the ambience of a flying boat as a vehicle for going about one's daily or nightly business was unbeatable. The Archimedes principle and the laws of fluid dynamics were certain to dictate that a long-endurance ten-man flying boat weighing 60,000 lb would be of a certain length, broad of beam and hence roomy.

At the end of each sortie, following touch-down, the crew would revert to becoming sailors. Once more the rules of the sea and seamanship came into play. Mooring a Sunderland could be much trickier that slipping the buoy. Once the crew had 'caught' the buoy, mooring the aircraft securely was not generally a problem. The crewmen in the bow – ignoring a few details – more or less followed the slipping procedure in the reverse order. Certainly, the task of the two bowmen at the time when the aircraft had approached right up to the buoy was crucial; would they be able to pass the short slip through the hawser loop above the buoy and get a couple of turns of the short slip around the bollard before the aircraft's continuing movement had pulled the short slip out of their hands? The more difficult task was that of the pilot. This is why.

Much depended on the combination of sea, wind and tidal conditions. It could also depend on the amount of space available for the pilot to manoeuvre the flying boat safely within the trots. How many other aircraft were there to avoid? What choice of buoys was there available? In which directions and at what speeds were the wind and tide? In a landplane, after touching down and clearing the runway, if you really felt like it you could abandon the aircraft on the taxiway and ask the ground crew to tow it back to the dispersal! You wouldn't even have to leave any aircraft crewmen on board. You certainly couldn't do that with a flying boat, no matter how much you felt you would like to when faced with difficult mooring conditions. This was when knowledge of seamanship and your skill at aircraft handling, and making the right decisions and giving the right orders at the right time, would count. To a slightly lesser extent it depended also on the skill of other members of the crew who on that day were manning the drogues in the galley, and on the agility and determination of the crewmen in the bow of the aircraft.

The ideal situation for entering the trots and mooring to a buoy at the first attempt, especially where there was a tidal flow of perhaps 2–4 kts to contend with, was to have a high degree of freedom in the direction in which to enter the trots and approach the selected mooring buoy. Preferably, there should be no other aircraft moored in the immediate vicinity, and certainly not in the preferred approach path. Anything less than this ideal would pose greater difficulties to the flying boat crew. The degree of difficulty would depend on the number and combination of unfavourable factors, piled one upon the other. The best situation, in addition to freedom in the approach direction and few other aircraft moored nearby was to have a surface wind speed in the trots of 10–15 kts, with its direction the same as the tidal flow. So if the tide was flowing from north-west to south-east we would wish for a north-west wind, or a direction fairly close to it. This would mean that ideally we would approach the buoy on a north-west heading. With engines at near idle and advancing into both a 2–4 kt current and a 10–15 kt wind, forward movement towards the buoy could be maintained at a very slow speed. It would probably be unnecessary to deploy the sea drogues through the port and starboard galley hatches. The pilot would have good directional control using aerodynamic forces coming from the rudder, and corrective asymmetric bursts of engine power to achieve even more directional control would be possible without fear of creating excessive speed towards the buoy.

Now consider the situation if a 10–15 kt wind was blowing from the north-west but the tide had now turned and the sea or river current was flowing from south-east to north-west. The pilot would prefer to approach into a fair to moderate breeze, to aid rudder control and gain other aerodynamic benefits from the headwind; but unfortunately the aircraft's approach speed towards the buoy would be greater by at least 4 kts because the water in which the aircraft was floating would now be moving towards rather than away from the buoy. To add to the pilot's dilemma, if he ordered deployment of the drogues these would probably either have no significant beneficial effect or might possibly make matters worse. They might not fully deploy if the following current was 4 kts, or could be less effective in assisting directional control when the pilot used differential engine thrusts. If an approach in this direction proved unsuccessful, the pilot might attempt a downwind approach in order to head into the sea or river current. In this case early use of both sea drogues would be essential. The pilot's main problem would be lack of rudder control and the aircraft's tendency to weathercock into wind. Directional control would have to be mainly by differential engine power, and unless the pilot was lucky or extremely skilful, this might increase the aircraft's speed towards the buoy to such an extent that the bowmen would be unable to 'catch' the buoy using the short slip.

An alternative, if the downwind approach proved unsuccessful would be to approach the buoy on a northerly heading with the north-west wind on the port bow. The tendency would be for the aircraft to want to weathercock to port (left). To check this, the pilot would be advised early in the approach to deploy the starboard (right) sea drogue. This would tend to act against the wind's tendency to pull the aircraft's nose to port and reduce the amount of port engine thrust required to hold a steady direction. This is turn would result is less aircraft speed through the water. Now that the aircraft was steering across the current, its movement towards the buoy due to the speed of the current would be reduced by about one-third compared with the previous down-current direction of approach. All would depend on how little engine power the pilot could get away with using, and how skilful he was in judging a crabwise approach towards the buoy. The aircraft's speed when it came up to the buoy would be critical. I have chosen to suggest an approach towards the buoy with port drift. This was because the crew in the bow could only erect a ladder on the outer side of the aircraft's nose on the port side. One of the two men in the bow would stand on the bottom rung, leaning forward over the water, hanging onto the aircraft with his right hand, in order to get the end on the short slip through the hawser loop atop the buoy as soon and as quickly as possible. This would give the other crewman the best chance to grab the end of the short slip from his colleague and make a couple of turns around the bollard before it was too late. This would be much easier if the aircraft reached the buoy with it on the left side of the aircraft's nose rather than on the right. Meanwhile, the crewman on the

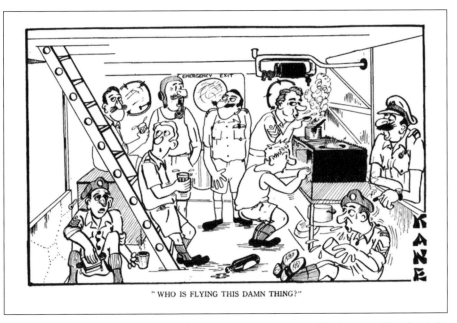

" WHO IS FLYING THIS DAMN THING?"

This cartoon, showing most members of a ten-man crew congregated in the aircraft's galley, is by 'Kane', formerly a ground-crew member of the FEFBW. Some of the characters depicted are easily recognisable to those who were on the squadron at the time!

ladder would have to scramble quickly up the ladder and into the aircraft to avoid his legs being trapped by the short-slip now attached and looped through the buoy.

I hope this has given the reader an impression of some of the main differences between operating flying boats and landplanes. Two major differences I have not discussed in this chapter are covered in Appendix 2. These relate to take-off and landing (or 'alighting') techniques, by day and at night. I hope, therefore, that I have given sufficient examples to show why those who flew 'boats' were so attached to them and why they gained so much satisfaction from the skills and knowledge that operating from the water demanded. They became sailors as well as airmen. Operating flying boats in the Far East was especially attractive because, in the lower latitudes, apart from localized tropical storms, the weather was usually fair or nearly idyllic. The spaciousness of the Sunderland with its two decks, many portholes and open hatches, made it an ideal viewing and photographic reconnaissance platform. Of course, flying in the depths of winter on Korean operations from Iwakuni over the Inland Sea, the Shimonoseki Strait and the Yellow Sea often placed heavy demands on Sunderland crews. This was both operationally and in terms of the kinds of weather they had to fly through day and night for periods of nine to twelve hours of more. It

Two crewmen preparing food in the galley. *Bill Whiter*

En Garde. A lookout at the open starboard
0.5 cannon hatch. *William Devine*

Manning the 0.5-inch cannon in the starboard beam hatch of the Sunderland. There was a second cannon on the port side. The ammunition belt can be seen being fed into the gun from its storage can forward of the hatchway. This gun had a hefty punch and a rapid rate of fire. *Courtesy RAFSA*

Two crewmen in the bow, one on the ladder leaning forward and about to pass the short slip through the hawser loop on top of the buoy. The crewman on the right will then grasp it and make several turns around the bollard. Notice that the pilot has steered the aircraft so that the buoy is just to the left of the aircraft's bow. *Bill Whiter*

After each sortie, Sunderland flying boats were refuelled by the aircrew, seen here with hoses from a refuelling barge, moored alongside the starboard side of the fuselage. Sgt Vic Kapl, air gunner and the crew's chief 'chef', is standing nearest to the camera. Sgt John Land, flight engineer, is farther away but facing in the same direction. *Author*

The trots and alighting area at RAF Seletar. On the day of the Queen's Birthday Flypast in June 1953, no fewer than thirteen Sunderlands were moored in the trots. Between eight and ten was a more usual number, taking into account permanent detachments at Iwakuni and Kai Tak. In this picture, an aircraft carrier, possibly HMS *Glory*, is seen steaming past the alighting area. *Author*

RAF Marine Craft moored alongside the pier at Seletar. The aircraft hangars can be seen in the background with FEFBW Headquarters offices in front of the right-hand hangar. *Tony Feist*

A rare sighting of a Royal Navy cruiser near Singapore probably HMS *Newfoundland.Bill Wilson*

is to the credit of RAF Sunderland crews that hardly any sorties were aborted due to weather. Engine failure was the most usual reason for the few 'early returns', but these were few and far between – except in my case in December 1953. The Sunderland, designed in the mid-1930s was not well equipped to combat moderate or severe icing. Because of this, in winter crews usually chose to fly below cloud to avoid the worst icing conditions. This placed added demands on crew navigation skills and teamwork because there was much high ground to be avoided around Korea, over Japan and along the route from and to Iwakuni through the Inland Sea.

As AVM Chesworth says in his Foreword, there has always been a certain 'mystique' surrounding those relatively few RAF aircrew fortunate enough to have operated flying boats. I hope this chapter, when read in conjunction with the others and the Appendices, will enable readers to understand why flying boat crews took great pride in being 'boatmen'.

Note

1. On each FEFBW squadron, five crews of ten or eleven individuals, each member identified by name, were formed, usually for periods of three to six months. Throughout the RAF, these are commonly referred to as 'constituted' crews. Because all RAF postings are and were made on an individual basis, within the three- to six-month period there would have to be occasional replacements of individuals when they reached the end of their overseas tours, and sometimes for other reasons. On FEFBW squadrons, each constituted crew was known by the letter of the particular aircraft (e.g. Charlie) that had been allotted to its care. Their flying pattern would therefore be determined to a significant extent by the maintenance (or servicing) cycle of that particular aircraft.

Chapter Seven

The Queen's Birthday Flypast, June 1953

After leaving Kai Tak at the end of the May 1953 detachment, we headed south to Seletar on the last day of the month. On 6 June at Seletar – four days after the Queen's Coronation – we flew RN302 'C' with David Cooke as captain in a formation of twelve Sunderlands in a *Queen's Birthday Flypast*. Indeed, it was the *first* Queen's Birthday Flypast. We flew around Singapore Island, passing over the RAF bases, the naval base, the city and its famous harbour. As reflected by reports and photographs in the *Straits Times* the next day, it was an impressive sight, just as we too had thought it when seen from the air. Having completed the flypast, the twelve aircraft headed for Seletar while slowly changing formation from 'Vics' to line astern.

Pilots spaced their aircraft about two hundred yards behind the one in front while slowly descending from our original height of about fifteen hundred feet. We flew northwards and then over the Malay Peninsula, gradually wheeling left to approach Seletar from the north-east. By the time we reached the Johore Strait we were down to 200 feet and still descending. We soon crossed the northern shoreline of Singapore Island and the boundary of Seletar airfield, by now down to less than 100 feet, heading directly towards the officers' mess about half a mile distant. It was lunchtime, and the day's work had ended for most officers on the station, including aircrews of 81 PR Mosquito Squadron who had flown earlier in the day. There was a large gathering on the mess veranda in anticipation of the return of the wing of flying boats. Pints of Tiger in hand, they looked towards the eleven 'white birds' approaching ever closer to near to zero feet. One closely behind another, they bore down on the officers' mess until, shortly before reaching it, the throttles were pushed forward to full power, each Sunderland passing low over the mess roof and climbing, while gently wheeling to the left. On the downwind leg aircraft turned crosswind at thirty-second intervals for a 'stream landing' on the Johore Strait.

That evening after nightfall, three Sunderlands, fitted with floodlights to illuminate the white underside of the wings, fuselage and tailfin, flew over

This shows the typical conditions under which fitters had to service Sunderland engines, on the water, in sun or rain. *'Bob', courtesy RAFSA*

Singapore city and dropped flares and fired Very cartridges over the harbour. The local radio and *Straits Times* described these as 'great white dragons'. It was a memorable Queen's Birthday, one of many that would follow.

The flypast excitement over, I took ten days' leave while I was still at Seletar. This enabled me to investigate more of the island and the city of Singapore that I had not had much opportunity to see before. I played squash almost every day – on the squash court the heat and humidity soon removed great chunks of skin from the soles of my feet! Much time was spent at the open-air swimming-pool on the base. I also took the opportunity to hire some clubs and try my hand at golf on the course that was laid out around the airfield; it was enjoyable but the results were less than encouraging! Apart from two weeks' leave we had taken in the UK during

Approaching the buoy in ideal conditions, in the face of about a 10–15 kt breeze. *Bill Whiter, courtesy RAFSA*

our prolonged ferry flight, described in Chapter 2, this was the first break I had taken since joining the squadron in June 1952.

On return to duty on 22 June, our crew had a temporary change of captain when F/L Les Tester took charge. Between 23 and 26 June we flew a series of air tests and loop swings in RN302, which, since the flypast, had been up-slip for routine second-line servicing. On 29 June we did some practice instrument flying (IF) for the benefit of the two pilots, who had to complete a certain number of hours' IF every month as part of their training

An RAF Marine Branch tender approaches with Sunderland Whiskey moored on the next buoy in the trots at RAF Seletar. Masts of the RAF Signals Unit communication station can be seen in the distance. *'Bob', courtesy RAFSA*

Sunderland DP198, an aircraft manufactured by Short Bros Ltd, Windermere, escorted by two Lincoln bombers. *Bill Whiter*

schedule. We also practised locating and homing onto ships using our ASV radar, and completed a nine-hour navigation exercise that also included open-sea bombing and air-to-sea gunnery.

An incident that had also occurred on 29 June 1953 involved another 88 Squadron crew who were at Iwakuni. Their aircraft, SZ599 (Fox) – the one F/O George Chesworth and our crew had flown from the UK to Singapore – had taken off from Iwakuni on a Korean War patrol. On the outbound transit to the patrol area, one of the crew members, F/Sgt Dixon, had fitted and was about to load ammunition into the two 0.303 in. Browning machine-guns in the nose turret when (according to the 88 Squadron History Book) a five-foot snake reared its ugly head inside the front turret, and in a flash F/Sgt Dixon was fitting guns to the rear turret! It was left to F/Sgt Ruddick to 'batter the reptile into insensibility'. At the end of their nine-hour patrol, the snake was taken ashore to sick quarters, where they were surprised when the medical officer pronounced it as still living. It was a rat snake, a class that normally lives on land, but due to recent excessively heavy rains over Iwakuni it had been washed out to sea and climbed up the mooring chain. The 88 Squadron History diarist remarked, 'What a cheek to board a Sunderland'; but perhaps it really wasn't so surprising, because the official badge of No. 88 Squadron depicts a snake! This incident reminded me of when, after similar heavy rains at Iwakuni, another crew member and I were in the bow section of our aircraft after landing, and having just secured the aircraft to the buoy we saw a long snake swimming towards us. We poked it with a boat hook but were horrified when it tried to clamber up the boat hook into the aircraft. We quickly shook it off and closed the turret.

Chapter Eight

Penang and Ceylon

A flying boat alighting area I have not so far mentioned was at Glugor on Penang Island (Pulau Penang). This was off the west coast of the Malay Peninsula near Butterworth, where there was an RAF airfield. We landed at Glugor relatively infrequently. My first visit was on 30/31 July 1953. Three 88 Squadron Sunderlands, A–Able, captain F/L Les Tester, F–Fox, captain F/O Len Stapleton and our crew in C–Charlie, captain F/L David Cooke, were to fly to Ceylon. We broke our journey at Glugor. My friend Stuart Holmes has reminded me that we were accommodated in Minden Barracks, on the island, then the home of the Manchester Regiment. Flying boats stopping at Glugor were assisted and provided with fuel by a small RAF Marine Craft Unit (MCU), later designated 1125 MCU. Their craft carried out all the usual seaborne duties for visiting Sunderlands of the FEFBW. Glugor was a weather diversion and an occasional refuelling stop as well as being a base for armament practice camps (APCs).

The MCU also supported and ferried RAF range control staff, detached from RAF Butterworth, to Song Song Bombing and Gunnery Range on Bidan Island, 17 nm to the north and five miles off the coast of Malaya. According to Brian Banks, a former ATC assistant who worked there in 1957, a few airmen made twice-weekly trips to Bidan to operate the range. They usually stayed there for a couple of nights, living in sparse accommodation – two huts within a wired-off compound just above the high-water mark. The sea was too shallow for the launch to take them to the beach, so a rowing boat was moored there for that purpose. On awaking each morning they would have a dip in the sea and decide whose turn it was to make breakfast. Among various duties they operated the VHF communications and triangulation equipment on Bidan and another nearby island, Telor. This equipment measured the accuracy of bombs and rockets dropped on or fired at a fixed target moored out at sea midway between the islands. Armament practice camps took place regularly for air-to-surface weapon drops and firing, mostly by aircraft from the RAF airfields at

Butterworth and Tengah. In 1952–4 my recollection is that, rather than using Song Song Range, the MCU more often towed targets at sea in a cleared weapons area in which Sunderlands were cleared to drop sticks of practice bombs, and to carry out practice air-to-sea gunnery on towed targets; but I could be mistaken.

In travel brochures, Penang is often referred to as the 'Pearl of the Orient'. It has always been an attraction to tourists. There are many inviting beaches, such as Batu Ferringhi, especially in the north of the island. On the east coast, not far from Glugor, is historic Georgetown, the oldest British colony in the Far East, dating back to 1786. Rather like Singapore, Georgetown is now a mixture of towering skyscrapers co-existing with kampong villages. In the 1950s there was, and there may still be, a bustling Chinatown district of Georgetown. Nature lovers can visit the famous botanical gardens there.

RAF Glugor was two and a half hours' flying time by Sunderland from Singapore. When we arrived there from Seletar on 30 July 1953, we were on our way to Ceylon to help to celebrate Ceylon Air Force Day. Because strong headwinds across the Indian Ocean were forecast for the next several days, 88 Squadron decided its three aircraft should depart Seletar a day early and stop overnight at Glugor to refuel, stay overnight and shorten the following day's flight. Our three aircraft flew independently to Glugor. Our captain, David Cooke, agreed to my request to carry out an airborne 'loop swing' over a small island to the south-east of Penang. I wanted to calibrate the accuracy of our loop antenna and prepare a new correction card before navigating the 700-mile crossing of the Bay of Bengal. During the transit flight from Seletar we flew low along the Malayan coastline, often at a couple of hundred feet or lower. We rarely reconnoitred this coastline, and took the opportunity to take in the scenery. On reaching the Penang area, I located the small island I was looking for, and initiated the loop swing, completing it in about twenty minutes. We landed on the sea at RAF Glugor after 4 hrs 20 min. We refuelled the aircraft from a refuelling barge which came alongside our starboard bow in the usual way. We then went ashore, and at about three o'clock a few of us left Glugor by taxi to do some sight-seeing around Penang island.

Dave Cooke and I first visited the famous Snake Temple, founded in honour of a Chinese monk, where green vipers, supposedly harmless, can be seen crawling over the walls. I have recently been told by David Croft (RAF Seletar Association Archivist) that there are two theories concerning these vipers. One is that their fangs have been drawn; the other is that they are rendered into a dozy state by the intensity of the incense. In any case these are said not to be a very dangerous strain of viper. We went on to see typical British colonial architecture at Fort Cornwallis, the site of the original landing by the Royal Navy in July 1786. Other places of local interest that unfortunately there wasn't time to see included the Penang Bird Park and the beautiful Kek Lok Si Temple with its amazing Kuan Yin Buddha, the 'Goddess of Mercy'. This towers over the temple and is the largest Buddhist temple in Malaysia. Any readers visiting this part of the Malay Peninsula would find a day or so on Penang Island well worthwhile.

Above Georgetown at a height of 2,500 feet is Penang Hill. This is really a collection of hills from the top of which you have a panoramic view of Georgetown and across the strait to the mainland of Malaya. Penang Hill has long been a place for holidaying; this is partly because it is cooled somewhat by a combination of the altitude and a steady breeze. The hill top is reached via a quaint single-track funicular railway with passing-places. Construction began in 1906 and was not fully completed until 1923. The 'carriages' are said in recent times to have been modernized, but basically it is the same railway that was conceived a hundred years ago. Apart from a rough 'jeep' track, it remains the only means of regular access to the top of Penang Hill. In the 1950s Penang was completely separated from the Malayan mainland except for a ferry; however, in 1985 an eight-mile oversea bridge was completed, connecting Penang to the mainland.

After an overnight stop at Glugor all three Sunderlands departed for Ceylon on 31 July. We in C-Charlie took off at 07.15 hrs. After passing Pulau We and the northern tip of Sumatra to port, we set off to cross the Indian Ocean, or that part of it called the Bay of Bengal. As on previous occasions I first obtained a long-distance running MF loop fix on Car Nicobar beacon to the north of us. This was followed by about six hours of taking sun sights with the sextant, accuracy checks of our magnetic compasses and frequent drift taking. In a 20–25 kt wind coming from a generally westerly direction, it was important to keep a constant check on its direction and drift angle, otherwise you could soon be blown several miles off track. As there was little or no low cloud beneath us as we cruised at about 4,500 feet, with so many 'white horses' on the sea surface, drift taking was easy. We reached China Bay in 9 hrs 30 min, an average groundspeed of only 116 kts.

After a day's rest, on the afternoon of 2 August 1953 we were to fly to the south-west coast of Ceylon. Another Sunderland, N-Nan of 205 Squadron, captained by F/O George Chesworth, had also deployed to China Bay from Seletar. That afternoon the weather was fine, and after taking off from China Bay all four aircraft flew in loose formation towards Colombo on the south-west coast of Ceylon. Shortly after arrival near our destination, we formed up into a box formation and at the appropriate time made several low-level flypasts over Ratmalana airfield, where the celebrations were centred. This was then the international airport for the capital, Colombo, and the airfield where the Ceylon Air Force had a base. Ratmalana was the staging airport for a daily BOAC Comet service to London. The display and flypast were to mark and celebrate the anniversary of the formation of the Ceylon Air Force.[1] Today at Ratmalana the Sri Lanka Air Force (SLAF) operates C-130 and AN-32 medium transports and a few Harbin Y-12 twin-turboprop light utility aircraft.

After completing the afternoon flypast we retired from the area to kill time and wait for nightfall. Once it was reasonably dark we switched on all the lights we could muster and re-formed into a not-too-close formation, including of course the 205 Squadron aircraft flown by George Chesworth. It was rare for Sunderland pilots to fly in close formation, especially at night. However, our aircraft were so well illuminated by floodlights fixed to the bomb racks that seeing the other aircraft wasn't really a problem. Indeed, a story is told that on this particular night formation, Sunderland A-Able was at one point flying so close to the 205 Squadron aircraft, N-Nan, that two SNCOs standing in the open port beam gun hatch were seen with a boat hook ready to fend off A-Able!

We overflew Colombo harbour also dropping 1.7 in. flares and firing off Very pistol cartridges as fast as we could. Flypast completed, we climbed and flew diagonally across Ceylon on a fine, starlit night until the lights of Trincomalee on the north-east coast eventually came into view. Before preparing to land, we switched our 'illuminations' on again and fired more pyrotechnics and Very cartridges as we flew over Trincomalee and China Bay, much to the enjoyment of a Royal Navy contingent we knew would be watching, whom we wanted to impress. The 'show' over, we invited George Chesworth to land first, on the understanding that he and his crew would set up a bar in the sick quarters building that served as a mess. It was the first time most of us had landed at night on the China Bay alighting area, but providing the flare-path of illuminated dinghies was well positioned it ought to be perfectly straightforward (readers unfamiliar with flying boat operating techniques may at some point wish to read about these in Appendix 2). As we expected, all went smoothly. Eventually, we were taken ashore, and after a quick wash and change we made our way the mess. There we saw that, aided by the commanding officer of RAF China Bay, F/L (Happy) H.P. Williams MBE DFC, George Chesworth and his crew had wasted no time in setting up a more-than-adequate bar. We settled down to do justice to it and to the food that had been prepared by the staff. By now it must have been close to eleven o'clock, but thereafter we enjoyed several more hours in company with the many outside guests whom the CO had invited, including a party from the Royal Navy.

Thankfully, we had the next day to recover from the evening's activities. On 4 August, all four aircraft took off shortly after daybreak and – now

A view of RAF Glugor in 1953. *Courtesy RAF Butterworth and Penang Association*

benefiting from strong tailwinds – flew the 1,448 nm across the Indian Ocean and down the Malacca Strait to Singapore in only 9 hrs 15 min, an average speed of 156 kts – quick for a Sunderland. As readers will have gathered, when aircraft cruised at still air speeds as low as 125 kts, a 30 kt headwind or tailwind could significantly lengthen or shorten any long-distance journey.

Note
1. Ceylon had been given its independence from Britain in 1948.

Chapter Nine

Operations around British North Borneo

By 1954 we were increasingly called upon to deploy to Sabah – then the British colony of North Borneo – to search for pirates and smugglers. We operated mainly from Sandakan, which is at the very north of the island. We also periodically called into Kuching and Jessleton, on the north-west coast. In addition, we occasionally landed at Tawau and Lahad Datu. These were both located on the south-east coast of Sabah. While Kuching and Jessleton were then small towns, Lahad Datu and Tawau were closer to being villages. They had all suffered terribly under Japanese occupation during the Second World War, and were finally liberated by the Australian Division in June 1945 after three and a half years' occupation. One of the British district officers, Mr Cole Adam, arrested and removed from Borneo by the Japanese, died in a prison camp in September 1945 on the very day of his release by Allied forces[1] after 44 months in captivity. Small towns and villages on the south-east coast were mainly agricultural centres prospering from rubber and hemp; Tawau was an important centre for tuna fishing.

All these towns in Sabah, now part of newly formed Malaysia, have been built up into thriving commercial and tourist centres. Indeed, Tawau province is the world's third-largest producer of cocoa, after the Ivory Coast and Ghana, and prawn farming is another of Tawau's main industries; it operates hundreds of trawlers. In 1953/4, Sunderland crews were increasingly deployed there to reconnoitre the sea areas and islands to the east of Borneo in co-operation with the police, who patrolled aboard motor launches. They, with our help, were trying to deter, locate and catch smugglers – entering Sabah from the Philippines – and pirates who boarded vessels transiting sea areas between North Borneo and Mindanao. The Sunderland's task was hampered by no direct VHF radio communication with the police launches; moreover, the police were not able to read messages sent in Morse code by our Aldis signalling lamps. Hence, when we found a boat we thought suspicious we had difficulty in quickly directing the police towards it. We were forced to return to the police launch, fly close beside it, then turn and head in the direction we wanted them to follow. I remember we once even considered writing a message on a sheet of paper, placing it in a bottle and dropping it into the sea beside the launch – we may even have done so!

In Sandakan, we were accommodated in the Sabah Hotel. This was located at the top of a hill to the south of the town. It is still there but, today, is a much modernized hotel compared with when we stayed there in the early 1950s. Sandakan had been the capital of British North Borneo at the outbreak of the Second World War. By the end of the war it had been very badly damaged by a combination of Allied bombing and action by the Japanese. As a result, North Borneo was made a British colony, and Jessleton (now renamed Kota Kinabalu) was named the capital. Sandakan is now the *second*-most important city in Sabah. It and the surrounding district nevertheless have a population of over 400,000 and it is one of the busiest and most modern towns in the country. When I visited it in 1953/4, it was no more than a small, developing town. Today, Kampung Buli Sim Sim, a small stilted village, apparently provides the only remaining vestige of 'old' Sandakan.

During one of our detachments to Sandakan we decided to go to a local dance. The dance-hall was a long wooden building with a thatched roof. It soon became obvious that young Europeans were seldom seen there and that many of the locals spoke little or no English. Most girls were chaperoned by their mothers or other older ladies. The girls with their chaperones sat on chairs around the dance floor waiting to be asked to dance. After a while we decided it would be courteous to leave because we felt our presence was not much appreciated by some who were obviously seeking more permanent partners.

When deploying to Sandakan we always called first at Labuan, an island on the west coast where there was a flying boat alighting area, an airfield and a small RAF unit. There was a regular shuttle from Changi by RAF Hastings and Valetta transport aircraft, to deliver supplies and spare parts, and move people from or back to Singapore. As Labuan was the only Borneo base where we normally refuelled, we always called there before flying on to one of the other alighting areas, either Sandakan or less frequently Kuching or Jessleton. Sometimes we would stop overnight at Labuan, where we were accommodated in the rather grand-sounding but actually very modest Airport Hotel. More than once we had to sleep in the hotel's annexe. This was a 'basher hut' and a real hell-hole, swarming with mosquitoes. When retiring, it was advisable to seek out and kill the many mosquitoes that would already have found their way inside your bed net. This wasn't easy because at night, the only electric light – powered by a generator well within earshot – couldn't have been more than 25 watts. Since the net itself usually had sizeable holes poked into it, despite your best efforts you were likely to have been well and truly bitten by morning.

A VIP tour of Sabah takes an unexpected turn

An unusual series of events occurred at the end of August 1954. Our crew flew in our own 88 Squadron aircraft RN293 ('F'), but for this trip the aircraft captain was F/L Alec Rawling, the Flying Boat Wing training pilot. On 25 August, we took off from Seletar and headed for Labuan. On the way, over the open sea, having first released a smoke marker as an aiming point, I aimed and released a fully armed 250 lb depth charge. It was only the second time I had been given the opportunity to drop a depth charge, although we had carried live DCs on every Korean sortie flown from Iwakuni. We felt a shock wave from the explosion as a huge fountain of sea water was thrown into the air. We landed at Labuan.

Later the same day we flew to Sandakan and checked into the Sabah Hotel. The next day we carried out some practice bombing; we must have carried the bombs in boxes with us from Seletar. We then flew for a further three hours on an anti-piracy patrol between Sabah and islands to the south and south-west of Mindanao. We assisted armed Borneo police in a fast motor launch, but were again hampered by not having radio communication with them. Our task was to search for suspicious craft and direct the police towards them so that they could board and inspect them. On the 27th we ferried the chief of police from Sandakan to Tawao. In March 1953, while I had been ferrying SZ599 from the UK to Seletar, there had been a major fire in Tawao that had destroyed much of the small town. Sunderlands of the FEFBW immediately answered a call for assistance, and rushed food, medical supplies and other necessities to the town.

After stopping for a short while at Tawau, we took off and flew the police chief to Lahad Datu where we disembarked for lunch. In the afternoon we flew our passengers first to Sandakan and then to Jesselton; the chief of police thanked us, and we took off for Labuan to refuel and stay overnight in the mosquito-ridden Airport Hotel annexe. On 29 August, we first flew to Sandakan, and there collected two Members of Parliament from Westminster (one Labour and one Conservative) who were on a 'fact-finding tour' of British North Borneo. We ferried them, with the Resident, to Tawau, later bringing them back to Sandakan. For some reason I cannot now recall, the captain decided we should refuel at Sandakan rather than at Labuan. This was very unusual – indeed, at first I thought it wasn't possible. Anyway, refuel we did, but it was a hair-raising experience because the coxswain of a most unsuitable-looking refuelling boat that came alongside had clearly never been asked to refuel a flying boat before. It took my mind back to the scary refuelling we had experienced at the French naval base at Cat Lai on a previous occasion. Somehow our aircraft came away unscathed, and we prepared to continue our tour the following day.

Labuan Airport Hotel in 1954. *Author*

We then again flew the MPs on their 'junket' to various locations around British North Borneo, and on the morning of the 31st returned, via Jesselton, to refuel at our usual port of call, Labuan. While we were having an early lunch at Labuan Airport Hotel we received a telephone call asking if we could help five people on board a 10-ton motor launch belonging to Liddell Bros & Co. (Sarawak) Ltd, a timber company. The boat had been missing for three days and had just been spotted out at sea by an aircraft owned by the Shell oil company that had just landed at Labuan. In case those on the stranded boat should require medical attention we telephoned

An RAF Hastings from Changi having landed at Labuan. *Author*

The control tower at Labuan airfield in 1954. *Author*

a local doctor, who somewhat hesitatingly agreed to come with us. Taken by motor boat out to RN293 ('F'), we started the engines and quickly took off from Labuan harbour. At 1.25 p.m., we located the launch – about thirty-five feet in length – and after a careful inspection of the sea state, Alec Rawling decided it was safe to land. After an uneventful touch-down we taxied towards the launch and hove to alongside. We were on the South China Sea, thirty-eight nautical miles west of Labuan Island.

The four local forestry workers and a European aboard the boat, the engine of which had broken down, had a little water left but no food. They said they did not need any medical attention. We gave them water and food, transferring it in an inflatable rubber dinghy that we carried in our aircraft. As no one gave us any indication by radio as to when the police or Coast Guard would meet us, after about thirty minutes, and using the dinghy to help us, we finally managed, after a considerable struggle, to get a strong towline to the boat, secured to our aircraft through the starboard rear door. Using at first two and then all four engines, we began to tow the boat towards Labuan on a course of about 090°, while awaiting developments. About three hours later we sighted a launch in the distance, but it never came closer than a mile or two and didn't respond to our Aldis lamp

Preparing to refuel at Sandakan for the first time. L to R: Sgt Griffiths (engineer), the author (navigator) and F/O Colin Sharpe (co-pilot) seemingly holding on precariously to the refuelling boat. *Author – 88 Squadron History Book, courtesy RAF Museum Reserve Collection*

A difficult refuelling; trying to position and secure the refuelling boat safely. Sgt Holliday (signaller), F/L Alec Rawling with the cap (pilot and captain) and the author in the bow of the aircraft. *Author – 88 Squadron History Book, courtesy RAF Museum Reserve Collection*

The 35 ft launch with a broken engine 38 nm west of Labuan with five crew on board. Three of the crew of 88 Squadron aircraft RN293 securing a towline from the aircraft to the launch. *Author – 88 Squadron History Book, courtesy RAF Museum Reserve Collection*

signalling. We decided to continue in the direction of Labuan, passing through rain squalls and at times choppy seas as we did so. The doctor by this time was sea-sick. He received medical attention in the form of sympathy and sick-bags. We then ran into another very squally period, the wind strengthening considerably and blowing from an awkward direction that made it difficult to maintain our course towards Labuan because the aircraft kept trying to weathercock to the north. However, we gradually emerged into calmer weather as a band of cumulo–nimbus clouds moved away; then the sky cleared, allowing the sun once again to beat down on us. We made better headway.

As dusk approached I became a little concerned because I had no Admiralty (seabed) charts of the South China Sea or of the immediate approaches to the Labuan group of islands. Not unreasonably, I feel, I had expected to arrive at Labuan by air rather than by sea – least of all salvaging a vessel. The launch in tow had no radio, and it was virtually impossible to communicate by shouting because of the noise of our engines – we simply couldn't keep shutting them down. With great difficulty, we managed to pass a message to the boat by writing it on a piece of paper and placing it in a bottle secured to the end of a long piece of cord which we paid out to the boat crew behind us; I had asked in the message whether we should pass to

RN293 heading east tows the 35 ft craft and stranded crew to safety at Labuan, a journey that took eight hours ten minutes, including two hours thirty minutes at night. *Author – 88 Squadron History Book, courtesy RAF Museum Reserve Collection*

the left or right of a particular flashing light that we could see, the geographical position and the flashing code of which were on my terminal approach (TAP) chart. After a short while we hauled in a reply and I hoped they had understood my question correctly and were giving me reliable directions.

It was now dark. I took loop bearings on the Labuan MF beacon and, by using the O2 hand-held compass, on the flashing light whose location I had identified. I simply had to trust the directions I had been given by the boat crew. The aircraft terminal approach chart for Labuan that I had with me was intended for instrument approaches by aircraft into Labuan airfield, but the cartographer had thoughtfully included a few rather indistinct indications of reefs and shallows on the chart. I had to assume they were not mere decoration or figments of his imagination! I therefore did my best to avoid these possible obstructions as well as I was able. (Map 123)

At long last, at ten minutes past ten in the evening, we arrived in Labuan harbour after safely weaving our way around islands to the south and south-west of the main island. We had towed the thirty-five-foot, ten-ton motor launch for 8 hrs 10 min, the last two and a half hours in total darkness. As he stepped ashore we thanked the local doctor for coming with us, although, as it turned out, his services were not required. The rescued crew of the boat thanked us profusely.

ALL OFFERS ARE SUBJECT TO GOODS BEING UNSOLD ON RECEIPT OF REPLY

MALAYAN TIMBER AND TRADING CO., LTD.
(INCORPORATED IN SINGAPORE)

P. O. Box 1791

30A, Raffles Quay

SINGAPORE, 1.

Our Ref.

Your Ref.

CABLES & TELEGRAMS

EMTETECO SINGAPORE
27360

TEL. No. 30770
27369

7th October, 1954.

The Officer Commanding,
88, Squadron Flying Boat Wing,
R.A.F. Maintenance Base,
Seletar,
SINGAPORE.

Dear Sir,

At the request of Montague L. Meyer (Far East) Ltd.,
(our Associated Company) who are the Managing Agents for
Liddell Bros. & Co. (Sarawak) Ltd., we are enclosing a Silver
Salver which they would like you to accept as a very small
token of their great appreciation for the very vital part
which one of your aircrafts played in going to the rescue
of their personnel from the launch which was going adrift
into the South China Sea.

Yours faithfully,

For and on behalf of
MALAYAN TIMBER & TRADING CO. LTD.

DIRECTOR

EJC/DS
Encl:

A letter, received by 88 Squadron shortly after its disbandment, which accompanied the Silver
Salver presented by the Malayan Timber and Trading Company Ltd as a token of appreciation
for the aircraft's part in going to the rescue of the crew of a launch owned by Liddell Bros & Co.
(Sarawak) Ltd. *Author – 88 Squadron History Book, courtesy RAF Museum Reserve Collection*

The following morning we took off from Labuan and headed towards Singapore. Immediately after take-off I stood between the pilots to try to pick out the route we must have taken by sea in darkness during the final stages of our approach to Labuan harbour. It seemed we must have passed over or very close to reefs or shallows that I could see below the surface of the clear azure sea now beneath us. I was thankful our unique rescue and salvage operation hadn't ended with both the boat and our aircraft being salvaged by some third party. That really *would* have been embarrassing.

On 20 September I flew in SZ578 ('B') with instructions from F/L Alec Rawling, the Wing training pilot who had been our captain for the boat-salvaging episode, to enquire and convey to the CO at RAF Labuan that if (as rumoured) there was to be a gift from the boat's owner, following our rescue and salvage exercise on 31 August, it should be presented to the 'Far East Flying Boat Wing' and *not* to 'No. 88 Squadron'. The Labuan CO told me he knew of no such gift. I so reported to Alec Rawling on my return to Seletar.

Three weeks later a magnificent silver salver was delivered to the Headquarters of Far East Flying Boat Wing at Seletar, engraved to *The Crew of No. 88 Squadron* – with it, a wooden crate containing a dozen bottles of champagne. Sadly, this quickly 'disappeared' without 88 Squadron members of the crew even hearing the 'pop' of a cork! We can only surmise where it went. I am still trying to locate the engraved silver salver, hoping against hope that it is safe in a Ministry of Defence depository – or on display in an officers' mess somewhere. So far I have found no sign of it. I would like to trace it because the gift of the salver marked a unique, if minor, event in aviation history – the salvaging of a vessel which was towed to safety by an aircraft.

Note

1. See http://www.tawauweb.com/history.html

Chapter Ten

Co-operating with RAF Marine Craft

When in Singapore, we occasionally trained with a Royal Navy ship or submarine, but such opportunities were few and far between. More frequently we enlisted the help of our colleagues from No. 1124 Marine Craft Unit at RAF Seletar with their RAF-manned seaplane tenders, pinnaces, and rescue and target-towing launches (RTTL). The coxswains and crews enjoyed occasionally venturing out into the South China Sea or Strait of Malacca for a few days rather than spending all their time in the Johore Strait off Seletar. I recall two memorable incidents involving RAF Marine Craft. On the first, our Sunderland crew had been homing onto an RAF pinnace using our ASV radar. After one such 'homing' we passed low over the vessel, only to find immediately afterwards that we had lost VHF radio contact with it. We flew low past the pinnace and saw that the crew were either waving or shaking their fists – possibly both. Our radio operator then admitted he hadn't wound in his HF trailing aerial, the end of which was now missing. On the end of this aerial cable would have been about twenty lead balls – the wire had struck the vessel and broken its VHF aerial as we flew overhead, lead balls and the metal cable hitting the deck and wheelhouse. We signalled the vessel by Aldis lamp to apologize and ask if there were any casualties. Fortunately, neither the wire aerial nor the lead balls had hit any of the crew. It was a salutary lesson for us; the result of our carelessness could have been far more serious. We gladly bought the pinnace crew two crates of beer after landing at Seletar.

On another occasion, I was ordered to act as the Officer in Tactical Command (OTC) of an 1124 MCU RTTL. I was to remain aboard for two days while we proceeded northwards at high speed off the west coast of the Malay Peninsula. On the first day we were to provide Sunderland crews with training in defensive patrols around a 'naval' vessel (simulated by the RTTL) in order to detect and prevent possible attacks by 'enemy' high-speed motor torpedo boats. I was to order co-operating Sunderlands by radio to carry out various patrols around us as we sped northwards through the Malacca Strait between Malaya and Sumatra. When that phase was complete, we were to act as 'mouse' in a cat-and-mouse game where Sunderlands were tasked to try to locate a high-speed launch (fitting our description) that was suspected of gun running along the west coast of Malaya. Our RTTL's task was to try to make their search as difficult as possible by hiding among other vessels – whether fishing boats or merchant ships – or close to the coastline or in river inlets. On the second morning we were trying to avoid being detected by searching Sunderlands, and entered the wide estuary leading to Port Swettenham, a few miles to the west of Kuala Lumpur. In the estuary were several large merchant ships at anchor, with various smaller motor craft occasionally plying between them or to the port. We decided to lie up there for a while.

Some time later, with no sign of any Sunderland, we decided it was time to head out to sea again. We had gone no further than a couple of hundred yards when there was a loud explosion from the stern of our RTTL. I turned to see a hatch flying into the sea after striking a metal stanchion near the stern that had been in its way. The coxswain immediately shut down both engines and we dropped anchor. Other members of the crew – who knew what they were looking for – went aft to inspect the damage. The hatch had covered the battery compartment where, below deck level and resting on lower decking fixed to the hull, were several very large batteries in a box-like compartment. These provided electrical power to the engines and the entire

RAF high-speed rescue and target-towing launch. *Courtesy RAFSA*

A Sunderland in close co-operation with craft of No. 1124 RAF Marine Craft Unit at RAF Seletar. *Courtesy RAFSA*

vessel. It appeared that – presumably through lack of ventilation – there had been a high pressure build-up of fumes of some kind (which we could smell), which had been unable to escape from the battery compartment. Eventually the pressure had become so great that, with tremendous force, it blew off the hatch, which had been secured to the deck. The hatch had then struck and bent one of the steel stanchions there to support a canvas canopy that could cover the deck when required. We were soon able to recover the hatch from the sea. It was very fortunate that no one was on the stern when the explosion occurred. Allowing twenty minutes or so to ventilate the vessel and allow the fumes to dissipate, the coxswain then started one engine, and we made our way slowly into Port Swettenham. There, the crew inspected the damage and the cause more closely before we set off to return to Seletar, 190 nm away and twelve hours' sailing time at slightly reduced speed. The next day we arrived at Seletar without further mishap.

Chapter Eleven

My Own Crew

In mid-August 1953, F/L Mike Colman, the only navigator aircraft captain on 88 Squadron, was posted to FEFBW headquarters as Wing navigation officer. F/L Dave Cooke, my long-standing aircraft captain, sadly retired on medical grounds and returned to the UK. This sequence of events resulted in my appointment as captain of Sunderland SZ571 (B-Baker). This came as a complete surprise – probably as much to others as it did to me. Apart from a new 1st pilot, our crew was otherwise to remain unchanged. My new 1st pilot was F/Sgt Nick Nicholas, a very experienced Sunderland pilot. I was pleased that F/O Sandy Innes-Smith, whom I knew well, remained as co-pilot.

During the third week of August, in my new role as aircraft captain, we flew two navigation and bombing exercises and two air tests. These were followed by a ferry flight to Kai Tak and then to Iwakuni. On 30 August I flew my first Korean sortie as captain and navigator, a night-time West Coast Weather operation. In September, we flew eight Korean missions: five Fox Blues, one Fox Red, and two Tsushima Strait patrols. For all except the last Tsushima patrol, our squadron commander, S/L Harold Francis, became my first pilot in place of F/Sgt Nicholas, although I still flew as the aircraft captain. I imagine he wanted to see how I was shaping up. I personally felt I had a great deal to learn; not only was I still relatively inexperienced as a navigator but I had no previous experience of, or guidance on, 'captaincy'. Indeed, in the 1950s, few navigators were lucky enough to be appointed an aircraft captain.

On 16 September, for the first time, we were ordered to fly a Task Force 77 replenishment group protection sortie at night in the Yellow Sea. This required us to report to TF-77 the location of what few shipping contacts we detected on our ASV radar. Naturally, we were unable to inspect detected ships visually, as it was dark. We recorded and reported the weather, similar to a West Coast Weather patrol. Just after we had completed the operational phase of our mission, No. 4 engine gave trouble so we closed it down and feathered the propeller. We transited to Iwakuni without difficulty on three engines, completing the full mission in 10 hrs 40 min. Between 13 August, when I first flew as captain, and the end of September, our crew flew 148 hours, of which ninety-eight were Korean missions from Iwakuni.

After flying a Korean mission on 2 October, we transited south on the 5th, arriving at Singapore the following day. On 26 October my crew, now in RN302 'C', flew several senior officers from HQ Far East Air Force from Seletar to Kai Tak, from where, on 30 October, we collected another senior officer from Air Headquarters Hong Kong and flew the entire VIP party to a US naval base at Buckner Bay, Okinawa.[1] At that time few Sunderland crews had the opportunity to land in Buckner Bay, so we were fortunate. We dropped off our VIPs and continued our journey to Iwakuni, where we landed shortly before nightfall. On 1 November, we took off at 05.30 from Iwakuni, landing 4 hrs 15 min later back at Buckner Bay, where we stayed overnight. The following morning, together with our VIP party, we took off at 07.00 hrs, and after staging overnight at NAS Sangley Point, Manila Bay, we continued south to Seletar the next day; thus ended our one and only mysterious visit to Okinawa.

Taken in April 1954, south of Ceylon, when Sunderlands of No. 88 Squadron escorted SS *Gothic*, carrying HM Queen Elizabeth II on her way back from a tour of Australia. In the background is HMS *Newfoundland*, a Colony-Class cruiser. We last spotted her in January 1953 when anchored at the outer breakwater at Gibraltar. She was then *en route* to join the Far East Fleet.

Later that month we flew four Operation Firedog missions in the Butterworth and Kuala Lumpur areas; I will describe Firedog operations later. On 11 November, an RAF Valetta transport, VX490, took off from RAF Changi with seven people on board. Some time later Changi air traffic control lost radio contact with this aircraft, and nothing more was heard. A series of Sunderland search and rescue sorties was immediately mounted, the first soon after contact with the Valetta was lost. My crew was ordered to take off at 06.30 on 12 November. We searched for eight hours but found nothing. Other Sunderlands flew on the 13th, and we again on the 14th, this time for 8 hrs 20 min. During this sortie we sighted yellow objects floating in the water. Thinking they could be lifejackets or other survival gear, we decided to risk an open-sea landing; we were actually in Indonesian territorial waters some way south of Singapore. When we reached what we has seen, we found they were only jetsam and not from an aircraft. It was subsequently concluded that the Valetta must have lost control or broken up when flying through a violent storm.

On 26 and 27 November we flew overnight to Sangley Point *en route* to Iwakuni. On arrival at 08.25 hrs, RN302 was so unserviceable I decided to return to Seletar straight away rather than wait for spare parts to be delivered. While the unserviceabilities were significant in total, they presented no hazard for a return flight to Seletar. We took off at 11.50 hrs, landing at Seletar after 9 hrs 5 min. During November 1953, we had flown 103 hrs 55 min.

Note

1. I learned from Tony Burt recently, after he had seen the declassified F540 diary of 88 Squadron, that the VIP party we were ferrying was visiting the USN at Buckner Bay in connection with 'a secret survey'.

Chapter Twelve

Mayday in December

On 3 December 1953 we renewed our attempt to deploy to Japan, taking off from Seletar in darkness at 00.55 hrs, again routing via NAS Sangley Point. We landed at 08.35. In addition to the flying boat alighting area at Sangley Point, the naval air station had an 8,000 ft long runway. Two USN patrol squadrons were based there. They patrolled sea areas between Formosa and the coast of Red China as far north as Shanghai. That was approximately the most southerly boundary of the Fox Red, Blue and Green patrols that we and our USN VP colleagues mounted from Iwakuni. It was while I was at Sangley Point that I watched a P4M-1 Martin Mercator take off. This was a very impressive-looking aircraft powered by compound engines comprising two Pratt & Whitney R-4360-4 Wasp Majors and two Allison J33-A-17s. Carrying a crew of fourteen, it was well armed and its role was signals intelligence gathering (SIGINT). The Mercator's take-off was spectacular – a very distinctive whine from the compound engines, a high rate of climb and lots of black smoke! This was a rarely seen aircraft.

At Sangley Point we were accommodated in batchelor officers' quarters (BOQ) and ate in the officers' club. On 5 December, after an early 'wake-up', we took off at 06.00 hrs and arrived in Iwakuni after an 11 hr flight. Within a few days of arriving at Iwakuni, our aircraft RN302 'C' developed several unserviceabilities. This forced us, on 8 December, to take PP144 'A' on a Fox Blue mission. Unfortunately, while over the Inland Sea, the No. 4 engine soon gave trouble; we shut it down, feathered the propeller and returned to base, landing after only forty minutes. There was no other serviceable aircraft available, so the RAF fell down on their mission that day – a rare occurrence: not a good day. Six hours later, my crew air tested our own aircraft, RN302 'C', and it was now serviceable, but too late to complete a daytime mission. That was the last occasion F/Sgt Nick Nicholas flew with my crew. For some reason – I forget why – the CO transferred Nick to crew 'A'. I was not happy about this because I had developed a good captain/ first pilot understanding with F/Sgt Nicholas, whose airmanship, seamanship and piloting skills I trusted implicitly. He was succeeded by F/L Jack Oliver, a qualified flying instructor (QFI) and an experienced pilot, though new to the squadron and to Sunderlands. I was pleased that at least Sandy Innes-Smith would remain as my co-pilot, because we had been flying together for many months. No doubt I would get to know Jack Oliver in the coming weeks.

On 12 December, we flew an 8 hr 50 min ASP Tsushima patrol in RN302 'C', and carried out a practice three-engine landing on return – just in case! Up at 04.30 on 15 December for our next mission, while carrying out our pre-flight checks we found that RN302 'C' was again unserviceable, so we returned to the buoy, moored, called for a marine craft and changed to PP144 'A'. We at last took off at 07.20 hrs and successfully completed a Fox Red in 9 hrs 45 min. The remainder of 88 Squadron had now returned to Seletar, but as an all-single crew we had volunteered to 'hold the fort' over Christmas. On the 18th, C-Charlie was again unserviceable when we were tasked for another Op Fox Red. We therefore took PP154 'X', which was one of No. 209 Squadron's aircraft. After transiting through the Inland Sea and past Shimonoseki we had to shut down the port inner engine due to a very heavy oil leak. Although Sunderland 'X' was heavy, we had no great difficulty in maintaining altitude on climbing power. We landed at Iwakuni after 1 hr 45 min. Four hours later we air tested PP154 'X' after the ground crew had fixed the oil leak. We flew for forty-five minutes and carried out a practice GCA.[1]

Three days later, on 21 December 1953, we were again late in taking off because we had to take the reserve aircraft, NJ177 'V', another 209 Squadron aircraft, as our own was unserviceable. Nevertheless, we successfully completed a Fox Blue patrol in 9 hrs 45 min. On 24 December, Christmas Eve, we flew another Fox Blue, this time at last in our own aircraft, RN302 'C'. For the last three missions in twelve days we had had to take other crews' aircraft. On this particular day, after 1 hr 30 min while transiting the Tsushima Strait and shortly before reaching the start of our Fox Blue patrol, there was an explosion followed by a fire in No. 3 engine, the starboard inner. The extinguisher doused the fire and we were able to maintain height and return to Iwakuni, landing on three engines after 3 hrs 10 min. That was my crew's third engine failure in sixteen days, all in different aircraft. Such a high incidence of engine failure was unheard of, and why it should be happening was a mystery. The weather was wet and cold, and in such conditions we had enormous sympathy for the RAF fitters and riggers who were having to work on aircraft in the open, either on the water or 'up slip', day and night, identifying and rectifying problems in very low temperatures, whatever the weather. They were a tremendous team of airmen who somehow always seemed to remain cheerful. They deserve a great deal of praise.

Forced down in the Tsushima Strait

Having flown on Christmas Eve we were off duty on Christmas Day, but on Boxing Day our crew went to base operations to be briefed by the duty USN operations officer for a patrol in the Tsushima Strait the following day. Our RAF maintenance crew said they would have our aircraft, RN302, C-Charlie, ready by the morning, having rectified the cause of the engine failure on the 24th. The next day, 27 December, we got out of bed at 04.45 and took off from Iwakuni as briefed at 06.15 hrs. As night slowly turned to day, and while monitoring our progress on the radar, we flew at 800 ft along the length of the Inland Sea to Shimonoseki below a layer of cloud. Climbing a little to pass over the city that was then just coming to life, we entered the Strait and our patrol area. The cloud continued to lift and disperse, and we began our patrol at about 800 ft. F/L Jack Oliver had by then moved to the left-hand seat, and F/O Sandy Innes-Smith crossed to the co-pilot's seat.

At 08.25 hrs, we were well into our patrol and heading north just to the east of Tsushima Island. I happened to be standing with my head in the astrodome, looking east along and beyond the starboard wing, when suddenly the No. 4 engine (the starboard outer) emitted a flash, accompanied by a mild explosion, followed by flames and black smoke streaming back over the wing as I watched. The pilots immediately shut down the engine, feathered the propeller and activated the fire extinguisher. After a short while, the fire appeared to have been extinguished. At least flames could no longer be seen outside the engine cowling.

Jack Oliver set the other three engines to maximum climbing power as recommended in the Pilot's Notes. At first the aircraft maintained height, but soon afterwards he complained that he was unable to climb the aircraft and it was now actually descending. It was at about this time that one of the flight engineers reported from the lower deck that No. 2 engine, the port inner, was losing oil and beginning to issue smoke. Possibly this engine was not delivering full climbing power, and this may have been why the pilots were finding it impossible to maintain height. As we would have used no more than 350–400 gallons of fuel since we had taken off, we were above the maximum recommended landing weight. We had a short discussion about whether to jettison fuel. I think we decided against this for two reasons: apart from a possible fire risk, there was too little time to jettison enough fuel to make a worthwhile difference to the aircraft's weight to arrest our rate of descent. We were now down to about 600 feet.

Jack Oliver said he would have to land very soon because we were still descending. It therefore seemed inevitable we were going to have to force-land, and we needed to set the aircraft up properly for landing rather than being in a semi-prepared state. Although I was the aircraft captain, Jack was a very experienced pilot; I was in no position, as the navigator, to doubt or question his judgement – or that of Sandy Innes-Smith, the co-pilot. The Pilot's Notes stated that a heavy aircraft should be able to maintain height on three engines if set to maximum climbing power with the dead engine feathered (as ours was). We had successfully returned to base on three engines only three days earlier, as well as on two further occasions that month alone. Although reasonably reliable for the 1950s (an average of one engine failure per 1,000 flight hours), that December in Japan the Pratt and Whitney R1830 engines had for some reason suffered a spate of failures, many more than usual, including on this particular aircraft. It was RN302's second engine failure that month. Having already shut down No. 4 engine, and since there were indications that all was not well with No. 2, the total power available must presumably have been insufficient to maintain height at our aircraft's present weight. (See map 128)

We transmitted a Mayday message on 121.5 MHz, giving our position, describing our emergency and our intention to land (or ditch) the aircraft on the sea. We were then heading north, parallel to the east coast of Tsushima Island, which was a mile or less to port. I think we were flying roughly into wind. The pilot sounded 'L', for 'Landing', on the aircraft's warning horn, and pre-landing checks were quickly completed by the crew, who then took up crash-landing positions. I removed the astrodome which provides a crew escape exit, and the flight engineer stowed the dome securely in his compartment. I then took up my own crash position.

The surface wind was about 10–12 kts and there was an appreciable long swell from the north or north-east, estimated to be 6–8 ft. These were not good conditions for an overweight landing on three engines. The recommended approach speed was 95–100 kts, using as little power as possible. The stalling speed would be around 83 kts. Our speed over the sea just before touch-down if correctly judged would therefore probably be a relatively fast 85–90 kts. On touching the sea the 1st pilot would need to prevent the aircraft's nose from dropping and burying itself deeply into a rising swell crest if we were thrown into the air after the initial and any subsequent touch-downs. We were landing roughly in position 34° 37' N 129° 30' E.

I was sitting on the upper deck floor, facing aft, behind the main spar, and had no view of the actual touch-down. As far as I can remember, we were thrown off the water three times. The second impact was especially violent, but my impression was that, fortunately, Jack Oliver had succeeded in maintaining a slightly nose-up attitude throughout, thus avoiding the serious danger of the aircraft burying its nose into the sea (as had happened to the unfortunate crew of PP-148, Foxtrot, at Iwakuni). We seemed to stop in a remarkably short time. I jumped onto the platform beneath the astrodome escape hatch and looked out.

No. 1 engine and propeller had been wrenched from its mountings and had fallen into the sea through the force of the aircraft's impact with the water. *Author*

My immediate concern was whether either of the wing floats had been ripped off, in which case the crew would quickly have to carry out 'broken float drill' – that meant most of the crew running onto and sitting on the wing on which the float was still in place, to prevent the other wing from entering the sea and allowing the aircraft to turn turtle. I saw that both floats were intact. However, as I looked to port I was astonished to see that No. 1, the port outer engine, had broken free from its mountings during one of the

The Albatross of 3rd Air Sea Rescue Squadron from Ashiya takes off using rocket assistance, carrying some of the crew of RN302. *Author*

The starboard tailplane had broken away from its mountings by the aircraft's impact with the sea or by the upward force of the water. *Author*

aircraft's impacts with the sea, and had disappeared; only a dangling trail of cables and pipes remained. I then looked aft and saw that apart from a small section of the leading edge, the remainder of the starboard horizontal tailplane was also missing. It, too, had fallen into the sea, presumably swept away by a combination of the vertical impact and being struck by the sea surface. There were no injuries to the crew, and a quick inspection showed that the hull was sound and without leaks.

Looking to our left (west), less than half a mile away was a coastal inlet about 400 metres or more in length, and at most 200 metres wide. The pilots manoeuvred the aircraft slowly into this coastal inlet, using the remaining serviceable port and starboard inner engines, both of which were still running. Normally, aircraft were taxied using the outer engines because they provide more leverage for turning without building up too much speed, the aircraft having no sea rudder. The inlet into which we taxied had rocky sides, and soundings with the lead-line indicated that the water was very deep. With some difficulty we managed to stop and, with the aid of our rubber inflatable dinghy, tether the aircraft to the shore near the western end of the inlet. We shut down both engines and started the auxiliary power unit to provide electrical power. We sent a message by HF W/T to Iwakuni, updating them on our situation. On further inspecting the aircraft it became evident that the main spar supporting the wings had fractured during the landing; RN302 'C' was clearly a Category 5 'write-off'. I told the crew to gather all documents, especially everything that was classified or sensitive, and to begin dismantling as many instrument and electronic modules, radio sets, the IFF, etc. as we could, for future use as spare parts at Iwakuni. We didn't know at this stage how we would recover these, but knew they would be useful.

Within an hour of landing, a USAF search and rescue Albatross amphibian, believed to have been from the 3rd Air Rescue Squadron based at Ashiya, circled overhead, landed on the sea in the entrance into the inlet and taxied towards us. By means of our inflatable rubber dinghies, some of our crew members paddled across and spoke to the SAR Albatross crew and agreed what should best be done. I considered we no longer needed a full crew, and several of our crew members were therefore put aboard the Albatross. The aircraft then took off, using rocket-assisted take-off (RATO) to get airborne in an incredibly short distance, possibly even within the inlet in which we had anchored.

Later that day, we were pleased to see the USS Destroyer, *De Haven*, DD-727, appear about a mile off shore and drop anchor. She had detached from Task Force 77. Ed Edwards, Boatswain's Mate 3rd Class, organized the launching of the captain's gig, a motor whaleboat, and the *De Haven*'s 1st lieutenant, Lt Hal Smith USNR, (see colour photo) together with Eric Brummitt USN, a medic, and Lloyd Gasway, engineer, came to see what assistance we needed. It was agreed they would take us (and the equipment we had removed from the aircraft) aboard the USS *De Haven* that night, and the next day they would tow RN302 out to sea. Assuming permission was given, they would then sink it in deep water to remove it as a hazard. That night we left a 'boat guard' on board to make sure the aircraft didn't drag its moorings.

The next day, 28 December, our aircraft was towed out to sea to a position roughly a mile offshore and about 250–300 yards from *De Haven*. This can be

The destroyer USS *De Haven* (DD-727), rescuer and host to most of the crew of Sunderland RN302 (Charlie) from 27 December 1953 to 1 January 1954, when we disembarked at Sasebo US naval base on the west coast of Kyushu, Japan.

RN302 being towed into position before being sunk by USS *De Haven*, seen in the background. *Author*

seen in photographs, two of which were taken by another RAF Sunderland that was fortuitously circling overhead. Dale Harbin, a USN radio operator aboard *De Haven*, told me recently, 'I remember we first tried sinking your seaplane from our motor whaleboat with Browning automatic rifles, but that was unsuccessful.' Dale continued, 'I was on the bridge during the decision to use the 3.5 in. gun; I remember Captain Sigmund asking the gunnery officer, "Can you hit it with one shot?" The gunnery officer avowed he could, so the Captain gave permission to fire.' The last we saw of RN302 was when a single 3.5 in. shell from USS *De Haven* hit the aircraft amidships. There was a

RN302 in position immediately before her destruction, photographed from another Sunderland, circling overhead.

Moments after Charlie had received a direct hit by a 3.5-inch shell from USS *De Haven*, a mile offshore from Shushi Wan, Tsushima Island, photographed from another Sunderland.

This photograph was taken by Jim Buzzard, Seaman 1st Class and gunner's mate aboard the destroyer USS *De Haven*. Jim took the picture from the motor whaleboat shortly after unsuccessful attempts were made to sink the aircraft using Browning automatic rifles.

The last picture was also taken by Dale Harbin just after RN302 had succumbed to a 3.5-inch shell. Note the piece of flying debris high above the burning aircraft.

second's pause and then a flash as RN302 exploded, soon disappearing below the waves under a pall of black smoke. Photographs taken by another RAF Sunderland circling overhead, and also by Dale Harbin and by Jim Bussard, Seaman 1st Class Gunner's Mate aboard USS *De Haven*, dramatically record the final moments of C-Charlie, RN302. Those of Charlie's crew, including myself, who were now aboard the USS *De Haven*, were made welcome by Captain Sigmund and his crew, and found sleeping accommodation. John Land, one of our two flight engineers, reminded me recently of the excellent food served aboard. We spent the next three days at sea, more or less having the run of the ship (see colour photo page 1).

USS *De Haven* (DD 727) was one of four destroyers in Destroyer Squadron 9 (DESRON 9). The three others were USS *Mansfield* DD 728, USS *Swenson* DD 729, and USS *Collett* DD730. DESRON 9 provided the escort for the aircraft carrier, CVA USS *Boxer* (with CV-21 aboard). After weighing anchor, we set sail in USS *De Haven* to rejoin the rest of DESRON 9 and Boxer which, with other vessels, made up Task Force 77.

From a distance, we watched a continual stream of fighter aircraft flying off and landing on the aircraft carrier.

On the second day of our stay aboard *De Haven*, we were resupplied at sea (RAS); a supply vessel came alongside while stores were transferred by jackstay as we sailed, a few feet between the two ships, at around 12–15 kts. On 1 January 1954, after three days at sea, we docked at the US naval base at Sasebo on the west coast of Kyushu. There, we bade farewell to our rescuers in USS *De Haven* and disembarked, together with the equipment we had removed from RN302. We were next taken by road to the American Itazuki airbase, whence Lt Cdr Jose USN flew us to Iwakuni in a US Navy R5D transport aircraft (Registration No. 50875). Although our stay aboard *De Haven* had followed from an unwelcome event – which nevertheless could have had far worse consequences – our rescue and the help we received from both the US Navy and the US Air Force was a heartening and encouraging experience of comradeship between different military services and Allied nations. I was interested to read recently that in December 1973, USS *De Haven* was transferred to the Republic of Korea and renamed *Incheon*. This somehow seemed fitting for a warship which had for more than three years defended the ROK against aggression at their time of need. I especially want to say how grateful I am to the many past crew members of *De Haven* who recently contacted me, telling me their recollection of the ditching and destruction of Sunderland RN302, and for forwarding some very interesting and historic photographs they had taken at the time.

In accordance with standard practice, a court of inquiry was set up on our return to Iwakuni to gather evidence on the circumstances of the loss of RN302 on 27 December. The two pilots, flight engineers, and I as the aircraft captain, told the court what had happened. I never learned what conclusions the court of inquiry came to, or what recommendations they may have made. The day after the inquiry was completed, on 16 January, we took off from Iwakuni in Sunderland PP137 (O-Oboe), as passengers – we now had no aircraft of our own; we were bound for Kai Tak and then Seletar. We were flying with F/L Peter Wildy (one of the court of inquiry members) and his crew. It wasn't long before No. 2 engine began to give some trouble. Pete Wildy shut it down and feathered the propeller, and we returned to Iwakuni on three engines. That was the fifth engine failure we had experienced in five weeks.

Our crew finally departed Iwakuni on 18 January 1954, and returned to Seletar after a two-month absence, on 22 January. I twice again flew to Japan for Korean operations before my tour in the Far East was over. The first was only eight days after I had returned to Seletar. On 4 February, flying in SZ578 'B' with F/O Stuart Holmes as captain, we were north of the Paracel Islands when we were diverted to the US flying boat base at Sangley Point,

Manila Bay, because of bad weather at Hong Kong. My next detachment to Iwakuni was in June 1954.

I remained there on operations until 11 August, when, crewed with F/L Jock Beer and F/O Stuart Holmes, I departed for Hong Kong. During June, July and early August 1954 I flew another twenty-seven Korean patrol missions, bringing the total to sixty-one. Strangely, after the repeated engine problems we had suffered in December 1953 and January 1954, I experienced no further engine failures throughout the whole of the remaining ten months of my tour.

Flying in the Korean theatre was never dull. It also gave me some experience of working with the US Navy, which controlled RAF operations from Iwakuni. This helped in 1979 to 1981 when, as a wing commander and Staff Officer Plans and Exercises in Naples, I was responsible for planning NATO maritime air operations and exercises in the Mediterranean flown by US, French, Italian, Greek and Turkish maritime patrol aircraft (and by any visiting RAF Nimrods from the UK). Later, I was promoted to Group Captain and appointed Acting Chief of Staff to the Commander Maritime Air Forces Mediterranean, Rear Admiral Wayne D. Bodensteiner USN. I greatly valued and enjoyed my experience of serving with the United States Navy.

Note

1. Ground-controlled approach. The American-manned military GCA on Iwakuni airfield was able to give USN and RAF flying boats an 'off-set' GCA from its installation.

The Destroyer USS *De Haven* (DD-727), rescuer and host to the author and some of the crew of Sunderland RN302 from December 27th 1953 to 1st January 1954 when we disembarked at Sasebo on the west coast of Jyushu, Japan. *Photograph source unknown*

Chapter Thirteen

Firedog Operations over Malaya

D uring my tour, I flew eight Firedog missions from Seletar. These sorties provided air support to the British Army fighting in the Malayan jungle during the so-called Malayan Emergency, which lasted from 1948 to 1960. Communist guerrillas of the Malayan National Liberation Army were trying to subvert and overthrow British government influence in Malaya. They attacked European-managed rubber plantations, tried to take over control of villages and endeavoured to turn the population against the legitimate local and national government. The Army called upon the RAF to assist in combating the threat, and Sunderlands were among a variety of RAF and RAAF aircraft variously employed in this task throughout a long and ultimately successful campaign.

Crews were briefed for Firedog operations by an Army Liaison Officer. The ALO usually allotted a target area several kilometres square. On one such Firedog flown by my crew on 22 August 1952, the target area, 25 nm west of Chukai, was no less than 80 sq nm (10 nm × 8 nm). However, this was exceptional: an area of 5–10 sq nm was more typical. Sometimes targets were not far from rubber plantations, but more usually deeper in the jungle. The objective was to hinder the movement of guerrillas (referred to as CTs – Communist Terrorists) within the designated area, typically for twelve hours during a one- or two-day period, while British troops reached or surrounded the area before working their way into it or setting up ambushes. In 1952–4 a Sunderland sortie might be preceded or followed by others flown by RAAF long-nose Lincolns or RAF Brigands from Tengah. Lincolns and Brigands usually dropped heavy ordnance, typically 500 lb per weapon.

Our ground troops usually had intelligence that the designated target area was where CTs were hiding. For such missions, Sunderlands normally carried about 240 20 lb fragmentation bombs. These then cost £4 10 shillings each! We also carried several thousand rounds of machine-gun and cannon ammunition. The bombs were loaded aboard still in their boxes, and for take-off were stacked both on the bomb-room floor and elsewhere along

" ITS NOT THE BOMBS I'M FRIGHTENED OF - ITS THE BITS FALLING OFF !! "

(Cartoon by KANE)

A Sunderland northward bound just off the west coast of Malaya, heading towards the target area. Dense jungle seen to the aircraft's starboard side was typical of a FIREDOG target area. *Bill Whiter*

Sgt Land, flight engineer, about to drop a 20-pound fragmentation bomb into the Malayan jungle target area, below. *Picture courtesy of John Land*

F/O David Germain, navigator. *Author*

Sgt Vic Kapl, air gunner and first-class chef. *Author*

Sgt Bob Nairn, air signaller. *Author*

All of these excellent crewmen flew with me at various times during my squadron tour.

the length of the lower deck, to spread the load, according to aircraft trim requirements. The target area could be up to two and a quarter hours' flying time from Seletar, sometimes in the vicinity of Butterworth or Kuala Lumpur. Rather than securing the bombs on racks (see picture), a small team of crew members in the bomb room would open sufficient boxes of bombs before each run. Bombs were dropped singly. As each was required, the arming pin was removed and it was carefully handed to another crewman who stood on the now lowered bomb-door frame; when the navigator gave the signal over the intercom to start bombing, bombs were released by hand, one by one, through the large apertures of the lowered bomb doors. This process continued every ten to twenty seconds throughout a bomb run; there was seldom anything definite to aim at. We flew low, sometimes only fifty to a hundred feet above the usually dense jungle canopy. It was like flying low over a mountainous 'sea' of trees whose tops rose and fell in unison with the land contour. We would climb as we turned to reverse our course on reaching the far boundary of the target area, and then descend again to try to gain even a glimpse of what lay beneath.

The task of the navigator was to position the aircraft as accurately as possible at the start of each bombing run and then call out, 'Start bombing NOW!' over the intercom, followed by 'STOP bombing!' when he considered the aircraft was approaching the far target area boundary. Finding the boundary of an area of primary jungle could be difficult, to say the least. Usually there was no physical boundary to mark it, such as a stream or track that could be seen through the tall and densely thick jungle canopy. The navigator usually had to take the aircraft to some specific pin-point on the map that *was* recognizable, and carry out timed runs, using a stop-watch, on specific headings at designated speeds until, by checking the stop-watch, he calculated when the aircraft was crossing the near boundary, and when it was about to reach the far boundary of the target area. Our own troops could be quite close to the target area, and we did not want, accidentally, to harm them. On 23 March 1953, when flying in RN302 'C' over the Bentong area with F/L David Cooke as captain and P/O Paddy Brogan as my 2nd navigator, on return to Seletar we were told we had 'dropped an appreciable number of bombs on a detachment of the Cameroons'. Fortunately for me, the matter was soon cleared up when the Cameroons rang up apologetically to admit that some of their number had strayed into the target area.

After each bombing run the next run would usually be gun strafing. The navigator would again carefully position the aircraft and give the signal to start and stop firing. The crew would fire hundreds of rounds from the four 0.303s in the tail turret, the two 0.5 beam cannon, and the two 0.303s in the nose turret, on each run.

Sunderlands were typically ordered to stay on task, bombing and strafing, for between four and five hours. The navigator therefore needed to calculate roughly how many bombs should be dropped on each run and tell the bombing team leader and gunners so that the aircraft neither released all its ordnance too soon – nor would have to take some back to Seletar. Including the transit from and back to Seletar, Firedog sorties could sometimes exceed eight hours. The last Firedog was flown on 17 September 1954 by F/O Stuart Holmes's crew in B-Baker. This was the 165th by 88 Squadron out of a total of four hundred flown by the three Flying Boat Wing squadrons.

NJ272 flying over low-lying jungle in southern Malaya. *Courtesy of the RAFSA*

Chapter Fourteen

Far East Sunderland Dress Code

R eaders may have noticed in photographs that Far East Sunderland crews can be seen in various states of dress or undress. Except for Japan and Korea in winter, and to a lesser extent in Hong Kong between November and March, daytime temperatures were usually in the 80s and 90s Fahrenheit, with high humidity. Most photographs in this account were taken in hot weather. Nevertheless, it occurs to me that the mode of dress we adopted for flying might require some explanation.

The first photograph, of pilot F/O Sandy Innes-Smith, was almost certainly taken while flying from Iwakuni between December and February. In wintertime, it could be very cold in and around Japan and Korea. When not flying, we wore RAF Blue uniform. Temperatures were typically in low single figures, and often below freezing at ground level. The Sunderland Mk V, like its predecessors, was unpressurized and unheated. There was no hot air or air conditioning on the flight deck, nor anywhere in the aircraft. It had rotating gun turrets with open gun ports in the nose and tail, and two beam

F/O Sandy Innes-Smith, well wrapped up against the cold around Japan and Korea in winter. I flew many hundreds of hours with Sandy as my pilot. *David Germain*

Sgt John Rowell, flight engineer, 'dressed' for warmer climes. John was another crew member with whom I flew for many months. *Author*

gun hatches (each more than a metre square) that were constantly open, once on patrol. There were other places on the flight deck and elsewhere around the aircraft where draughts freely found their way into the fuselage.

Provided that the primus stoves had been alight for a while, the galley was the only place in the aircraft where the temperature increased to a comfortable level in winter. This was where crew members would congregate periodically during a winter sortie, to warm themselves, or perhaps get a hot drink or a bowl of soup or stew. When it was really cold even the navigator might occasionally tear himself away from his table and go to the galley to warm up for a few minutes. A regular supply of hot drinks and warm food was essential on sorties that typically lasted for between nine and twelve hours, in temperatures sometimes near to or below zero degrees Centigrade.

There were eight crew positions where there were plugs for electrically heated suits. We had each been issued with an electrically heated Kapok inner suit to wear under our outer flying-suit. However, as I described earlier, we learned that because of the already heavy load on the aircraft's ancient electrical system, it was unwise to allow more than four or at most five crew members to plug in their suits at any one time. Hence, on a night-time West Coast Weather patrol over the Yellow Sea, at altitude, and when all gun positions were continually manned, if the tail and nose gunners and the two beam gunners were connected to electrically heated suits all the time, at most one or perhaps two other crew members could have their suits plugged in. Because of this I tended to wear two pairs of socks, my 'long johns' and sometimes my pyjamas underneath my flying-suit.

I think it was in the autumn of 1953 (or it may have been earlier) that additional winter clothing was issued. This included a loose-fitting, long, padded anorak with a hood having a wire-strengthened opening with fur around it – to catch blowing snow! In addition, we had thick white socks and tall, Mukluk winter boots with insulated inner soles. These certainly helped, but were rather bulky for moving around the aircraft.

Hence, flying in wintertime in Japan could be testing. Apart from the cold, sometimes it snowed and more frequently rained. When a Sunderland was moored and it rained, the windows and upper hatches on the flight deck leaked like sieves. Consequently, as soon as we climbed on board it was invariably necessary to sweep rainwater that had collected on the upper flight deck (sometimes half an inch in places) down the forward stairs to the bow and bilges. The astrodome had to be open throughout pre-flight checks, and since the navigator's table was more or less beneath the open hatchway,

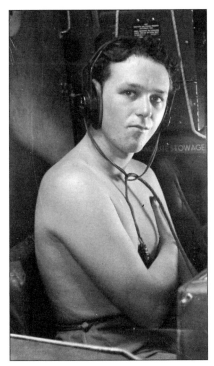

Sgt Air Signaller Pete Brookes, one of the younger air signallers on the squadron who flew in our crew.
Author

the navigator, too, could be cold and perhaps wet before even getting airborne. It was also difficult to keep the navigation charts, flight plans and log sheets dry. The flight engineers and at least one of the pilots (in addition to whichever crew member was attending to the mooring in the bow), were worse off because they had to be on the aircraft's upper surfaces, turning over the engines and doing other outside checks for up to half an hour before take-off, and while refuelling after landing.

As a result, in winter you could find crews dressed in all kinds of clothing in an effort to keep warm and dry. It was at times when the weather was really cold *and wet* at Iwakuni that flying on 'boats' could be far from pleasant; but we had to balance that against the better times, in summer and farther south in the much hotter temperatures of Hong Kong, Borneo, Singapore and Ceylon.

In summer, it was really pleasant to come aboard. The only problem when the aircraft had been standing on the water in temperatures of 85–95°F with a high percentage of humidity was the likelihood that you and your clothing would be bathed in perspiration within minutes. In hot climates, whether in Singapore, Hong Kong, Borneo or Japan, we generally found it impractical to wear even a lightweight flying-suit for much of the time. It was sodden with sweat in minutes. The only practical solution was to wear, at most, KD[1] shorts and a short-sleeved KD shirt, preferably made of Aertex material. More often than not, KD shorts and a sleeveless vest or no top at all were more practical once aboard the aircraft. Hence you will have seen this style of dress in many of the photographs; for example, photographs of the radio operator and the flight engineer were taken during the crew's detachment to Hong Kong in the 'hot and sticky' season. Once airborne in a hot climate, the aircraft soon cooled down, and there was always the possibility of walking aft and standing by an open beam gun hatch to cool off. When flying at altitude at night in a hot climate, it was comfortable to wear and work in a KD shirt and shorts or slacks, or even a lightweight flying-suit. It was just a case of 'dressing for the occasion'.

Note
1. Khaki drill RAF uniform, usually short sleeved.

Chapter Fifteen

Sunderland Navigation – a Question of Teamwork

The navigator of a Far East Sunderland flying boat in the 1950s was responsible for the safe navigation of the aircraft. However, he depended on the willing co-operation of other members of the crew, as well as on his own skill. The later addition of a second navigator slightly reduced the need for other aircrew on board to provide regular assistance to the navigator. *Note. DR navigation is discussed in detail in Appendix 3.*

Because of the dearth of outside navigation aids in the Far East in the 1950s (and earlier), and because of the very basic navigation equipment fitted to the aircraft, the frequent measurement of 'drift' was fundamental to accurate dead-reckoning (DR) navigation. Drift could be obtained directly in one of three ways: the navigator himself could measure it using the drift recorder, in which case he had to ask the pilot to level the wings and hold a steady course. When the navigator wanted to obtain a three-drift wind (often hourly) he would have to ask the pilot to change onto three different headings in succession, and on each to level the wings and hold the aircraft as steady as possible.

Another way to obtain an accurate measurement of drift was for the navigator to obtain a back bearing on a flame float dropped at low altitude, into the sea. In this case, he would have to ask one of the other crew members, an air gunner, flight engineer or air signaller in the galley or manning one of the beam look-outs, to go to the rear of the fuselage, to prepare and launch a flame float. At the same time the navigator would have asked one of the air gunners to man the rear turret and take a bearing on the flame float with his gunsight, reading off the resultant azimuth angle on the calibrated turret ring. Throughout this drift-taking process, the navigator would again ask the pilot to level the wings and hold a steady course.

Likewise, for the navigator to find the local wind velocity using the wind-finding attachment (WFA) would require another crew member to prepare and drop a marine marker or smoke float though the launcher at the rear of the aircraft. While the navigator zeroed and operated the WFA equipment, the pilots would have to orbit the aircraft at low altitude and, with the greatest possible accuracy, steer it towards and when the aircraft was exactly overhead the pyrotechnic in the water, tell the navigator, who would then switch on, and after about a three-minute orbit, switch off the WFA as the aircraft passed overhead the marine marker for the second time. The navigator would then calculate the wind velocity from the change in grid co-ordinates.

The navigator also relied on crewmen who were manning gun turrets and look-out positions, as well as the two pilots, to report on their own initiative such navigationally useful information as possible pin-points (few and far between), and whenever islands, coastlines and shipping first came into view. Also of interest to the navigator would be apparent changes in the surface wind direction or speed – judged by visible changes in sea state, white horses and wind lanes – changes in visibility, and changes in cloud amounts or weather, all of which might herald changes in wind velocity and ambient temperature.

Every hour, and sometimes more frequently, the 'nav' would need to check the accuracy of the aircraft's compasses, a key component in the DR navigation triangle of velocities. He would do this by using the astro-compass; this required the pilot once again to hold a particular course very accurately with level wings for one to two minutes. At the same time (assuming a 2nd 'nav' was not carried) the navigator would ask another aircrew member to go to the direct reading compass master unit in the aft section of the fuselage, to monitor the readout and call out over the intercom the exact heading on the MU when the 'nav' asked for it. This would enable the navigator to make an accurate comparison between all the compass readings in the aircraft, and the actual heading according to the astro-compass bearing on the sun or other celestial body.

When a navigator was reliant on astro-navigation for fixing, as was often the case when over an open ocean by day or at night, each astro-sight would require the pilot to hold the wings level, to maintain a steady course and try to minimize any speed or height changes and accelerations during the two or three minutes that it took the navigator to take each single 'shot'. The 'nav' would often take two sights, separated by probably two to three minutes, and at night, three or four sights over a total period of twelve–fifteen minutes. Especially at night, the crew could assist the 'nav' in cloudy conditions by alerting him if there was a sudden break in cloud cover through which he might be able quickly to snatch one or two star or moon sights; otherwise he might not know that the opportunity was there.

Every hour, both the navigator and the air signaller manning the W/T operator's station were required to note in their respective logs and report

F/O Sandy Innes-Smith holds a steady course while the navigator takes a drift reading. (*Author*)

the aircraft's position to base or the controlling authority by radio, usually at specific times. This required the navigator to be 'on the ball' with preparing an accurate latitude and longitude position (and any other required information) at the right time; for this he usually appreciated a reminder from the W/T operator a few minutes beforehand in case he was busy doing some other navigation task. The navigator might also need to obtain an updated weather forecast from base or elsewhere. For this he would ask the signaller or pilot to call on an appropriate radio channel. Hence the W/T operator and navigator, whose stations were close to one another, worked as a team.

In some areas – not usually in the Far East – but possibly on a transit flight to the UK, it was possible for the 'nav' to ask the W/T operator to obtain HF DF bearings for use as position lines.

Turning to radar; it was invariably important that whichever air signaller was operating the ASV radar – sitting behind the navigator – he should work closely with the navigator. The navigator would point out to the air signaller on a topographical map the land masses or islands that he would like the operator to look out for and on which particular points the 'nav' would like to have radar ranges and bearings when they were detected and identified.

In situations such as when navigating along the length of the Inland Sea in Japan (with a coastline and high ground not far distant on either side of the aircraft) or finding the entrance to Kowloon harbour, the alighting area at Hong Kong, the navigator and radar operator would at times be in the radar tent together, the navigator standing beside the air signaller at his set. Together they would watch the radar PPI, discuss what they could see while taking bearings and ranges and comparing them with a topographical map to ensure the aircraft's safety in conditions of poor visibility or at night, beneath or while flying in and out of low cloud and below the aircraft's Safety Height.[1] Close teamwork within the crew was vital.

Last, and least important, was the navigator's periodic need to eat and drink. The Sunderland crew complement was ten, and there were ten positions to be manned when the aircraft was at action stations. However, for much of the time, the nose gun turret was not manned (the two pilots were already covering the forward 180° arc). This left one crew member 'spare'; he most usually manned the galley preparing hot or cold drinks and at least one full hot meal during the sortie that would typically last eight to twelve and a half hours. Usually within every crew there was one member who volunteered and was happy to act as the crew's cook. On the crew with which I flew for most of my tour, this was Sgt Vic Kapl. He was an excellent air gunner, but equally skilful in the galley – a very popular crew member! Nevertheless, when Vic was otherwise engaged in the rear turret, others stepped in willingly and took their turn.

On most sorties a solo navigator could never find enough time to organize and prepare a meal for himself, let alone for the rest of the crew. Except for the two pilots, other crew members could generally rotate around different crew positions, usually leaving one spare, whereas the navigator was more or less continuously 'at work'. Hence, as a navigator I was reliant on and grateful for the drinks and meals provided to me by other crew members. Throughout a sortie at frequent intervals I was asked if I would like a mug of tea or coffee, or a glass of water or a soft drink; and what would I like to eat for lunch or breakfast? Would I also like soup or fruit? It was an excellent service, allowing me to give full attention to navigation; meals were always brought to me at my 'nav' table. It serves to illustrate the kind of consideration that was typical of Sunderland aircrews.

Hence, navigation in Far East Sunderlands was a team effort, involving the entire crew, although it was the navigator who held the prime responsibility; he decided the best aids to use and when, he initiated all the actions, calculated the data, plotted the results and took all the necessary follow-up action. The navigator tuned into and took his own MF loop bearings, obtained his own Loran position lines and fixes, and often operated and interpreted the ASV radar without the help of others.

Nevertheless to obtain many of the most essential navigation data inputs and ensure their accuracy and hence safe navigation, the navigator was reliant on the co-operation and immediate and unquestioning help of all other members of the aircraft's crew.

I therefore express my thanks to all with whom I flew for their help and co-operation. Without their willing assistance my task would have been more stressful and difficult, and on some occasions, safe navigation less certain.

Note

1. Typically, the height of the highest ground within a radius that increased at a rate of 30 mph, plus 1,500 feet.

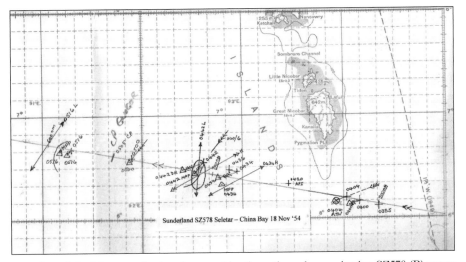

Sunderland SZ578 Seletar – China Bay 18 Nov '54

A section of the Mercator plotting chart used by the author when navigating SZ578 (B) across the Bay of Bengal on 18 November 1954 en route to China Bay, Caylon, and thence to the UK.

Chapter Sixteen

Trouble in French Indo-China

In Chapter 1, I described a short detachment to Cat Lai in French Indo-China on 6 and 7 December 1952. I now want to look back at an even earlier visit, in August 1952, when we were there briefly to discuss and plan the one-day French naval exercise that we took part in on 6 December. My purpose is to illustrate the difficulties a Sunderland crew could sometimes face when mooring.

It was on 26 August that our crew, in PP155 (D-Dog), captained by F/O Misty Donaldson,[1] flew to the French naval airbase at Cat Lai. We arrived overhead at 10.30 hrs. Before landing, the French air traffic controller warned us to exercise care when landing because logs had been seen floating through the alighting area on the tidal and fast-flowing Dong Nai River. I believe the surface wind was 10–12 kts, but (crucially) its direction was from about 215°T, while the downstream flow of the river was from the east, almost the opposite direction. During the approach and landing, our pilots kept a keen eye open for anything floating ahead of the aircraft. The landing was uneventful. However, as we slowed and made a 180° turn towards the mooring buoys, we realized how quickly the river was flowing on that day and at that particular time. There must have been very heavy rainfall in the previous twenty-four hours because the water level was high and the river current was probably about 4 kts, possibly faster.

When a Sunderland was on the water, if both inboard engines were shut down and the outer two were at idle, and if there was no water current and little or no wind, the aircraft would move forward at a fast walking pace; hence, the frequent need to deploy drogues into the water from the galley hatches to slow down the aircraft sufficiently to enable the two crewmen in the bow to 'catch' the buoy as the pilot manoeuvred the aircraft to bring it close along the port side of the nose. To steer the aircraft accurately into that position, the pilot needed to use the aircraft's rudder[2] and, in addition, to deploy one or two sea drogues as well as differential power from the outboard engines. However, excessive engine power could gather too much forward speed to allow the bowmen to catch the buoy successfully with the short slip (rope) and make a turn around the bollard. This was why, unlike at Cat Lai, most flying boat mooring areas were purposely *not* located in fast-flowing rivers.

In the situation we faced that day, the speed at which the river was flowing made it essential to approach the buoy against the current. The problem was that this placed the aircraft with the wind on its starboard beam or quarter. This gave Misty Donaldson poor rudder control during the final stages of the approach to the buoy, into the tidal flow; the natural tendency was for the aircraft to try to turn into wind (like a weather vane). This could only be corrected by more differential engine power, which would help to regain directional control but increase the aircraft's speed through the water. If Misty had approached the buoy into wind to gain effective steering control using the rudder, the aircraft would be moving at an angle to the fast-moving current, and the speed towards the moored buoy would have been at a fast walking pace *plus* perhaps 3–4 kts – far too fast to catch the buoy. It was also proving difficult to deploy the drogues in any way that materially helped to control or slow down the aircraft.

Misty, his co-pilot and the two crewmen in the bow and on the drogues had a major problem on their hands. We went up and down the river and around the mooring area, repeatedly, wrestling with the fast current and the wind, approaching from different directions and using various combinations of techniques to approach the buoy. My flying logbook states that it took us *four* hours to get ashore (that probably included an hour's refuelling time); it must have been well over two hours before we were able to secure the aircraft to the buoy! Misty Donaldson was a very experienced flying boat pilot, so this says something about the scale of difficulty he faced.

If we had had the support of a powerful and manoeuvrable RAF Marine Craft launch and an RAF coxswain – without any language difficulties – we might have manoeuvred so that the boat took the aircraft in tow while facing into the current; but the French naval motor boat had poor manoeuvrability, too little engine power, very ineffective steering using a long tiller (rather than a steering wheel), and a French-speaking coxswain not used to dealing with this situation. No flying boats were permanently based at Cat Lai, and the much larger Latécoère 631 docked at a jetty which *we* were not permitted to use.

Having at last secured ourselves to the buoy, we closed down the two outer engines. The French motor boat then proceeded to come along the *starboard* side of the aircraft (instead of the port); the coxswain was weaving all over the place just behind and under the wing, seeming to have very poor control over both the steering and the boat's engine; the craft appeared to have only three speeds – fast forward, neutral or fast reverse. We shouted and waved to the coxswain to get away from the aircraft, but in no time at all he collided the bow of his boat with the rear end of our starboard float and stove it in!

Shortly afterwards, the coxswain approached along the port side and proceeded to do almost the same to the port float, but struck it a more glancing blow, causing less damage; although the boat's hull also caught one of the bracing wires, it didn't snap. After a few more heart-stopping moments we managed to grab hold of the bow with a boat hook and secured it alongside our port front door.

Fortunately, the coxswain of the refuelling barge had better control of things, and what we feared might result in an even worse disaster passed off without incident. We went ashore, where there were profuse apologies by French naval officers for damaging our aircraft and commiserating with the difficulties we had experienced in mooring – all in the interests of *entente cordiale*! They said they would repair the float overnight; we imagined them riveting a thick steel plate onto the broken float to make it 'shipshape', but in practice they completed a very professional temporary repair.

Once ashore, we must have completed our business and were then asked if any of us would like to go into Saigon, about five miles distant by road. I seem to recall that Harold Francis (our CO), one other officer and I said we would like to visit the British Military Attaché's office in Saigon to draw some local currency. A French Navy *capitaine de frégate* (commander)

The French Navy inspects damage to the starboard float and considers how best to make a temporary repair. *Author*

offered to take us in his jeep; he said that he would be remaining in the city but that he would take a sailor with us who could then drive the jeep with us back to Cat Lai. The three of us squeezed onto the back seat of the jeep. The commander, who was driving, stopped at the guardhouse at the naval base entrance. Shortly afterwards, a sailor armed with a French automatic carbine like a Sten gun, emerged from the guard house and sat in the right-hand seat at the front. The commander, who continued as the driver, remarked that it was necessary to be armed because of the possibility that Communist guerrillas might set up an ambush on the road to Saigon – something we had not even considered!

We were driven along a dry, dusty and pot-holed road, storm drains on either side, and beyond them, paddy fields tended by traditionally dressed, mostly female farm workers. The sailor sat silent, loaded gun across his knees. We arrived safely in Saigon and the commander gave us directions to the British Embassy, telling us the sailor would wait for us where we had parked. When we were ready, he would drive us back to Cat Lai. He said something in French to the sailor, who replied, '*Oui, mon Capitaine*', stamped to attention and saluted.

We found the Embassy and the Attaché, obtained our money, walked a short while and then returned to the jeep where the sailor was waiting. We said, 'Cat Lai, *s'il vous plaît.*' The sailor saluted, laid the loaded gun on the floor between himself, now in the driver's seat, and S/L Harold Francis, who sat in the right-hand front seat. My other companion was in the left rear seat and I on the right. We sat beneath the jeep's canvas roof, which was supported by metal stanchions. The sailor started the engine and we set off along the fairly straight, dusty gravel road; we were soon doing about 50 mph. After a couple of miles we came to a left-hand bend that clearly needed to be taken at no more than 40 mph, but the driver made no attempt to take his foot off the accelerator. Halfway round the bend, he tightened the turn but still didn't slow down. The jeep then slewed sideways at right angles to our intended direction of travel, and rolled. I was soon aware of being thrown in all directions and seeing a dusty and stony road passing in front of my eyes as my forehead scraped the road. We appeared to roll once, possibly twice. When all movement had stopped I found I was standing on the road *behind* the jeep, which had righted itself. I was unable to move my head because my neck was held fast between two collapsed metal stanchions that had once supported the jeep's canvas roof.

The other three – including the driver – were fortunately free. S/L Francis had a grazed face that was bleeding, but no one had any serious injuries. The other two officers and the driver came to my rescue, lifting me bodily off the ground to extract my neck and head from its trapped position between the collapsed stanchions. My forehead was bleeding quite heavily,

The neat overnight repair carried out by the French Navy on our damaged starboard float. *Author*

but that apart I felt OK. None of the workers in a nearby paddy field made any attempt to assist us. The loaded gun lay on the road. Meanwhile the sailor driver, apoplectic at what he had done, repeated all the while, '*Mon Dieu, Mon Dieu, pardon Monsieurs, pardon Monsieurs.*' We calmed him down and he picked up the gun. We began to think about our situation; we were somewhere in the countryside between Saigon and Cat Lai where the commander had belatedly told us there was a possible threat of being attacked by terrorists.

It couldn't have been longer than a couple of minutes since we had rolled over when, fortuitously, a six-wheeled French armoured car appeared around the bend that we had just failed to negotiate, coming from the direction of Saigon. Immediately behind it was a military bus – the periodic, escorted shuttle bus between Saigon and Cat Lai naval base. After much Gallic shrugging of the shoulders and more cries of '*Mon Dieu*', we climbed aboard the naval bus. I was offered a piece of padding (I think from a first aid kit) to hold on my bleeding forehead. We set off for Cat Lai; a Frenchman in the seat in front of me had turned round and was looking at me, shaking his head and blowing out his cheeks in typical French fashion.

We were taken to the Cat Lai naval medical centre, where the three of us received medical treatment. My head wounds probably looked the most fearsome, but they were fairly superficial; I was injected by a naval doctor (presumably with anti-tetanus and I don't know what else), who then spent the best part of half-an-hour picking pieces of gravel out of my head with tweezers. He bathed and disinfected the wounds, cleaning them thoroughly. He then covered my forehead with a red-coloured antiseptic, which quickly dried, forming a protective layer across the wound. Their care and medical attention were excellent. The doctor insisted I go to bed in the medical centre for a couple of hours – presumably to guard against the onset of shock or the effect of the injections, although I was feeling perfectly OK and had little pain. A nurse brought me some French magazines to read and offered me a drink and something to eat. As I glanced at the magazines from my bed, something in the corner of my eye caught my attention; it was a rat climbing up the curtain – it left the room through an open, shuttered window!

We heard later that the sailor who had joined us from the guardroom, and later became our hapless driver, was actually in the cells, on 'jankers'.[3] When he was issued with the weapon and ordered to accompany the commander to Saigon, he wasn't expecting to be told to drive the jeep back to Cat Lai. When, on reaching Saigon, the French commander ordered him to do so, he was too frightened to say that he wasn't a qualified driver.

Before leaving Cat Lai, it is worth recording that I think it was when we flew there in early December 1952 that I saw and had the opportunity to go on board and look around a six-engine French flying boat, the Latécoère 631. This happened to be there when we arrived. It was moored to a jetty, purpose-built for this aircraft, which was a regular visitor, bringing supplies from France. Apparently it flew from Marseilles Marignane to Cat Lai in three stages, quite often refuelling at China Bay in Ceylon. The 631 had a wingspan of 188 feet (57.4 m), and its six 1,500 hp Wright Cyclone engines enabled it to cruise at about 150 kts over a range in excess of 3,000 nm. The fuselage had a very large cross-section, probably similar to one of today's wide-body airliners, and there was a long nose section ahead of the cockpit. The flight deck, too, was extremely spacious. Each of the two pilots had a large-diameter wheel mounted on the control column. The cockpit area was surrounded by large windows, giving the pilots an amazingly wide panoramic view. It was like a ship's bridge. The aircraft, which first flew after the German invasion of France in 1942, was originally intended to carry passengers across the Atlantic; indeed, this is what it did for a while after the end of the Second World War. However, after one disappeared without trace – with its crew and passengers – on one such transatlantic flight, by 1952 it was mainly being used as a freight carrier. The Latécoère 631 was only marginally smaller and lighter than the Glenn Martin Mars flying boat, which was two tonnes heavier and had a 12 ft greater wingspan.

S/L Harold Francis DFC, OC No. 88 Squadron, with a grazed face as a result of the Jeep accident. Behind him, enjoying the joke, is F/O Paddy Brogan (navigator).

The author with a bandaged head from the Jeep accident, being ferried by a French Navy motor launch out to PP155 (D-Dog) to return to Seletar.

A Latécoère 631 similar to the one we boarded at the French naval base at Cat Lai, French Indo-China, in December 1952. It was used mainly in support of the French Navy, transporting supplies and personnel from Marseille Marignane to Cat Lai, in three stages, including via RAF China Bay, Ceylon.

Notes
1. Our Squadron CO, S/L Harold Francis, was also with us on this trip.
2. I'm speaking about the aircraft's normal fin and rudder – it had no steerable rudder in the water.
3. 'Jankers' is slang for punishment; that was why he was in the guardroom, probably in a cell.

The flight deck of the Latécoère 631, more like the bridge of a ship than the cockpit of an aircraft.

Chapter Seventeen

RAF Seletar and Singapore

Ihave so far said little about RAF Seletar and Singapore. Although in total I spent longer here than in Japan or Hong Kong, most periods that I was in Singapore were intermittent and quite short. I think this was why my recollection of life in Singapore is somewhat hazier than at some other locations in the Far East. Apart from Firedogs and a few search and rescue operations – both of which I've described – Seletar was mainly the base from which we conducted routine training flying; readers would find this less interesting than some of the other operations we flew. This is not to imply that training flying bored me personally – I never tired of flying in the Sunderland, no matter what we were doing. Nevertheless, I will try to elaborate on life at Seletar and in Singapore, in so far as I can recall it after more than fifty years.

I liked Seletar. An unusual feature of the base was that all the roads on the station were named after well-known London streets; they included Piccadilly, Park Lane, Battersea Road, Maida Vale and many more. The roundabout just inside the main gate was Piccadilly Circus. From my perspective Seletar had a happy atmosphere and – at least during my time – a good community spirit. However, I have read elsewhere that some of the airmen were less than happy to be there, no doubt with good reason. Of course, it had been the scene of the famous 'strike' by RAF personnel in January 1946; however, that was well before my time, and it would be inappropriate to review the reasons and the outcome here. Nevertheless, in 1952, daily pay for RAF personnel was pretty low by any standard. Airmen, airwomen and junior NCOs especially were certainly much worse off than I as a junior officer and an aircrew member receiving additional flying pay – but even the flying pay supplement was minuscule in real terms compared with today.

Seletar was home to a variety of units, with vastly different roles. Apart from the three flying boat squadrons, there was 81 Squadron flying PR Mosquitoes and Spitfires. There was the Base Flight equipped with, among other aircraft, Beaufighters. Also based there were a Signals Unit, No. 390 Maintenance Unit and No. 1124 Marine Craft Unit.

RAF Seletar airfield showing the single runway and the flying boat alighting area in the Johore Strait to the north-east. *Ted Wilkins*

Unlike Hong Kong and Japan, Singapore has no clear-cut seasons. While both Hong Kong and Japan are very hot and humid in summer, this is followed by a few months in which it is cooler (in Hong Kong) and cold (in Japan). The average daytime temperature in Singapore is 86°F (30°C) throughout the year, typically peaking at 95°F (35°C) during the late morning and early afternoon and falling to an average 74°F (23°C) at night. Humidity can be 90%, which is uncomfortable. It can rain on more or less any day of the year, and when it does it nearly always comes as heavy showers of varying duration, often accompanied by thunder and lightning. The monsoon season is from December to March. The statistically dryer months are between June and September. Rainfall can average anything between 40 and 60 inches a year.

As a single man, I had no special ties with Seletar. For those on the squadron who were married it was quite different. Most had their wives with them in Singapore, and many had children, too. We had not yet reached the stage when it became common for the children of servicemen to be packed off to boarding school; in the 1950s this was unaffordable. It was not uncommon for service children to have attended six or more schools during their education. Most married officers lived in married quarters on the base,

Overflying the Sunderland hangars and slipway. *Don Jones*

but some were in houses dotted around the Island. A few shared a house –
especially if they were under 25 and not, therefore, receiving Marriage
Allowance. Most stayed in cheap hotels until they could find a suitable house
or were allocated a married quarter. As an unmarried officer and a member
of an all-single crew, after two or three weeks at Seletar I was usually about
to be detached to some other location, whether it be Japan, Hong Kong,
Borneo or Ceylon. Hence, for many single men flying on one of the
Sunderland squadrons, Singapore was in a sense a transit base.

   While in Singapore, I spent most of my time on the base at Seletar. All
ranks made good use of whatever facilities were there. We did not expect to
go gadding about every day of the week. Whether or not we wished to do so,
our level of pay prevented extravagance, and few owned cars. We had a bar
bill limit of £10 a month. When they were not night-flying, small groups of
officers would meet in the evening for dinner. Afterwards we would chat
while drinking a beer on the veranda, or go to the camp cinema. At weekends,
husbands might bring their wives to the mess, and we would join them in the
ladies' room. Ladies weren't allowed in public rooms other than at mess
functions, such as dances, which happened once or twice a year at most.

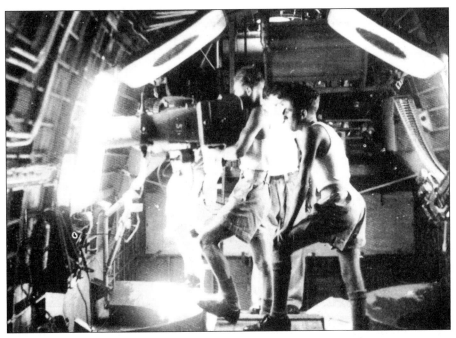

A long-focal-length F52 camera mounted in the port beam position. *Courtesy RAFSA*

Scenes from Chinatown, Singapore, in the 1950s. *Mike Rees of the RAFSA*

Six Sunderlands flying in formation over Singapore harbour. *Courtesy RAFSA*

View from overhead Far East Flying Boat Wing hangar, slipway and RAF Marine Craft pier at RAF Seletar. The compass base is at the bottom of the picture. *Courtesy RAFSA*

'W' Whiskey shortly after the beginning a take-off run. Note the high attitude of the nose and the large amount of spray between the floats and the hull, and also beneath the tailplane until the aircraft has risen well up onto the step. The speed here is about 40 knots. In this picture, the aircraft is probably taking off from Glugor, Penang, or possibly from China Bay. *A Carrie* (See photo 182c, d, e & f in colour section)

ML797 'P' with beaching legs and tail trolley fitted about to be brought up the slipway at Seletar prior to the 'paying-off' ceremony in May 1959. *A Carrie*

HRH the Duchess of Kent and the young Duke of Kent seen about to go on board an SZ578 that took them on a short tour in the South China Sea area in 1953. The wardroom interior of the aircraft was fitted out with tasteful décor for the journey, and was temporarily renamed Powder Puff. I later flew this aircraft from Seletar to Wig Bay at the end of my overseas tour. (*Bill Devine*)

But how did the airmen fare? Mike Rees,[1] an airman who was posted to 390 Maintenance Unit, said about his two and a half years on camp at Seletar in 1959, five years after I had returned to the UK, 'Life as a single man seemed to revolve around the lack of money, and the main preoccupation was how long the duty-free Tiger and Anchor beer would last in the NAAFI. West Camp airmen used to get really annoyed when East Camp airmen came over when their own beer quota had run out.'

While at RAF Thorney Island, where I completed my basic navigation training as an officer cadet navigator, I think I was paid about £8 a week. Hence, as a newly commissioned aircrew officer, I – and most other aircrew officers – arrived in Singapore on our first squadron tour with little or nothing in our newly acquired bank accounts. At that time, most RAF servicemen didn't expect and couldn't afford to have a car. A few, as I did in the UK, had motor bikes, but we weren't able to bring them with us when posted abroad; we relied almost exclusively on shared taxis or buses. For the most part, cars were owned only by those who were married and by older single men who had had a few years to save up enough to buy a second-hand car and could afford to run it.

Married officers – especially those living off base – needed transport to get to and from work; for them a car was a necessity. With their marriage and overseas allowances, a modest second-hand car was just about affordable. Those few aged less than 25 who were married found it extremely difficult to survive financially, and this must have put an enormous strain on their young marriages. This was especially true of those on Sunderland squadrons who were away from Singapore for at least a third of their tour. Out of necessity, unlike today, few service officers married before they were 25. Not only did they first have to seek the permission of the station commander, but they would receive no marriage allowance and no entitlement to live in married quarters until they were 25. As to cohabitation, that was completely off limits, and the quickest way to find you were on a troopship sailing towards the UK. Same-sex partnerships had not even been thought of – and any that might have existed were cause for immediate discharge from the service.

RAF Station Seletar was approached through a small village, Jalan Kayu. The main gate was unprepossessing, but this belied what lay beyond. On the base a visitor would at once notice the flowering trees and shrubs, neatly manicured grass, white-painted kerbs, and well-maintained roads and monsoon drains. The staff of the Air Ministry Works Department (AMWD) looked after all buildings on the base – including hangars, offices, the officers' and other ranks' married quarters and the barrack blocks.

When anyone of any rank moved out of a married quarter at the end of their tour of duty, they were 'marched out'. Similarly, those newly occupying a quarter were 'marched in'. Station routine orders designated the day, time and which officer was to accompany one of the AMWD staff and the barrack warden on an inspection of the house being vacated or occupied. In the presence of the occupant whose tour was ending, they inspected the house with eagle eyes, a 'wet finger and a fine toothcomb', looking for the slightest damage to the property, its contents and its decoration – and for any sign of dirt or grime. Every item on a long inventory of cutlery, china, bedding, furnishings, garden tools, etc. had to be neatly displayed by the occupant in its proper place as stated in the inventory. Furniture had to be in its appointed room, and like everything else was rigorously inspected for any stains, damage or dust. The garden, too, had to be neat and tidy. The occupant would have to pay for anything that was missing or damaged except if it was judged to be 'fair wear and tear'. If the house wasn't spotlessly clean the occupant would have to pay for it to be cleaned. On a 'Marching In', it was imperative for the new occupant to be very diligent in spotting any damage or anomalies in the inventory, otherwise they could find themselves paying for cracked cups, a missing knife, a stained sofa or a damaged wardrobe when they vacated the quarter, two to three years later. Single men had a weekly 'bull' night and inspection of their barrack block and bed-space. These, too, had to be kept spotless.

Some people were rather scornful of the AMWD, and of course it wasn't perfect; but the situation we have in the UK, today, after successive government and Treasury-led financial cuts of the Armed Services, have made the situation ten times worse than ever it was in 1983 when I retired from the RAF. Many servicemen, servicewomen and their families are angry, and understandably so, because of the poor state of repair and lack of investment in armed forces barracks and married quarters. This was never the case in the 1950s, when six or seven times as many military establishments were supported by the AMWD, even though the UK economy was financially in a far worse state than today during the so-called 2008 Credit Crunch. It is true that married and single living quarters were then not fitted out with all the appliances and labour-saving conveniences that everyone expects today. However, the fabric of buildings was never allowed to deteriorate, and essential repairs and decoration were in general dealt with promptly.

Most officer and SNCO aircrew regularly played one or more sports – especially those who were unmarried. Wednesday afternoons were set aside for organized or individual sports. If you were on the station and not officially 'at work' or on duty, all ranks were *expected* to play a sport – and the majority did. Obesity was rare. I played squash and swam on most days, and took part in athletics and sometimes golf, as detachments allowed. The Services recognized that their men and women should be fit – not fat.

As to other spare-time activities, occasionally several of us would share a taxi into Singapore. The taxi engine would 'pink' all the way to the city because taxi drivers invariably had their carburettors set to a fully weak mixture! Once in the city we might walk past St Andrew's Cathedral, the Padang and the Cricket Ground, onwards to Collyer Quay and through Change Alley. If we were feeling especially flush, we might go to Raffles Hotel, into the Long Bar made famous by Somerset Maughan, and after a couple of beers, take 'tiffin' there. The Malay dish Nasi Goreng was one of my favourites. Of course we would have liked to be members of the Tanglin Club with all its facilities, or the Cricket Club on the Padang, but these were unaffordable for servicemen.

It was interesting to walk through Chinatown (I believe only one street now remains), Little India and Arab Street, all fascinating in their different ways. We might go shopping and 'people watching' in Orchard Road. Today, it has huge, air-conditioned stores. Once in a while several of us might go to Bugis Street in the evening, famous for its far-from-obvious transvestites and open-air eating-places. Another favourite was to see a film at a 'midnight matinée' in the city on a Saturday night, and enjoy the luxury of the cinema's air conditioning.

On the RAF station at Seletar the airmen had the NAAFI and Malcolm Clubs at which to eat, drink and play darts, snooker, billiards or the juke box.

The two clubs also ran dances. There was an excellent open-air swimming-pool where most people swam several times a week. The pool was a good place to meet the few 'eligible' girls, and to socialize. There were the Yacht Club and Golf Club. The golf course was on the airfield, and one of the fairways ran parallel to and close behind the officers' mess. On Saturday and Sunday mornings, early, before the hottest part of the day, the course often became very busy. It was not unknown for a hooked drive from one of the tees to end its trajectory ricocheting around the balcony of a first-floor bedroom – followed by a bellowed 'FORE' or 'SORRY!' from the golfer. The officers' and sergeants' messes organized various social functions – dining-in nights, dances and other parties – which many aircrew on 'boats' missed because of detachments to other parts of the Orient. There were other clubs on the base, too. Everyone made use of the Astra cinema which was very popular.

Mention of the Astra reminds me that one evening after nightfall, several of us were sitting on the officers' mess balcony outside the ante-room, overlooking the airfield. We were about to walk to the Astra cinema, ten minutes away from the mess. To our left was the main runway where two 81 Squadron Mosquitoes were carrying out night-time circuits and landings. As we stood up to leave for the cinema, one of the aircraft, landing towards the north-east, had touched down and was nearing the end of its run, clattering along on the PSP[2] runway. Suddenly, there was a bang, followed by a loud scraping sound and sparks as the Mosquito came to a halt. An RAF medical officer (MO) who was sitting on the balcony near us, leapt off his chair and was last seen running into the darkness at high speed across the mess lawn, towards the airfield runway and the crippled Mosquito. We gave him a loud cheer. Our group then left the mess and walked towards the cinema. As we passed close by the medical centre, not far from the cinema, an ambulance pulled up. The rear doors opened and two men in flying-suits, presumably from the Mosquito, emerged, carrying the MO whom we had last seen running towards the airfield. In the darkness and his haste to rescue the crew, he'd fallen into a deep monsoon drain near the runway, breaking his leg. The Mosquito crew, who had by then climbed unharmed from their aircraft, fortunately heard him shouting for help and rescued him!

RAF Seletar was effectively bisected by the single runway into west and east Seletar. Two aircraft hangars, one used by No. 81 Squadron, the air traffic control tower, an airmen's mess, a sergeants' mess, a NAAFI and at least two accommodation blocks, plus part of No. 390 Maintenance Unit and other small units and facilities that I can't recall, were in the western half of the station. All the other units and the station headquarters, as well as the officers' mess, additional sergeants' and airmen's messes, a NAAFI, Malcolm Club and the main Astra cinema, were to the east of the runway. The three Sunderland squadrons' headquarters and engineering wing were near the waterfront. Nos 205 and 209 Squadrons had their headquarters at the front

RAF Seletar with a No. 81 Squadron Mosquito in the foreground. *Courtesy No. 81 Squadron*

of two large hangars (see pages 184 and 186), whereas 88 Squadron (the last to arrive at Seletar) had to be satisfied with a 'basher hut' several hundred yards from the slipway, not far from the compass-swinging base. As I have already described, 88 Squadron was transferred from Kai Tak to Singapore after the outbreak of the Korean War.

Singapore was an exciting city to visit. Moreover, I always felt safe there despite the Emergency in Malaya, only a few miles distant. In 2007, the Jurong Town Corporation, at a cost of many tens of millions of Singapore dollars, declared its intention to develop Seletar as an Aerospace Park and a centre of excellence for the Singaporean Aerospace Industry. This has already been followed by further investments by well-known major aerospace companies. New and large hangars, and other manufacturing and office buildings, have been built or are under construction. There is also the magnificent Seletar Country Club with a golf course, sailing and other sports facilities. While it is therefore no longer a military base, its close connection with aerospace, begun in 1923 when the British government decided to open a naval base nearby and establish an airfield and flying boat base at Seletar, will continue into the foreseeable future.

Notes
1. Mike Rees, RAF Seletar Association website
2. Seletar was one of the few RAF airfields to have a PSP (metal tracking) runway. When the runway was extended towards the Johore Strait after the Second World War, PSP was used for the extension. It gave out a loud metallic clatter whenever an aircraft ran over it.

Chapter Eighteen

The Beginning of the End

The end of deployments to Iwakuni

Although an armistice was signed on 27 July 1953 ending offensive operations in Korea that had begun on 25 June 1950, there was more than a year-long post-Armistice period during which all UN forces (land, sea and air) either remained in their wartime locations or continued non-combat operations. RAF Sunderland and USN VP squadron patrols continued until some date in late August 1954. I was on detachment at Iwakuni from 7 June until 13 August 1954, and flew during the last month of RAF Far East Flying Boat Wing operations from Iwakuni. Most were sorry to see the end of detachments to Japan. We regretted that the intensity of flying during of our deployments had not allowed us enough time to travel far from Iwakuni to see more of Japan. Most Japanese people working on the airbase and with whom we came into contact in shops and bars in Iwakuni town were friendly and helpful. We have to remember that it was then only seven years since the war had ended and the atomic bomb had exploded above Hiroshima, less than twenty miles away. Many Japanese families living in Iwakuni and some working on the base had lost relatives on that day, or earlier during the war.

Even after the armistice was signed in July 1953 and until September 1954, operations by Sunderland Mark Vs and our USN counterparts operating PBM-5 Mariner flying boats and PB4Y-2 Privateer landplanes had continued at the same rate as we had done since mid-1950.

After the loss of RN302 near Tsushima, our crew was temporarily without an aircraft. In February 1954 we acquired SZ578 (B-Baker) and a new captain, F/O Stuart Holmes. At around this time the squadron CO appointed me squadron navigation leader. In this new role, when not flying with our crew, I periodically flew with other 88 Squadron crews to see for myself how other squadron navigators were performing. I had to recommend their annual proficiency assessments to the CO, and felt it only fair to see them at work and not to assess them solely on the basis of their logs and charts (I had to check the navigation accuracy and activity rates and award a mark to each navigator's log and chart for every sortie of any consequence).

Although, at that time, we were not aware that this was to be the final Sunderland detachment to Iwakuni for Korean operations, what turned out to be my last visit there began on 7 June and ended on 11 August 1954. On the last twenty-three days of June I flew eleven Fox or Tsushima patrols totalling 122 flying hours. This was followed in July by a further twelve patrols totalling 127 hours. My last Korean sortie was on 4 August 1954. This was a nine-hour ASP Tsushima. That brought my tally for Korean missions to sixty-one and 576 flying hours spread over seven detachments. To provide readers with an overview of the pattern of flying during a typical Far East flying boat tour, I have included an analysis of my own tour, which is probably representative of many Far East Flying Boat Wing crews. This is at Appendix 1.

The cessation of flying in support of the United Nations in Korea heralded the beginning of the run-down of the Far East Flying Boat Wing. It was almost inevitable that one of the three squadrons would have to go because the ending of detachments at Iwakuni slashed the operational task of the Sunderland Wing by one-third. Historically, 88 Squadron had more often been a light-bomber squadron, whereas 205 and 209 were former Royal Naval Air Service squadrons and, later, RAF maritime patrol squadrons; so they were bound to have precedence over 88 when it came to one of the squadrons being disbanded.

The disbandment of No. 88 Squadron

For the third time in thirty-seven years, the expected disbandment of No. 88 Squadron was ordered to take place on 1 October 1954. A squadron disbandment party for all ranks was held at the Seletar Malcolm Club. Four hundred and fifty-six pints of beer were drunk at a cost of about six 'new' pence a pint! No. 88 Squadron had first formed in 1917 and went to France equipped with Bristol Fighters for reconnaissance and artillery spotting. By the war's end it had shot down 164 enemy aircraft destroyed. The squadron was disbanded in 1919. '88' re-formed in 1937 with Fairey Battles. On 20 September 1939, while patrolling near the German front line in Belgium, Sgt F. Letchford, the air observer (navigator/air gunner) of an 88 Squadron Battle, successfully used the aircraft's 0.303 in. machine-gun to shoot down a German Me109, the first RAF air-to-air kill of the Second World War. However, the squadron suffered heavy casualties during the German invasion of Belgium and France, and eventually returned to England after losing virtually all of its aircraft. In 1941, the squadron was the first to be re-equipped with Boston light bombers. They became engaged on shipping strikes and other bombing operations, including during the ill-fated Dieppe

Raid by six thousand predominantly Canadian troops on 19 August 1942. The squadron was briefly disbanded in April 1945, but formed again on 1 September 1946, this time with Sunderlands at RAF Kai Tak, whence they flew courier and transport missions between Hong Kong and Japan. However, the squadron role changed to maritime reconnaissance over the Yellow Sea and the Sea of Japan following the outbreak of the Korean War on 25 June 1950. As I have described, they flew these operations from Iwakuni, 88's base in Japan. Later, Sunderlands of 205 and 209 Squadron, then based in Singapore, joined 88 Squadron in these operations on a rotational basis. In September 1950, 88 Squadron moved its main base to Seletar, becoming the third squadron of the FEFBW. The squadron's disbandment for the third time in 1954 signalled the beginning of the run-down of the Far East Flying Boat Wing. Some time later, 205 and 209 Squadrons would combine into a single squadron (No. 205/209 Squadron) continuing at first to fly the Sunderland. Gradually, the number of Sunderlands was reduced and replaced by land-based Shackletons operating from RAF Changi, Singapore. No. 205/209 Squadron then operated two different aircraft types – one a flying boat, the other a landplane – from different bases.

On 1 October 1954, with my overseas tour due to end in December, I was temporarily posted to No. 205 Squadron. This was a rather strange experience – like being a 'new boy' again. However, I and others in the same position were made welcome and became additional members of 205 or 209 Squadron crews. Early October was taken up mostly with helping to 'wrap up' 88 Squadron, destroying what was no longer required, packing away historically interesting material, and sending official papers of any note to be archived. Equipment was returned to stores. We also had numerous rehearsals for the disbandment parade. Most of us had become somewhat unaccustomed to formal parades and drill, having routinely sought to avoid these whenever possible over the previous two years.

The disbandment parade for No. 88 Squadron – which was later yet again to re-form, this time as a Canberra B(I) 8 bomber squadron in Germany – was held on 10 October 1954. Air Marshal Sir Clifford Sanderson KBE, CB, DFC, Commander-in-Chief Far East Air Force, was the reviewing officer. Except for one or two absentees, all squadron members took part. The parade ground was the slipway between the aircraft hangars and the waterfront at Seletar. We wore No. 6 Dress with medal ribbons. The squadron parade commander was S/L Harold T. Francis DFC, the squadron's CO.

We marched onto the parade ground to music played by the Central Band. The squadron was positioned in the centre of a three-sided open square of parading station personnel. We faced the reviewing officer and a couple of hundred seated guests. No. 88 Squadron paraded in two flights, commanded respectively by the squadron flight commander, F/L Les Tester DFM, and the deputy flight commander, F/L Len Stapleton. Each flight was composed of airmen, SNCOs and officer aircrew of the squadron. There was a supporting squadron made up of four flights of personnel of No. 205 Squadron, Flying Boat Wing Headquarters, Technical Control, and Maintenance Base Seletar. White-painted and polished Sunderland Mk Vs were positioned to provide a backdrop. Guests included relatives and friends of squadron personnel, together with Army, Royal Navy and Royal Air Force top brass and several United States Navy and Air Force officers. After the Commander-in-Chief inspected squadron personnel, there were the usual parade formalities, drill movements and a General Salute. The two 88 Squadron flights, led by the squadron CO, marched past the C-in-C to the tune of 'Auld Lang Syne'. The parade over, we were 'dismissed' for the last time as members of 88 Squadron. I have listed below the names of aircrew officers who were on the final parade. I am sorry that I have not been able to locate the names of the six or seven SNCOs or WOs who were then crew members of the five aircraft, A, B, C, D and F.

No. 88 Squadron Commanding Officer	S/L H.T. Francis DFC
Squadron Adjutant	F/O Peter G. Sinclair
No. 1 Flight Commander	F/L Leslie H. Tester DFM
Supernumerary Officers	F/L E.W. (Jock) Beer (captain of D)
	F/L N.A. (Sandy) Innes-Smith (captain of C)
	F/O S.W. (Stu) Holmes (captain of B)
	F/L J. (Jack) Oliver (1st pilot)
	F/L A.W. Thomas (1st pilot B)
	F/O D.K. (Derek) Empson (Navigation Leader)
No. 2 Flight Commander	F/L L A (Len) Stapleton (captain of F)
Supernumerary Officers	F/O K.C. (Keith) Readyhoof (1st nav of B)
	F/O J.O. (Bob) Cook (1st nav C)
	F/O D.J. (Dave) Germain (1st nav D)
	F/O K. (Keith) Watson (1st nav A)
	F/O A.K. (Keith) Mosely (2nd nav A)
	F/L E.F. (Eric) Herbert (2nd nav D)
	F/O C.D. (Colin) Sharpe (2nd pilot)
	P/O P.J. (Pete) Baker (2nd pilot)

The last noteworthy function involving 88 Squadron while it remained a flying boat squadron was a guest night held in the officers' mess at RAF Seletar on the evening of 22 October. The squadron was invited to be guests of the mess. Drinks were 'free' – paid for by members through the mess guests' account. The station commander of Seletar Maintenance Base, G/C King, was present. After an excellent dinner, the port was circulated and the loyal toast drunk to Her Majesty. W/C Burgess, OC Far East Flying Boat Wing, and a former pilot of the famous wartime Gloster Gladiator fighters based in Malta, *Faith*, *Hope* and *Charity*, made a speech. He included apt remarks that indicated that someone had been telling tales out of school! He wryly applauded the efforts of F/L Len Stapleton, deputy flight commander of 88 Squadron and captain of Sunderland F-Fox, whom he congratulated for his attempts to improve Anglo-American relations by (unofficially) flying two United States Navy Nursing Sisters in his aircraft from Hong Kong to Iwakuni – it showed there was not much that went by undetected! He ended by saying, 'Whatever is said about 88 Squadron, it was definitely the squadron for getting the job done.' This was met by cheers from 88 Squadron members and catcalls from the rest. S/L Harold Francis, our CO, replied and thanked squadron members for their support, co-operation and forbearance. A toast was proposed, 'to 88 Squadron'.

From left to right, front row: F/O Derek Empson (nav ldr), F/L Jack Oliver, F/O Stuart Holmes, F/L Len Stapleton, F/L Les Tester (flight commander) and S/L Harold Francis (CO No. 88 Squadron). SNCO aircrew are standing behind.

On 10 October 1954, AM Sir Clifford Sanderson KBE, CB, DFC, Commander-in-Chief Far East Air Force, the Reviewing Officer, inspected No. 88 Squadron ground crews and aircrews on the Disbandment Parade.

After we rose from dinner, bottles of champagne miraculously appeared and were consumed to the accompaniment of music played on the bagpipes and drums of the RAF Seletar Band. At midnight, the squadron's CO was 'chaired' on an improvised Sunderland tail beaching trolley, from the mess to his married quarter not far away on Seletar base, where his wife, Lillian, was relieved to see him return in one piece. Little did she know that on the way, a rebellious former member of the squadron had tried to set light to a copy of the *Straits Times* on which her husband had been sitting to protect his mess kit uniform from the somewhat grubby trolley. However, before a conflagration was allowed to take hold, the offender was tossed ignominiously into a storm drain and the fire was extinguished. Having deposited the CO at his residence, the towing party returned with the trolley, but were prevented by the president of the mess committee from towing it up the steps into the officers' mess.   The party continued until about three o'clock, when most people drifted off to bed and the last official function of No. 88 Flying Boat Squadron came to an end.

Posted to No. 205 Squadron

In October 1954, following the disbandment of No. 88 Squadron, as I have mentioned, I was posted to No. 205 Squadron for the remainder of my tour. This finally ended in November. Finding myself at a loose end on the morning of 4 October, I grabbed the opportunity to fly in a Station Flight Beaufighter and navigate it from Seletar to Kuala Lumpur and back. F/L Griffiths was the pilot. I had wanted to fly in a Beaufighter since I was a boy. I used to see them pass low overhead my home when I lived near Sevenoaks in Kent throughout the Second World War. Beaufighters were then operating over that area, mainly as night-fighters. Commonly nicknamed 'whispering death', the 'Beau' had a very distinctive and pleasing engine note, just as the Sunderland had. The opportunity to navigate a Beaufighter was too good to miss.

During the short period I was with 205 Squadron, I mainly flew with F/L Rex Harrison as captain; ours was a somewhat mixed crew: some, including me, were ex-88 Squadron, while the remainder were already members of 205 Squadron. In October, we flew only 23 hrs 40 min. Most of this was practice bombing and gunnery at an armament practice camp at Penang, which we completed by flying there and back from Seletar rather than deploying to Glugor.

Farewell ferry flight to the UK by Sunderland

The end of my tour came in November 1954, and I could hardly believe my good luck when I was told I was to navigate Sunderland SZ578 'B', a former 88 Squadron aircraft, to the Short Bros & Harland base at Wig Bay in Scotland. Rex Harrison, with whom I had been flying for a month since my posting to No. 205 Squadron, was to be the captain, and F/L Pete Wildy the co-pilot. A point of historical interest is that in 1953, SZ578 was the aircraft that had been used to ferry the Duchess of Kent on her Far East tour. For this, the aircraft had been modified internally to provide greater comfort for the royal passenger in the wardroom and – it was rumoured – in the 'heads'! The aircraft had temporarily been named 'Powder Puff'. Disappointingly, by the time we came to fly it back to the UK it had been demodified!

I planned more of less the same route as for my first ferry flight to Wig Bay in 1952. The only difference was that we staged from Malta to Marseille Marignane in France, before flying to Pembroke Dock and thence to Wig Bay. We took off on 18 November and arrived at Wig Bay eighteen days later on 6 December 1954, a flight time of 67 hrs 5 min. The 1 hr 35 min flight from Pembroke Dock to Wig Bay in SZ578 (B-Baker) was my last ever sortie in a Sunderland. The next time I stepped inside a Sunderland fuselage was fifty-four years later, on 12 February 2008.

'Boat happy'. F/L Rex Harrison, captain of SZ 578, is ringed by a solid white circle, F/L Pete Wildy, co-pilot, by a dotted white circle, and the author, F/O Derek Empson, the navigator, is ringed by a dashed white circle. Other members of the crew are believed to be Sgt Holloway, Sgt Brian Lavender, air signaller 209 Sqn, Sgt Charlie Elliott, flight engineer 88 Sqn, Sgt J. Griffiths, air gunner 209 Sqn, Sgt D. Tweed, flight engineer 88 Sqn, and Sgt R. Hood. The marine craft is the type normally used to ferry aircrew and servicing personnel to and from aircraft moored on the trots. The coxswain is in the bow. These craft were fast, manoeuvrable and very seaworthy. However, with only a canvas screen in front of the coxswain, you could sometimes have a dousing by the time you reached the aircraft in choppy waters. Crew names were kindly provided to the author by Tony Burt and obtained from the Squadron F540.

Chapter Nineteen

Reflections

That brings to a conclusion an account of some of my experiences as a navigator of Sunderland flying boats over Far Eastern seas between 1952 and 1954. This was my first squadron tour in the Royal Air Force. At the beginning I was a newly qualified navigator with very limited experience. I then had just 450 flying hours; only 110 were in a Sunderland, of which a mere twenty-three hours were navigation training. By the end of my tour I had accumulated almost two thousand hours and flown more than a quarter of a million miles. The various crews I flew with had taken part in a variety of operations in many different locations throughout the Far East. We had also flown from Singapore to Scotland and back. I ended the tour by navigating a Sunderland to the UK, taking my few personal possessions with me. The only regular deployment location in the Far East I never flew to was Christmas Island, south of Java. Coincidentally, this was where, on 21 June 1954, Sunderland SZ599, by then being flown by 209 Squadron, was damaged beyond repair while landing in difficult sea conditions not dissimilar from those our crew had experienced on 27 December 1953 when attempting to land RN302 on the sea to the east of Tsushima Island. SZ599 was the last Mark V off the production line and was the aircraft our crew had flown from Wig Bay to Seletar early in 1953, described in Chapter 2.

The events I have described took place at various times during my thirty-month tour, and in total they occupied about a third of that period. The remainder of the two and a half years was made up of similar types of flying and deployments. During their tours of duty, most Far East flying boat crews will have had experiences similar to many that I have described in this book; they were not unusual, and in a sense, therefore, my story could be *theirs*, too.

I have tried to shed light on typical demands that navigation placed upon flying boat crews in the Far East fifty and more years ago. Aids to navigation then were vastly inferior to and different from today. Modern navigation aids and avionics systems provide quantum improvements in accuracy and 'user-friendliness' compared with those upon which air crews were dependent in the 1930s, '40s and '50s. While, therefore, I have often focused on the task of the navigator, I hope I have adequately stressed the contribution that, in my view, all members of Sunderland crews made towards safe navigation. While navigators carried the *responsibility* for safe and accurate navigation, they required the frequent and willing co-operation of other crew members – assistance which, in my experience, was unhesitatingly given.

I hope that those with whom I flew will forgive me for rarely being able to describe their involvement in the events I have recounted. In some instances their experiences could well have made more interesting reading than my own; however, after fifty-six years it has been difficult to recall, with certainty, my own actions, let alone those of others. Although I have researched with some care the incidents I describe, I can but apologize for such omissions and inaccuracies as there may well be. Like other such accounts, mine won't have included everything that took place, and I'm sure readers will understand the difficulty or impossibility of checking details with former crew members, most of whom I have been unable to contact, or who, sadly, in some cases have passed on. Nevertheless, I was fortunate to receive help from a small number of RAF Sunderland crew members and others whose names I have mentioned in the Acknowledgements. I am sure their contributions will have made this account more informative and readable. Despite its shortcomings, I hope readers – whatever their background and interest – will have begun to understand why 'being on boats' – a mixture of airmanship, seamanship and teamwork – meant so much to those of us who were fortunate to fly and operate in them.

Operations by RAF Sunderland flying boats in the Atlantic, North Sea and English Channel following the Second World War were very different from those in the Far East. Sunderland operations in the Eastern Atlantic and Mediterranean focused on the demands of the Cold War. To that end, not only the types of sortie flown but the equipment was in some respects different. UK-based aircraft were engaged in combating the potential and growing threat from powerful Soviet submarine and surface naval forces. They flew and practised techniques and tactics designed to protect NATO surface naval fleets and merchant shipping, and to detect and – if it came to war – to destroy Soviet Bloc submarines. Sunderland Mk Vs in the NATO area were equipped with sonics equipment to detect submerged submarines. This equipment was located in the wardroom on the lower deck. They also had a ground position indicator and plotting table in an additional crew station behind the 1st pilot's seat. And finally, those based in the UK carried the quick-fixing aid Gee. Sunderlands in the Far East were not fitted with sonar, Gee or a GPI, and they saw few Soviet naval forces. Indeed, crews saw comparatively few Royal Navy surface ships and submarines in the Far East, despite the fact that in 1952 the Royal Navy had 212 ships on active duty and more than three hundred in reserve. What a change from 2009! Those that we did see were mostly operating in the Korean theatre, and like us, were part of the United Nations Force there.

The role of Sunderlands in the Far East, as this account has described, was therefore quite different from that of their sister squadrons in the UK. Indeed, from June 1950 until August 1954, a third of the operational effort of the Far East Air Force Sunderland fleet was as an integral part of United Nations maritime forces engaged in the Korean War. This involved daily reconnaissance patrols in the Yellow Sea and Tsushima Strait, searching for and photographing mostly merchant vessels, especially those taking supplies to North Korea, which was subject to a United Nations embargo. It also required frequent weather reconnaissance sorties at night in the Yellow Sea, and occasionally surveillance protection to UN naval task forces, mainly Task Forces 77 and 95, when aircraft carriers were being refuelled at sea. In Malaya, Far East Sunderlands were engaged in Firedog overland operations to assist the British Army fighting Communist terrorists in the Malayan jungle. Sunderlands were in addition almost solely responsible for search and rescue around Hong Kong, Singapore, Malaya and throughout the South China Sea and Malacca Strait. There were no SAR helicopter squadrons. Sunderlands assisted police forces combating smuggling and piracy between the Philippines, British North Borneo and Brunei, and occasionally around Singapore. They were workhorses that were likely to be called upon to undertake more or less any operation, at any time. This included ferrying royalty and other VIPs around the region; flying top-secret missions to transport senior British scientists, such as Sir William Penney, to atomic bomb tests; and taking the Bishop of Singapore to visit his 'flock' on Christmas Island, south of Java. These operations were shared between the fifteen Sunderland crews of Nos 88, 205 and 209 Squadrons. Most took place in areas where radio navigation aids were sparse, and many were based on alighting areas where flying boat maintenance facilities were minimal or non-existent. Many flying hours were spent on 9–12 hr transit flights between Singapore, Ceylon, Hong Kong, the Philippines and Japan, much of the time across open ocean areas requiring reliance on celestial navigation and other dead-reckoning navigation techniques, described in Appendix 3. These demanded high standards of navigation in addition to first-class piloting, airmanship, seamanship and other aircrew skills. Each crew member was certified to service certain equipment; they had to be knowledgeable enough to identify the most common faults and be able to replace certain units when unserviceabilities occurred while away from their main bases at Seletar, Kai

Tak and Iwakuni where maintenance crews of the Far East Flying Boat Wing were permanently based or deployed. Periodically, aircraft were flown by crews to the UK for major overhaul by Shorts, and on these occasions a fitter and rigger usually accompanied the crew.

For those who study aviation history, I have included an analysis of the different types of missions, numbers of sorties and average durations flown by the crews with whom I flew during my tour of duty. This analysis is probably fairly typical of many other Far East Flying Boat Wing Sunderland crews. This is at Appendix 1. The only point to consider is that I generally flew with an entirely – or mostly – unmarried crew, and we therefore spent rather more time away from Seletar than most other 88 Squadron crews. This can be seen from what were almost certainly above-average periods of time spent at Iwakuni and Hong Kong.

While many good accounts have been written about operations by Sunderland aircraft in the Battle of the Atlantic and post war in the NATO theatre, descriptions of Sunderland operations between 1946 and 1959 in the Far East are few and hard to find. May 2009 marked fifty years since all RAF Sunderland operations ceased – and about eighty years have passed since RAF flying boat operations began. I therefore feel this to be an appropriate moment to put on record Sunderland operations in the Far East as seen by one who was engaged in them for two and a half years in that period.

The Sunderland was undoubtedly one of the finest aircraft of its time, first designed and built in the late 1930s. The Mark V was introduced in February 1945 (some were converted Mark IIIs), and was the last new mark to enter service. I therefore feel it important for historical reasons to include in this book details of the aircraft's flight performance, and photographs of the layout of the Mark V showing where the ten crew members worked, and the equipment they used to fulfil their operational tasks. I have compiled this information and illustrated it using photographs I took in February 2008 at the Imperial War Museum, Duxford, of Sunderland ML796, the first production Mark V aircraft. Technical details are included in Appendices 2 and 4.

I feel it is important to retain records and photographic images for the benefit of aviation historians, enthusiasts, the youth of today and, not least, former Sunderland crew members and their families who cannot now view the inside of a fitted-out Sunderland; nor are these data and images readily to be seen in other places. Of the relatively few Sunderlands now exhibited around the world, the equipment fit of Sunderland ML796 at Duxford, as shown in this book, comes closest to that of a former RAF front-line aircraft. A few items of equipment (e.g. the variation setting control) and some instrumentation (such as the correct marks of altimeter and the loop antenna and bearing scale) are not fitted on the flight deck. That said, I

PLANNED SERVICING

(Cartoon by KANE)

OPERATIONS WING

The author receives the 'keys' of Operations Wing, RAF Luqa, Malta, when he assumes command from his predecessor, W/C Mike Tinley, in spring 1964. The Tactical Evaluation Team descended on Luqa unannounced three days later, to test the station's operational readiness over a continuous ninety-six-hour period!

would estimate that 95% of the aircraft is authentic Mark V, a tremendous achievement for which all praise is due to the staff at Duxford who have lovingly completed a first-class restoration of this aircraft. They received it as a shell; it was a former night club at La Baulle in France. Since, understandably, the public are not generally admitted aboard this aircraft, it is hoped this book will provide a worthy substitute and show the Sunderland Mark V internally up to the standard of ML796.

My intention in writing this book was to provide readers with an opportunity to come as close as possible to experiencing what it was like to fly as a crew member aboard a Sunderland in the 1950s. I hope I have gone some way towards meeting that goal. I feel privileged to have been a member of a Sunderland crew. The teamwork and friendship I experienced during those two-and-half years were exceptional. It mattered not whether you were an officer or a SNCO, but how conscientiously you carried out your responsibilities and worked with every other member of the crew. We had to

W/C Derek Empson and his wife, Margaret, a former WRAF officer, photographed in front of a 203 Squadron Nimrod MR1 in autumn 1976 on the apron at RAF Luqa, Malta, just before flying back to the UK in an RAF Britannia at the end of his tour as Officer Commanding Operations Wing.

know and to follow the rules of seamanship as well as airmanship. Operating from the sea added a new dimension, demanding greater participation by the crew in the day-by-day maintenance, serviceability and operation of the aircraft as compared with landplanes. Unlike landplanes, the aircrew refuelled the aircraft and carried out all the engine runs once the aircraft was in the water. Flying in and navigating Sunderlands in the Far East taught me a great deal. It was an unforgettable experience and without doubt the most memorable and exciting period of my Royal Air Force flying career.

My last flight in a Sunderland was on 6 December 1954. A little under five years later, on 15 May 1959, ML797, the second production Mark V, flew the last official RAF Sunderland mission from Seletar. On 20 May, the same aircraft, piloted by F/L Jack Poyser, a former member of No 88 Squadron, flew a farewell sortie around Singapore, including over the busy harbour. This was the last flight by a Sunderland of the Royal Air Force. The aircraft had its beaching legs and tail trolley attached, and it was pulled out of the water. On 22 May, a paying-off ceremony with an RAF guard of honour took place on the slipway at RAF Seletar. This brought to an end the era of the Sunderland and the operation of flying boats by the Royal Air Force, probably for all time.

The author receives congratulations from Rear Admiral Wayne D. Bodensteiner USN, Commander Maritime Air Forces Mediterranean, on the occasion of the author's promotion to group captain in 1980, when he was the Admiral's Chief of Staff and Staff Officer Plans and Exercises at the NATO COMARAIRMED Headquarters at Agnano, Naples, Italy.

Statistical Analysis of a Far East Flying Boat Tour

This Appendix contains charts showing the numbers and percentage share of different types of sortie and associated flight hours flown by my particular Far East Sunderland aircraft during my two-and-a-half-year tour. This pattern of flying is likely to be fairly typical of many other Far East Flying Boat Wing crews who served on Nos 88, 205 and 209 Squadrons. Data showing the number of flight hours and sorties, and the bases from which they were flown, may be slightly skewed due to the fact that I flew in crews mostly or totally composed of unmarried aircrew. Understandably, there was a tendency to avoid over-long or undesirably frequent detachments away from Singapore by crews with a high proportion of married men, in order to reduce separation from families who were based at Seletar. Crews such as mine that were made up mostly or entirely of single men didn't object to this operating policy in the least.

During thirty calendar months, I flew 300 Sunderland sorties, amounting to 1,856 flying hours. Of these, 280 sorties and 1,766 hours were with No. 88 Squadron; the remainder were with No. 205 Squadron after '88' disbanded in October 1954. I flew a further 110 hours during twenty-three sorties while at No. 235 OCU RAF Calshot during my conversion training between March and May 1952, bringing my total Sunderland flying hours to 1,966 hours and 323 sorties.

The 1,856 hours flown in the Far East gives an average of sixty-four flight hours per month. This included three months on the Singapore to UK and return ferry flight, between December 1952 and March 1953, when we averaged only thirty-seven hours per month due to unserviceability, bad weather or high sea states that prevented flying. Further analysis shows that I flew more than eighty hours in nine calendar months, more than ninety hours in six months, more than one hundred hours in three months, and more than 120 hours in two months (127 hrs 10 min was the highest monthly total). The majority of months in which flying hours exceeded

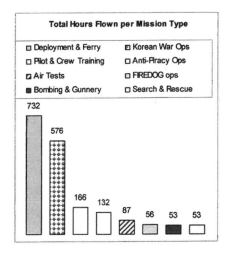

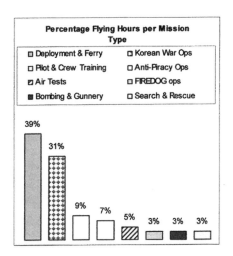

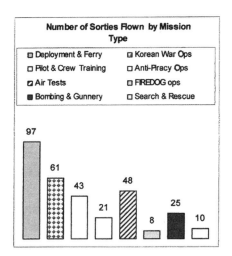

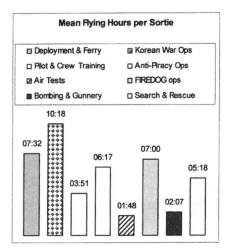

Charts Illustrating the Share of Flying between Different Missions.

Note: The breakdown of Korean War missions and flight hours was as follows:

Fox Red, Green or Blue:	29 sorties	292 hrs 20 min	47.5%
ASP Tsushima:	25 sorties	228 hrs 00 min	41.0%
West coast weather (night)	5 sorties	45 hrs 40 min	8.2%
East coast replenishment	2 sorties	20 hrs 15 min	3.3%
Total	61 sorties[1]		

ninety hours included Korean operations from Iwakuni, Japan. In six 'quiet' months I flew less than thirty hours. These were when I was either on leave (our annual entitlement was six weeks, though I usually took between three and four weeks), when I had no aircraft (January 1954), and when I was for a few weeks medically unfit for flying.

Analysis shows that crews of which I was navigator flew 148 hours at night, just 8% of our total flying. The majority of night flying was on three main types of sorties. The first were transit flights from Singapore to Hong Kong; these were flown overnight in order to arrive well before nightfall when the airfield and alighting area at Kai Tak were closed. Transit flights from Seletar to Naval Air Station (NAS) Sangley Point, and to Labuan, were also normally flown at least partially overnight. Another main source of night flying resulted from pre-dawn take-offs and post-dusk landings during Fox patrols, and to a lesser extent Tsushima patrols flown from Iwakuni in winter months. Lastly, West Coast Weather, and east and west coast task force replenishment patrols over the Yellow Sea or Sea of Japan were night-time missions flown in support of United Nations naval and air forces in Korea.

The high number of air test sorties (in the bottom left-hand chart) will be noticed. This is indicative of the relatively high number of engine-associated unserviceabilities resulting partly, no doubt, from ageing engines and some other systems, and from aircraft having to remain on the water and exposed to the elements for most of their life. They were brought ashore and pulled into a hangar only for minor inspections and certain other pre-planned servicing and, whenever possible, for engine changes. However, there were no hangars for Sunderland aircraft at Kai Tak or Iwakuni. First-line servicing was nearly all carried out while aircraft were at their moorings.

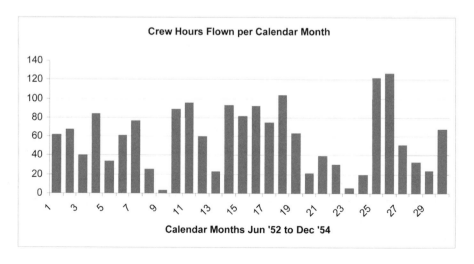

Deployment locations during the Far East tour

Using my flying logbook as a reference, I have calculated approximately how many days were spent operating from the various different flying boat bases in the Far East during my tour. The numbers of days in Table 1 are in some cases difficult to calculate exactly because of the complication of overnight flights between some bases. However, as near as I can judge, the numbers of days and the resultant share are as shown in the table.

Table 1 – Numbers of Days and Percentage of Tour in Various Locations

Location and country where detached or based2	*No. of days*	*% of tour*
Seletar (Singapore) and Glugor, Penang (Malaya)	325	37.7%
Iwakuni (Honshu Island, Japan)	270[3]	31.3%
Kai Tak (Hong Kong)	105	12.2%
UK Ferry: Seletar, China Bay, Korangi Creek, Bahrain, Fanara, Malta, Gibraltar, Pembroke Dock, Wig Bay (via Bizerte instead of Gibraltar and Malta on the return flight)	97	11.2%
Sangley Point (Philippines) and Buckner Bay (Okinawa)	24	2.8%
Labuan, Sandakan, Tawau, Lahad Datu, Kuching and Jessleton (now named Kota Kinabalu) British North Borneo	20	2.3%
China Bay (Ceylon, now Sri Lanka)	14	1.6%
Cat Lai (French Indo-China, now Vietnam)	8	0.9%

Sunderland airframes flown during the tour

Table 2 lists the eighteen different Sunderland airframes I flew during the course of my thirty calendar months' tour with the Far East Flying Boat Wing. In March to May 1952, I flew in five more airframes while at 235 OCU Calshot ('G', 'H', 'J', 'K' and 'P'), but I do not have their registration. I flew eighteen different aircraft in the Far East even though the general principle was that each constituted crew was allotted a particular airframe for three to six months. The airframes I flew are listed by registration number, identifying side letter, the squadron to which the aircraft was assigned, dates or periods during which I flew in that aircraft, and notes of interest concerning that particular airframe. Where an aircraft registration is followed by an asterisk (*) this indicates that the same aircraft had been flown on an earlier date and is listed higher up in the table. Each squadron normally had five aircraft on its unit establishment, but one from each of the three squadrons could at any one time be undergoing a Primary Star or Minor Inspection up slip or in a hangar at Seletar, or being ferried to or from the UK before or after a Major Inspection.

Table 2 – Sunderland Airframes and Dates Flown, June 1952 to December 1954

Reg. no.	Ltr	Sqn	Remarks
			(Main dates flown, captain/1st pilot and notable incidents)
PP155	D	88	25/6/52 to 24/9/52; then returned to Shorts, Wig Bay. Captain F/O Donaldson. In-flight engine failure while transiting from Iwakuni on 14/7/52 (RTB). Floats damaged by French Navy marine craft at Cat Lai on 28/8/52.
RN303	C	88	26–29/6/52 and 16/10/52 to 27/10/52. F/O Donaldson and S/L Francis.
PP148	F	88	27/10/52 to 8/12/52. Captain F/L Laidlay. Engine changed after ferry flight from Kai-tak to Seletar. Aircraft crashed Cat 5 on landing at Iwakuni on 25/3/53.
PP144	A	88	10/12/52. Captain F/L Laidlay. Air test and loop swing only.
RN303*	C	88	12/12/52 to 22/1/53. Ferry to Shorts at Wig Bay. Captain F/O Chesworth (205). Engine shut-down (carburettor) on 21/12/52 before landing at Bahrain.
SZ599	F/Y	88/209	5/2/53 to 21/3/53 and 2/8/53. Ferry Wig Bay to Seletar. Captain F/O Chesworth (205). Engine failure on take-off from Pembroke Dock on 14/2/53. A/c became 'Y' on 209 Sqn. Damaged Cat 5 on landing at Christmas Island, 21/6/54. This was the last Mark V off the production line, on 14/6/46.
RN302	C	88	23/3/53 to 2/8/53. Captain F/L Cooke. 27/3/53, radar and VHF unserviceabilities. Landed at Yoshimi in bad weather while redeploying from Kai Tak to Iwakuni. On 25/4/53, engine failure – shut down and returned to base (RTB).
SZ571	B	88	13/8/53 to 6/10/53. Captain F/O Empson. 1st pilots F/Sgt Nicholas and S/L Francis. No. 4 engine shut-down on 16/9/53 after Operation Fox Blue completed successfully.
RN302*	C	88	16/10/53 to 27/12/53. Captain F/O Empson. 1st pilots F/Sgt Nicholas, F/L Oliver, F/O Innes-Smith. On 24/12/53, fire in No. 3 engine, shut down and RTB. On 27/12/53, fire in No. 4 engine, shut down. Had to ditch at Shushi Wan, east coast of Tsushima Is. A/c Cat 5. Sunk by gunfire from USS Destroyer *De Haven* off Shushi Wan, Tsushima Is. on 28/12/53.
PP144*	A	88	8/12/53 engine failed on Operation Fox Blue. 15/12/53 Operation Fox Red. Captain F/O Empson, 1st pilot F/O Innes-Smith.
PP154	X	209	18/12/53. Captain F/O Empson, 1st pilots F/L Oliver, F/O Innes-Smith. Engine failure on Operation Fox Red. Severe oil leak. Air test later the same day.
NJ177	V	209	21/12/53. Captain F/O Empson, 1st pilot F/O Innes-Smith.
PP137	O	205	16/1/54 to 18/1/54. Captain F/L Wildy. On 16/1/54, No. 2 engine failed during transit from Iwakuni to Kai-Tak (A/c returned to Iwakuni).
PP154*	X	209	22/1/54. F/L Woodroffe. Kai-Tak to Seletar ferry.
SZ578	B	88	4/2/54 to 13/3/54. Capt F/O Holmes. Weather diversion to Sangley Point when *en route* to Kai Tak from Seletar.
PP137*	X	209	23/3/54. Captain F/L King. Air test and loop swing at Iwakuni.

Reg. no.	Ltr	Sqn	Remarks
RN273	L	205	20/4/54 to 25/4/54. Captain F/L Harrison. To Glugor for live SAR.
SZ566	C	88	14/5/54. Captain F/O Innes-Smith. Navex, live DC drop and circuits.
SZ578*	B	88	18/5/54. Captain F/O Holmes. Air test, bombing and night circuits.
RN293	F	88	20/5/54. Captain F/L Stapleton. Navigation exercise at Seletar.
EJ155	D	88	25/5/54 to 14/7/54 (various dates) and 27/7/54. Captain F/O Beer. Former Mk III.[4]
VB887*	A	88	6/6/54 to 7/7/54 (various dates). Captain F/L Tester.
SZ572	C	88	15/7/54. Captain F/O Innes-Smith. Operation ASP Tsushima.
RN293*	F	88	17/7/54, 21/7/54 and 30/7/54. F/L Stapleton. Fox Green, Tsushima and Fox Green.
SZ578*	B	88	20/7/54 and 23/7/54. Captain F/O Holmes. Fox Green (both dates).
EJ155*	D	88	4/8/54 to 13/8/54. Captain F/O Holmes. Ferry Iwakuni, Kai-Tak, Seletar.
RN293*	F	88	25/8/54 to 1/9/54. Captain F/L Rawling (Wing). Ferry MPs around Sabah. 31/8/54 landed on South China Sea and towed a 10-ton boat 38 nm to Labuan (8 hrs 10 min by sea, 2 hrs 30 min at night).
SZ578*	B	88	20/9/54 to 26/9/54. Captain F/L Beer. Anti-piracy patrols from Sandakan, Borneo.
NJ193	P	205	4/10/54 to 31/10/54. Captain F/L Robinson. Seletar and Glugor for bombing and gunnery.
SZ578*	B	205	15/10/54. Captain F/O Innes-Smith. BABS and circuits.
SZ578*	B	205	9/11/54 to 6/12/54. Captain F/L Harrison, co-pilot F/L Pete Wildy. Navigated SZ578 (B) to Wig Bay (Shorts Bros & Harland maintenance base) from Seletar. The last Sunderland in which I flew. In 1953, SZ578, then temporarily named 'Powder Puff', had been used to ferry HRH the Duchess of Kent around the Far East.

In-flight engine failure rates

In thirty months and 1,856 flight hours, my crew experienced eleven in-flight engine failures. Four occurred at some point during operational missions from Iwakuni in a twenty-three-day period in December 1953; the last of these engine failures ended in the loss of the aircraft (on the 27th). RN302 suffered two engine failures (plus another possible partial failure) in December 1953. The other two failures in that period were in different airframes. Two of the four failures caused a fire in the engine, but each was successfully extinguished. A fifth engine failure occurred on 16 January 1954. The other six in-flight engine failures experienced by crews with whom I was flying occurred at various times over the remaining twenty-eight months. After an engine failure on 16 January 1954, crews with whom

I flew throughout the remainder of 1954 experienced *not a single engine failure in ten months*, a total of 542 flight hours, equating to 2,168 hours per engine without failure. This makes the very high failure rate at Iwakuni during December 1953 and January 1954 even more atypical. Indeed, all eleven in-flight engine failures occurred in the first nineteen months of my tour, between June 1952 and January 1954. Including the period in December 1953, when the engine failure rate was exceptionally high, the mean hours between in-flight engine failures was 169 flying hours (on average, a failure every one to two months).

If the four engine failures suffered by aircraft from Iwakuni in December 1953 are discounted – after which the failure rate reverted to 'normal' – the remaining seven were spread over 1,848 flight hours (the number flown on my tour minus those sorties on which the four December 1953 failures occurred). This would result in a failure rate of one every 264 aircraft hours. Since the Sunderland had four engines, this is an average for an individual engine of one every 1,056 flight hours (or about 1,250 engine running hours, taking into account start-up and pre- and post-flight taxiing time) over a thirty-month period. If the four failures in December 1953 are included, the failure rate rises to one failure every 169 flight hours, or one per engine per 676 hours, or about 875 engine running hours including start-up, pre-flight and post-flight taxiing time. At the former rate, an FEFBW crew could expect between seven and eight in-flight engine failures in a thirty-month tour, or at the latter rate, eleven failures per tour. These data are based on the experience of only one of fifteen Sunderland crews over a thirty-month period. However, the flying hours and failures were spread over eighteen different airframes and more than seventy-two engines. Airframes on which there were engine failures during a sortie are indicated in Table 2.

Crew lists

Table 3 below lists the aircraft and crews, and the names of those with whom I mostly flew and was proud to fly while on the strength of 88 Squadron. There were some additional short-term crew changes that are not listed in the squadron F540 and are not shown here. I am grateful to Tony Burt for obtaining details in the table from the National Archives. However, the F540 did not record that after 8 December 1953, F/L Jack Oliver superseded F/Sgt Nick Nicholas as my 1st pilot. Also, from the time I became squadron navigation leader in February 1954, the F540 does not list me with a particular crew, whereas my flying logbook shows that until May I flew almost exclusively with F/O Stuart Holmes's crew. Throughout June and August 1954, when I was continually at Iwakuni, I flew in turn with the crews of 'A', 'B', 'C', 'D' and 'F' as part of my function as navigation leader. In Chapter 2 I list separately those with whom I flew to and from the UK between December 1952 and March 1953. In Chapter 18, I also list the crew members with whom I flew when we took 'B' SZ578 from Seletar to Wig Bay at the end of our Far East tour in November 1954. In Table 3, the aircraft captain is listed first. Abbreviations are (P) pilot, (N) navigator, (E) engineer, (S) signaller, (G) air gunner.

Table 3. Aircraft and crews with whom the author usually flew

June 1952		August 1953	
'D' – PP155	F/O A.H. Donaldson (P)	'B' SZ571	F/O D.K. Empson (N)
	F/O L.A. Stapleton (P)		F/Sgt R.J. Nicholas (P)
	P/O D.K. Empson (N)		P/O C.D. Sharpe (P)
	Sgt J.H.S. Rowe (E)		Sgt C.B. Elliott (E)
	Sgt J. Murray (E)		Sgt J.H. Rowell (E)
	Sgt J.D. Dixon (S)		F/Sgt J. McRobertson (S)
	Sgt V. Kapl (G)		Sgt J. Murray (S)
			Sgt P.J. Slatter (S)
October 1952	F/L A.M. Laidlay (P)		F/Sgt J.D. Dixon DFM (G)
'F' – PP144	P/O N.A. Innes-Smith (P)		Sgt F.C. McMillan (G)
	Sgt S.A. Blurton (P)		
	F/O D.K. Empson (N)	October 1953	
	P/O K.C. Readyhoof (N)	'C' RN302	F/O D.K. Empson (N)
	Sgt J.D. Smith (E)		F/Sgt R.J. Nicholas (P)
	Sgt G.G. Griffiths (E)		F/L J. Oliver (P)
	Sgt D.C. Byers (E)		F/O N.A. Innes-Smith (P)
	F/Sgt H. Filby (S)		P/O A.K. Mosely (N)
	F/Sgt C.J. Hogg (S)		Sgt G.G. Griffiths (E)
	Sgt K.I. Brearley (S)		Sgt C.B. Elliott (E)
	Sgt N. Silk (S)		Sgt W. Holliday (S)
	Sgt L .Whiskie (G)		Sgt E. Longmore (S)
			Sgt J.D. Dwyer (S)
March 1953			F/Sgt Vipond (G)
'C' RN302	F/L D.E. Cooke (P)		
	F/O N.A. Innes-Smith (P)	February 1954	
	F/O D.K. Empson (N)	'B' SZ578	F/O S.W. Holmes (P)
	P/O D.J. Germain (N)		F/O N.A. Innes-Smith (P)
	ME J. Davidson (E)		F/O D.K. Empson (Nav Ldr)
	Sgt J.D. Land (E)		F/O K.C. Readyhoof (N)
	F/Sgt H. Filby (S)		Sgt J.D. Land (E)
	Sgt K.I. Brearley (S)		Sgt G. Robert (E)
	Sgt B.M. Nairn (S)		F/Sgt J. Robertson (S)
	Sgt V. Kapl (G)		F/Sgt S.C. Wooley DFM (S)
			Sgt PJ Slatter (S)

Notes

1. Four sorties were curtailed due to engine failure.

2. The only deployment base within the Far East that I never visited was Christmas Island, south of Java (Map 1).

3. Detachments to Iwakuni ended in August 1954 (the Armistice was signed in July 1953 but operations continued for a further thirteen months). By the end of the last detachment in August 1954, I had spent 270 days at Iwakuni, equating to 33.3% of the period June 1952 until August 1954, when deployments to Japan ended. Each of the flying boat squadrons shared the Korean War task equally. Taking into account that three, or sometimes four, aircraft and crews were detached to Iwakuni, an equitable share should have been between 20% and 26% per crew. The fact that our crew was there for 33.3% of my tour up to August 1954 (31.3% over the whole tour) is explained by the fact that I served in largely 'unmarried' crews (see Appendix 1, first paragraph). My crew also spent twice the theoretical 'equal share' of SAR standby duty in Hong Kong (it should have been about 6.67%). This was largely through our own choice.

4. In July 1944, EJ155, formerly a Sunderland Mk III with 330 Norwegian Squadron, attacked and damaged a German U-boat (U-387). By 1954 the aircraft had been converted to a Mk V. It served with 88, 209 and 205/209 squadrons and returned to the UK in November 1955.

ML797, the second production Mark V and based at Seletar, photographed on 15th May 1959 while on the last officially tasked sortie by an RAF Sunderland; the end of an era. *Bill Whiter*

Selected Operating and Technical Data – Sunderland Mark V

Performance data are derived from Short Bros Ltd, 235 OCU Notes and 1952 Pilot's Notes.[1]

Dimensions

i)	Wing span	112 ft 9.5 in.	(34.40 m)
ii)	Overall length	85 ft 4 in.	(26.00 m)
iii)	Height to top of fin	32 ft 10.5 in.	(10.00 m)
iv)	Wing area	1,487 ft²	(138.15 m²)
v)	Maximum internal fuselage width	9 ft 10 in.	(3.00 m)

Aircraft weights and loadings

Empty weight	37,000 lb (16,783 kg)
Removable equipment	4,300 lb (1,955 kg)
Crew	1,800 lb (818 kg)
Depth charges, fuel and oil	16,900 lb (7,680 kg)
Maximum for take-off	60,000 lb (27,250 kg) [65,000 lb/29,520 kg in temperate climates]
Maximum for landing	54,000 lb (24,525 kg)
Wing loading (fully loaded)	35.6 lb/ft² (175 kg/m²)
Power loading (fully loaded)	12.5 lb/hp (5.68 kg/hp)

Engine data

i) Four Pratt and Whitney Twin Wasp (2-row radial air-cooled) R-1830-90B/90C/90D engines. NACA-type cowling rings with controllable gill flaps. 100 octane fuel

ii) Hamilton Standard Hydromatic fully feathering, 3-blade, constant-speed metal propellers, diameter 12 ft 9 in. (3.88 m)

iii) Maximum take-off limit, 5 minutes at 2,700 rpm +9 lb/sq.in.

iv) Maximum continuous climb, 2,550 rpm +5.5 lb/sq.in.

v) Maximum rich mixture, continuous, 2,325 rpm +3 lb/sq.in.

vi)   Maximum weak mixture, continuous, 2,000 rpm +1 lb/sq.in.

vii) Combat limit, 5 minutes at 2,700 rpm +7.5 lb/sq.in.

Flying limitations

The following maximum speeds were permitted:

i)	Flaps in	200 kts IAS
ii)	Flaps one-third out	120 kts IAS
iii)	Flaps two-thirds out	115 kts IAS
iv)	Flaps fully out	110 kts IAS

Flap settings and indicated speeds for maximum climbing performance

i)   Initial climb after take-off, flaps out one-third, 110–115 kts

ii) Then to 6,000 feet, flaps in, 125–130 kts

iii) Above 6,000 feet, 120–125 kts

Approach and landing

i)   Speed was reduced to 115 kts IAS, fuel mixture auto-rich, propeller speed control levers set for 2,550 rpm, flaps two-thirds out, gills closed

ii) At weights up to 50,000 lb an engine-assisted approach at 95 kts IAS was recommended, with touch-down at 80 kts in a level attitude

iii) In calm sea conditions, at night, or at aircraft weights above 50,000 lb, the approach was made at around 95 kts IAS until at 300 feet. The control column was then gently eased back and power on the inner engines was increased to maintain a speed of 80–85 kts IAS and a rate of descent of 200 ft per minute. When the step touched the water, power was eased back, first on the inner throttles (Nos 2 and 3 engines), and then the outer throttles (Nos 1 and 4 engines)

Stalling speeds

		60,000 lb	54,000 lb	45,000 lb
i)	Flaps in	88	83	74
ii)	Flaps fully out	73	67	63

Maximum range

i)   Still-air range at 116 kts at 2,000 ft with 2,552 imp gal = 2,591 nm (22 hrs 20 min)

ii) Still-air range at 134 kts at 2,000 ft with 2,552 imp gal = 2,339 nm (20 hrs 0 min)

Speeds for maximum range and endurance

i)   For maximum range, the aircraft was flown in Auto-Lean and with not more than +1 lb/sq.in. boost. Engine rpm were adjusted to maintain the recommended speed. If at the maximum practical rpm (approx. 1,550) the recommended speeds were exceeded, boost was reduced to maintain the recommended speed. Recommended speeds were:

a) Fully loaded   120–125 kts IAS
b) Lightly loaded   110–120 kts IAS

ii) Cruising for maximum endurance:

a) Fully loaded   110 kts
b) Lightly loaded   105 kts

Fuel tank capacities

i)	2 × front inner tanks	529 gallons each	Total 1,058 gallons
ii)	2 × front middle tanks	355 gallons each	710 gallons
iii)	2 × front outer tanks	132 gallons each	264 gallons
iv)	2 × rear inner tanks	111 gallons each	222 gallons
v)	2 × rear outer tanks	149 gallons each	298 gallons
		Total all tanks	2,552 gallons
		Approximately	17,100 lb

Fuel consumption

i) Approximate total consumption in gallons per hour in *rich* mixture at 2,000 feet:

2,550 rpm at a boost level of +5.5 boost lb/sq.in.   440 gallons per hour
2,325 rpm at a boost level of +2 lb/sq.in.   250 gallons per hour

ii) Approximate total consumption in gallons per hour in *weak* mixture at 2,000 feet:

2,250 rpm at a boost level of -0.25 lb/sq.in.   148 gallons per hour
2,250 rpm at a boost level of -3.0 lb/sq.in.   121 gallons per hour
1,950 rpm at a boost level of -0.25 lb/sq.in.   128 gallons per hour
1,950 rpm at a boost level of -3.0 lb/sq.in.   106 gallons per hour
1,650 rpm at a boost level of -0.25 lb/sq.in.   112 gallons per hour
1,950 rpm at a boost level of -2.0 lb/sq.in.   101 gallons per hour

iii)   Approximate climb rate and fuel consumption in the climb:

Fuel allowance for warming up, taxiing
    and take-off   Fuel used 43 gallons
Climb from sea level to 5,000 ft – 8 min,   Dist. 17 nm – Fuel used 60 gallons

Climb from sea level to 10,000 ft – 22 min, Dist. 45 nm – Fuel used
132 gallons

Total fuel consumed from start-up to
5,000 ft   Fuel used 103 gallons

Total fuel consumed from start-up to
10,000 ft   Fuel used 175 gallons

iv)   Approximate air nautical miles per gallon (anmpg) fuel consumption, cruising for range with or without weapons:

Indicated air speed	110 kts	0.95 anmpg	Weapons[2] loaded
Indicated air speed	110 kts	1.19 anmpg	Weapons released
Indicated air speed	115 kts	0.98 anmpg	Weapons loaded
Indicated air speed	115 kts	1.20 anmpg	Weapons released
Indicated air speed	120 kts	1.01 anmpg	Weapons loaded
Indicated air speed	120 kts	1.19 anmpg	Weapons released

v)   Approximate fuel consumption in gallons per minute and gallons per hour, cruising for endurance at 2,000 feet, with or without a full load of depth charges. Consumption is expressed in gallons per minute (gpm) and gallons per hour (gph):

110 kts IAS	A/c outbound	1.94 gpm, 116 gph	Weapons loaded
110 kts IAS	A/c inbound	1.76 gpm, 106 gph	Weapons loaded
110 kts IAS	A/c inbound	1.62 gpm, 97 gph	Weapons released
105 kts IAS	A/c outbound	2.0 gpm, 120 gph	Weapons loaded
105 kts IAS	A/c inbound	1.72 gpm, 97 gph	Weapons loaded
105 kts IAS	A/c inbound	1.58 gpm, 95 gph	Weapons released

Radar

Mk 6 anti-surface vessel (ASV) radar. Wavelength 10 cm with twin synchronized rotating under-wingtip scanners providing 360° cover in azimuth. Capable of detecting a submarine schnorkel (snort) in Sea States 3 or less. Also used for navigation.

Sunderland Mark V construction or conversion

Short Brothers Ltd, Rochester	46
Short & Harland Ltd, Belfast, N. Ireland	53
Blackburn Aircraft Co. Ltd, Dumbarton, Scotland	50
Total:	149

Note. Some of the above Mk Vs were originally built to Mk III standard at other factories and later converted to Mk Vs. One example that I flew from Seletar in 1953/4 was EJ155, built at Short Bros Ltd, Windermere. Others were built by Blackburn Aircraft Co. Ltd, Brough, Yorkshire.

Mean consumption rates used for fuel planning

The maximum range at 116 kts (mean) in *temperate* conditions was 2,550 nm, some 22 hrs flight duration and 1 anmpg. By halfway through a 1,420 nm ferry flight, we usually knew whether a weather or sea-state diversion was likely. Even in the tropical Far East, the tendency, therefore, when a diversion was extremely unlikely, was to let the speed creep up to 125 or 130 kts. We normally had at least three hours' fuel in hand, and never knowingly allowed ourselves to arrive at the destination with less than our planned reserve fuel. Patrol flying was treated differently during all stages of the sortie because tactical activity while patrolling, even when following pre-planned tracks (e.g. in the Yellow Sea or Tsushima Strait) could vary the duration of a sortie by as much as two hours, depending on the number of ships detected, all of which had to be carefully reconnoitred and photographed. On patrol sorties we therefore generally controlled the aircraft's speed to conserve fuel. But for ferry (transit) flights, once the fuel weight had reduced to the state where the aircraft would happily cruise at 125–130 kts, the pilots usually allowed the speed to build up. When flying for range, speed would normally be reduced as the aircraft became lighter, from 125 down to 120 kts, by reducing rpm and boost. Provided we were certain we had adequate fuel for all circumstances (including loss of an engine), we usually preferred to arrive at the destination sooner rather than later. Therefore, the mean indicated airspeed at our cruising altitude over a typical ferry sortie was usually somewhat higher than that recommended for range flying in the Pilot's Notes. Consequently, our average fuel consumption was also higher than that implied by sub-sub-para. iv) above.

Fuel planning data passed to me by the flight engineer for my last Sunderland ferry flight from Singapore to the UK in November and December 1954 indicate that with a full crew and luggage (as for a ferry flight), and no depth charges carried, and when the tanks were filled with 2,552 gallons, the fuel volume assumed to be usable was 2,250 imperial gallons. The mean fuel consumption assumed by the flight engineer over an 8–11 hr sortie, used for flight planning purposes, was 166.67 gallons per hour (approximately 0.82 nmpg). This gave an endurance of 13 hrs 30 min and a potential still-air distance of approximately 1,850 nm. Mean true airspeeds (i.e. in still air) from take-off to landing generally averaged around 137 kts. For shorter transit flights when only 2,200 gallons were often carried (i.e. for sorties expected to be 6–8 hrs duration), and with 1,900 gallons of assumed usable fuel, the mean consumption rate for planning purposes was assumed to be about 160 gallons per hour (approximately 0.86 nmpg). This resulted in an endurance of 11 hrs 52 min and a still-air distance of 1,625 nm. These fuel consumption planning figures included an allowance for fuel used for start-up, taxiing, take-off, climb, cruise, descent, landing, taxiing and mooring.

During the last one to three hours of most routine ferry flights over distances of typically 1,350 to 1,450 nm (e.g. Iwakuni to Hong Kong, and Singapore to China Bay or Sangley Point), I recall that in practice the air nautical mpg often approached or exceeded 1.0 air nautical mpg. The achievement of 1 anmpg was usually possible at lighter weights with reasonably careful use of power and cruising at 125 and 130 kts IAS at altitudes between 5,000 and 9,000 feet. Navigators generally preferred to cruise somewhere within this altitude band on long-range transit flights in order to benefit from increases in true air speed (TAS) as altitude was increased; this was provided that these gains in TAS would not be nullified by headwinds at higher altitudes.

Take-off technique
The take-off technique for a flying boat – and specifically for the Sunderland Mk V – was quite different from that of landplanes. The recommended technique was – at the beginning of the take-off run – initially to hold the control column hard back and gradually increase power on the two outer engines to take-off boost. The pilot kept the wings level using the ailerons. The nose at first rose steeply, but gradually lowered as the aircraft gathered speed. When spray was seen to be clear of the inner engine propellers, the throttles of the two inboard engines were opened to take-off boost, and the control column (surmounted by a three-quarter-circular wheel) was gradually eased forward to a position slightly aft of neutral. The pilot aimed to keep the aircraft directionally parallel to the flare-path dinghies that marked the take-off run, watching ahead for any obstructions. Any tendency to swing was checked initially by throttling back the appropriate outer engine until rudder control was gained. The nose slowly lowered with increasing speed as the hull of the aircraft slowly lifted higher in the water as lift from the wings increased. When the hull had risen onto the 'step', the sea surface offered less and less drag, and directional control became increasingly responsive to the rudder. Speed through the water then built more rapidly. As take-off speed was reached at 80–85 kts (depending on the aircraft's weight), the control column was steadily eased backwards until the aircraft left the water. The take-off run could be anything from 1½ to 3 minutes, depending on the aircraft's weight, the ambient temperature, the wind strength and the sea state. One-third flap remained selected until 110–115 kts IAS was reached, depending on the aircraft's weight.

Day and night landing techniques

Under normal daylight conditions at weights not exceeding 50,000 pounds when the sea surface was anything other than glassy calm or the position of the sun was dazzling the pilot's view of the alighting area, or when a layer of mist or fog obscured the sea surface, the pilot would make an engine-assisted approach starting at about 600 feet, with two-thirds flap selected, speed levers set to 2,550 rpm, and mixture in auto-rich with the engine gills closed. The pilot established and maintained 95 kts IAS during the descent towards the water, gently flaring just before touch-down and then allowing the speed to decay to 80 kts IAS for touch-down. After the step touched the water, the throttles were progressively closed and the control column was eased gently backwards to resist any tendency of the nose to dig into the sea.

When conditions were glassy calm, or if the surface of the sea could not clearly be seen due to fog or glare from the sun, and in the hours of darkness or at weights above 50,000 lb, the pilot set up an approach from 600 feet at 95 kts IAS until reaching 300 feet. He aligned the direction of approach to be parallel to the flight path, marked by a single line of moored pram dinghies surmounted by battery-powered lights. Flap, mixture and gill settings were the same as for a normal daytime approach. Once at 95 kts, the pilot slowly eased back the control column, at the same time gradually opening the inboard throttles to maintain a speed of 80–85 kts IAS and a rate of descent of 200 feet per minute. The attitude of the aircraft was adjusted so that the aeroplane on the artificial horizon indicator was fractionally above the horizon bar. This attitude, the 200 fpm rate of descent and 80–85 kts IAS were maintained until the hull touched the water; any temptation to flare the aircraft before touch-down had to be resisted. When the step of the hull touched the water, the pilot slowly closed the throttles of first the inner and then the outer engines, the control column being gently eased back to resist any tendency of the nose to dig into the water.

If the aircraft had to alight in a confined area, flaps could be set fully out, but only if it was certain that the alighting would not be baulked and a missed approach was not required. For missed approaches at light loads, the aircraft would climb away with flaps fully extended, but at heavy weights it would not climb until the flaps were raised. If the aircraft was not at a light weight, it was important to select the flaps 'in' immediately upon opening the engines to full take-off power.

Notes

1. Pilot's Notes issued to crews were produced by HM Stationery Office. It is possible to obtain reprints from Air Data Publications, St Annes on Sea, Lancashire.
2. A full load of depth charges.

Appendix Three

Dead-Reckoning Navigation Techniques used by Far East Sunderland Flying Boat Crews in the 1950s

Introduction

In the absence of quick-fixing radio navigation aids ('navaids') navigators of Sunderland Mk V aircraft of the Far East Flying Boat Wing in the 1950s (and generations of maritime patrol air navigators during the Second World War), practised and relied on dead-reckoning (DR) techniques to navigate their aircraft safely over the sea beyond the coverage of quick-fixing aids. As the accuracy, coverage and reliability of modern navigation aids have now largely rendered manual DR navigation techniques redundant, this Appendix reviews for younger generations of flyers and others interested both in aviation and in the evolution of air navigation, some of the main DR techniques in use in the 1940s and 1950s. To illustrate some of these techniques, I have sometimes referred to them in other parts of this book. The Appendix is intended for those who would like to gain an insight into past DR navigation techniques and the order of accuracy achieved. The information I am about to give is based solely on my own recollection after fifty years; I was not able to refresh my memory from navigation notes or manuals then in use. May I therefore apologize for any mistakes that I may inadvertently have made.

The need for dead-reckoning navigation[1]

For much of the time on the majority of sorties in the Far East, Sunderlands were flying beyond sight of land and out of coastline range of the anti-surface vessel (ASV) Mark VIC PPI[2] radar. The main purpose of this radar was to detect ships and submarines, but it could be used and was extremely valuable as an aid to navigation. Nevertheless, a general lack of radio navigation aids meant that DR navigation was not only necessary but was the only safe way to keep track of your geographical position. In the Far East there were no shore-based quick-fixing aids such as there were in the UK and in mainland Europe at that time (e.g. Gee, Rebecca/Eureka). ASV Mk VIC was the only equipment on board with the capability of 'quick fixing' in certain areas of the Far East. The only computer-like device in the aircraft was the analogue air position indicator (API), which I shall describe later. This was a tremendous boon to navigators; I hate to think what navigation must have been like before it was invented and fitted to Sunderland aircraft. The API must have doubled or trebled the accuracy of DR navigation, and made a navigator's job ten times less stressful. DR navigation is fundamentally navigation by continually solving and plotting the three vectors that make up the 'triangle of velocities': 1) True Course (now usually called 'heading') and True Air Speed in knots; 2) Wind Speed and True Direction; and 3) True Track (direction relative to True North) and Groundspeed (G/S in knots). Vector No. 3 is the result of the interaction between Vectors 1 and 2.

DR navigation in the Far East in the 1950s required the use of various techniques according to circumstances. Throughout this Appendix I shall at times draw attention to particular DR navigation procedures typically used (certainly by me) on certain of the routes commonly flown by Far East Flying Boat crews. These routes include crossing the Bay of Bengal at the northern end of the Indian Ocean, flying between Singapore and Hong Kong, the Philippines or British North Borneo; also between Hong Kong or the Philippines and Iwakuni. Patrols in the Yellow Sea also required careful DR navigation, not least to avoid infringing Chinese territorial waters and airspace. Several hours' flying on all these routes would have to be navigated without quick-fixing and radio aids or recognizable coastline features. Accurate DR navigation was essential.

The importance of drift measurement
One of the most important necessities for accurate DR navigation (in addition to a well-calibrated direct reading compass) was frequent drift measurements by the navigator. 'Drift' is the difference in degrees of azimuth between the aircraft's track and its heading (or 'course', as we referred to it in the 1950s). If, for example, the measured or calculated drift is 5° port, by definition the aircraft will drift towards the left; therefore, the track direction will be 5° to the left and less than the course (or heading) direction. Hence, if the aircraft's course is 270° True, its track will then be 265° True. For starboard (or right) drift the opposite is the case.

What is actually happening if drift is to port is that the aircraft, flying at a velocity determined by its air speed and True Course, is flying through an air mass which itself is moving bodily towards the left (relative to the aircraft's heading) in a direction and at a speed which is the mean wind velocity.

An analogy is to imagine the coxswain of a motor ferry boat who wishes to cross a river at right-angles from one bank to a landing-stage on the opposite bank when the current is flowing from right to left. Rather than pointing the boat directly at the far landing-stage on the opposite bank, the boat's coxswain will have to aim off and steer a course at some angle pointing to the right, towards the direction from which the tide is flowing. If the coxswain judges this angle correctly, the boat will track across the river over the river bed at right-angles from the near bank directly to the landing-stage opposite; hence, the boat's track will be to the left of its course and it will have port (or left) drift. The drift angle will be the difference between the course and the track. The correct course will depend on the speed of the boat and the speed and direction of the current, which we know in this case is running at right-angles to the boat's intended track. The faster the tide or the slower the boat, the larger will be the correct or mean drift angle that will enable the boat to track in a straight line to the opposite landing-stage. Hence, in the air, a slow aircraft experiencing a cross-wind will require a larger drift angle to maintain a given track than will a faster aircraft wishing to fly the same track.

I should add that an air mass, more so than water flowing down a river, in any one geographical position, is in practice constantly veering or backing to varying degrees in direction while, simultaneously, the speed of movement over the sea or land surface is constantly increasing or decreasing (gusting). Hence, any wind velocity that the navigator calculates is the *average* of many different instantaneous velocities, measured over time. The most frequent means Sunderland navigators used to measure 'drift' (by day) was the drift recorder (or sight). This can be seen just behind the author's left elbow in the photograph on page 8. The drift recorder had a periscope pointing vertically downwards towards the sea or land surface below. Provided the surface below was not obscured by cloud or fog, the navigator looked through the drift sight eyepiece and periscope, and aligned a graticule with the average direction of the forward-to-aft movement of waves or land seen passing beneath. The navigator could also insert a soft pencil into the holder which was attached to a pantograph arrangement. This allowed the navigator to follow the movement of waves through the periscope, using a pointer linked to the pencil holder. Thus he could draw pencil lines onto the Perspex screen, which was backed by red parallel lines. After asking the pilot to hold the wings of the aircraft steady and on course, the navigator tracked sea movement by visually following individual wave crests, at the same time aligning the graticule by eye or by using a pencil to mark the ground-glass screen. Satisfied that the graticule was aligned with the average direction of movement of the sea below, the navigator would read the scale on the upper periphery of the ground-glass screen (colour section page 3) the angular difference between the aircraft's fore-and-aft axis (indicated by zero) and the average direction of movement of the sea surface below. This was the 'drift', either to port (left) or to starboard (right). Applying the drift to the aircraft's true course would tell the navigator what the aircraft's track had been during the drift-taking. He would then compare this with the intended true track (i.e. relative to the direction of the true North Pole) and, if there was a mismatch, alter course to fly parallel to the intended track or to converge with it.

The drift recorder had another facility which can be seen on page 3 colour section. There were two circular scales, on one of which you set the aircraft's height in feet above the sea or land surface below. The other scale was time in seconds. When viewed through the periscope, in addition to the parallel lines used to align the drift angle, there were two slightly converging lines, at not quite 90° to the drift lines, one at each end of the drift lines. After the navigator had aligned the graticule with the drift he could – by using a stop-watch – time the number of seconds it took for a wave to move between the left-hand and right-hand almost-perpendicular lines. By taking the mean of several readings and then referring to the circular scales to the left, he could read the mean groundspeed of the aircraft. This speed and the drift could then be plotted on the navigator's Dalton computer (described later) to calculate the mean wind velocity.

Another method of measuring drift, but only when the aircraft was at low altitude (around 250 feet or less), was to ask another crew member to launch a 'flame-float' (through a special launching tube) into the sea. As soon as it hit the sea, it self-ignited and burned for about three minutes. At the same time the navigator would ask the pilot to maintain a steady course with wings level, and also ask the tail gunner to sight and track the flame-float through his gunsight. After the flame-float was a mile of two aft of the aircraft and about to disappear from his view, the gunner would read the gunsight's azimuth angle on the calibrated turret ring. The navigator could also compare this with a back-bearing he himself could simultaneously take using the astro-compass, mounted in the astrodome (this is covered later). By either or both methods, this was the measured drift angle, port or starboard. This method of drift-taking could be used by day and at night, including for calculating two-drift or three-drift winds (described later). Generally speaking, this method was not often used on long-range transit flights which we tended to fly at between 2,500 and 9,500 feet to maximize true air speed, which increases with altitude for any given indicated air speed.

A third method that I sometimes used while flying on low-level shipping surveillance or weather reconnaissance sorties by day in the Yellow Sea (on Fox Blue, Fox Red and Fox Green missions), especially when we were not many miles from the coast of Communist China, would be to mount the astro-compass in the astrodome and sight a back-bearing on the aircraft's prop-wash on the sea surface. This avoided launching flame-floats. I would also ask the tail gunner for a drift estimate, using his gunsight. This technique was only possible when the sea was relatively calm and you were flying at 30–50 feet. At this height, a downwash from the propellers was visible on the sea surface unless the sea was rough. This was not something you could safely do at night, whereas the flame-float method was a legitimate technique for night-time use.

Three-drift and two-drift winds
Knowledge of the average prevailing wind velocity (W/V) is fundamental to accurate DR navigation. Often the most practical way of calculating the W/V – at least in daylight – was to obtain a 'three-drift wind' (for which you needed to be able to see the sea surface). This was done by measuring drift using the drift recorder, then making an alteration of course 60 degrees to port or starboard, taking another drift measurement; then altering course 120 degrees in the opposite direction and maintaining that course for the same length of time while taking a third drift angle; finally, turning 60 degrees back to the original course. With these three drift angles, and using a Dalton computer – a kind of circular slide rule, explained later – the navigator could calculate the wind velocity and the aircraft's consequent groundspeed. By applying this wind velocity vector to the aircraft's 'no wind' or air position indicated by the air position indicator (explained in a moment), the navigator could plot the aircraft's DR position. He could also calculate the groundspeed and predict the expected drift on any course (heading). The three-drift winds taken while crossing a wide expanse of ocean would help me to calculate how far the aircraft had progressed along track, and with that information, calculate the ETA. Another benefit of three-drift winds was that each wind-finding manoeuvre only extended a journey time by two or three minutes. You could similarly obtain two-drift winds when altering course by between 60 and 120 degrees, so as to obtain a reasonably good heading 'cut'; for example, sometimes at turning-points. The diagram below shows an aircraft obtaining a three-drift wind. It is initially steering 105°T; the navigator takes a drift measurement, then alters heading (or course) 60° port onto 045°T and takes a second drift. The navigator then alters heading 120° starboard onto 165°T and takes a third drift. Finally the aircraft resumes its original course of 105°T. As soon as the navigator had calculated the wind velocity from the three drifts, he would alter heading to regain track or fly a parallel track.

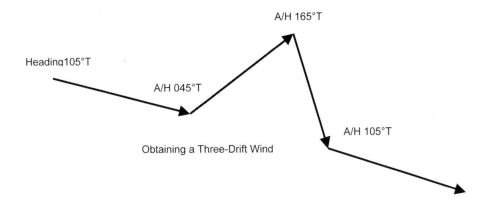

A/H 165°T

Heading 105°T

A/H 045°T

A/H 105°T

Obtaining a Three-Drift Wind

The wind-finding attachment (WFA)

Another wind-finding method was to use the wind-finding attachment, seen higher up in the photograph on page 8, stowed in its canvas bag. The WFA received inputs from the air position indicator. The process began by dropping a marine marker or flame-float into the sea. Because it was essential to be exactly overhead the sea marker when starting and stopping the WFA, it could only be used when flying at 500 feet, or preferably lower. The WFA (or 'Woofer') was said at low altitudes to be more accurate than a three-drift wind. To achieve greatest accuracy, it required the aircraft to complete a 360-degree orbit after releasing a marker into the sea, home visually to be *directly over the marker, and at that instant, switch on the WFA*, having already zeroed the counters. The aircraft was then required to execute a further three- to four-minute orbit and home, visually, directly overhead the marine marker once more. The WFA was at that moment switched off, the northing and easting counters were read and the wind velocity calculated. It was not a very popular technique because it was time consuming. It was more frequently used while on low-level patrols than it was while in transit.

Wind velocity estimation by wind lanes and 'white horses'

A third method of estimating the wind direction and speed was by observing the sea surface, but only when flying below 1,500 feet. With practice and by reference to a guide table issued to Sunderland crews (the Beaufort scale), it was often possible to estimate with reasonable accuracy the wind direction and speed at the sea surface. You observed what are known as wind lanes and waves on the sea surface. Wind lanes are caused by wind constantly disturbing the sea surface in a particular average direction. As wind strength increases, wind 'lanes' become more pronounced, wave heights increase and at a certain speed the crests begin to break, causing foam (white horses). As wind speed increases further, spume or spray will also be blown downwind from breaking wave crests, easily visible from the air. The Beaufort scale describes different sea conditions, which can then be related to different wind speeds and sea states, as set out in the Beaufort table. This enables a fairly accurate estimation be made of the strength of the surface wind by noting how widespread and pronounced the 'white horses' are, the roughness of the sea, the height of the waves and the amount of blowing spray and spume.

Wind lane estimation is useful to aviators as a continuous guide to the prevailing wind direction and strength *at the sea surface*. When reliant on DR and flying at low altitude, it provided crews with a cross-check against wind velocities found using the drift recorder, wind-finding attachment and fixes. It had to be remembered that wind lanes and white horses indicate the wind velocity *at the sea surface*. Usually, the wind speed strengthens with altitude, and the general tendency is for the direction to veer (change in a clockwise direction) with increases in height, at least for several hundreds of feet, depending on the characteristics of the prevailing air mass.

The effect of weather on celestial or astro-navigation

Due to the absence of other long-range and quick-fixing aids, celestial navigation – usually referred to by aviators as 'astro-navigation' – was one of the main methods of obtaining position lines in Sunderland aircraft (and in Hastings and Valetta transports) in the Far East in the 1950s. In daylight, this necessitated frequent 'shots' or 'sights' of the elevation of the sun (or the moon if it was visible). At night, you could usually – if not below or in cloud – 'shoot' the stars and planets to obtain two- or three-position line fixes. Hence, astro-navigation was probably practised to a greater extent by navigators in the Far East than by those in most other theatres. We should not forget that, on joining a Far East squadron, inexperienced navigators needed to learn to recognize celestial bodies in the night sky quickly. When perhaps some of the sky was obscured by cloud, a navigator might need to seize an opportunity for a one-minute astro-sight on a recognized star or planet through a short-lived gap in cloud cover. He would then have to back-calculate the intercept difference between the celestial body's assumed position elevation and the measured elevation. Since we were operating in latitudes between the equator (just to the south of Singapore) and latitude 38° N, navigators would also have to adjust to the different appearance of the night sky compared with the more northern latitudes in and around the UK.

There were other practical considerations to take into account, depending on which particular operational area a navigator was flying in and the time of day or night. As an example, when heading north or south at night between Singapore and destinations such as Cat Lai (French Indo-China), Hong Kong or Sangley Point (Philippines), the aircraft would at certain periods of the year have to fly through the Intertropical Front (ITF), or Intertropical Convergence Zone (ITCZ), as it later became known. This typically consisted of gradually thickening and more extensive layers of cloud, generally in a wide, east–west band, with very turbulent, embedded cumulonimbus with strong up-and-down drafts and electrical activity. The band of cloud could be anything from 25 to 75 miles wide. The ITF or ITCZ was usually penetrated by transiting Sunderlands at between 2,000 and 8,000 feet. We rode out the strong updrafts and downdrafts like a roller coaster, sometimes losing or gaining several hundreds of feet as we did so. The Sunderland was a sturdy aircraft and rode these conditions well. Such heavy turbulence and cloud could make it impossible to use the sextant for astro-navigation for anything from fifteen minutes to an hour. You might find it possible to squeeze in a one-minute shot on the moon – immediately recognizable – if the opportunity arose at night. At the same time, lightning (and night effect, described later) could render bearings from any MF beacons that might be within range unreliable. Since passing through the ITCZ often signalled a significant change in wind direction and strength, not only was the whole exercise exciting, it tested every aspect of a navigator's DR navigation skills. Of course we used our ASV radar to detect the core of storms in our path and did what we could to weave around and between the worst of them – but sometimes you just had to steer a course into the thick of it and ride it out.

The bubble sextant Mk IXA

Navigators measured the elevation of celestial bodies relative to the true horizontal (or horizon) using the bubble sextant Mk IXA. The navigator viewed the celestial body through an eyepiece and, by rotating a knurled wheel (8) on the right side of the sextant, moved a sighting mirror whose gearing ensured that the angle of elevation was slowly and progressively changed by very small amounts (i.e. minutes of arc). Once the navigator had the celestial body correctly in view, he started the 'sight' and a clockwork motor (14). He took the sight over a period of one or two minutes. The navigator continually moved the angle of the mirror to keep the celestial body's image in the centre of a clearly visible air bubble simultaneously in view and suspended in a clear oily liquid; the sighting bubble effectively acted as a spirit level and defined the true horizontal, tangential to the earth's surface, the imaginary plane from which the celestial body's elevation angle of arc was being measured. However, the bubble 'spirit level' was affected by aircraft accelerations due to turbulence and involuntary minor changes in aircraft speed, heading and height while the 'sight' was being taken. The bubble sextant included a selectable one-minute or two-minute device (7 and 14 in the photograph below) which averaged the measured angle as the navigator tracked the celestial body through the eyepiece for the chosen length of time. The navigator then read the averaged arc of elevation of the star, planet, sun or moon, through a small window on the side of the averaging device (15 in the right-hand photograph, below).

The averaging device also helped to cancel out or reduce elevation arc measurement errors resulting from the fact that a navigator was unable to track a celestial body with perfect precision for the entire length of time of the 'sight' due to turbulence and aircraft accelerations. Sights (or shots) were averaged over one or two minutes (as preferred by the navigator). Calculations were completed by the navigator by referring to Greenwich time-based data in a Nautical Almanac, and in some circumstances using Admiralty Tables or another book which simplified the navigator's task somewhat, called HO249.

The Perspex astrodome through which the navigator sighted the sextant and measured the elevation of celestial bodies was calibrated for imperfections in light refraction, and might require the navigator to apply a small correction to the elevation measured by the sextant. When all corrections had been applied, the navigator completed various mathematical sums and was then ready to plot a single position line on his chart. This position line (P/L) was at right-angles to the direction in azimuth of the celestial body that had been sighted. Hence, if the azimuth of the sun or other body was due south (180° T) from the aircraft, a position line derived

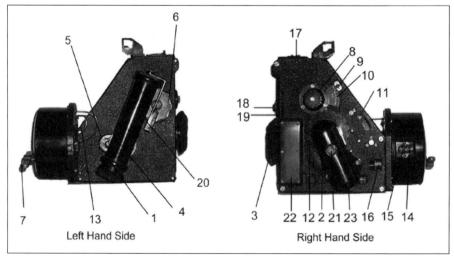

The Mark IXA Bubble Sextant.

from the body's elevation in degrees and minutes of arc above the horizon would result in an east–west position line (090/270° T).

Position lines were calculated and plotted using the Marc St Hilaire intercept method. The actual location of the position line on the chart was determined by first calculating what the elevation of the chosen celestial body (the sun, for instance) would be if the aircraft were to be located exactly at a convenient, nearby, latitude and longitude (for example 07° N 107° E). This was known as the assumed position (AP), and the navigator would plot this position and the predicted azimuth of the celestial body (taken from tables) on his chart (for example, azimuth 145°T). Preferably before taking the astro-shot, the navigator would choose a convenient position for the mid-time (e.g. 10.27 GMT) around which he intended to take the sight. After taking the astro-shot, the elevation of the celestial body from the AP was then compared with the average elevation angle when measured and averaged using the sextant. The difference between the two angles of elevation determined the difference in distance between the aircraft's *actual* position and a position line passing through the known AP on the chart. If the sextant-measured angle of arc was *greater* than that calculated for the AP, the aircraft's true position line was parallel to the AP position line but distanced from it in the direction of (towards) the celestial body's azimuth by an amount in nautical miles equal to the difference of the two elevations in minutes of arc. Hence, if the body's measured elevation using the sextant was 50° 27' of arc, and the AP elevation was 50° 05' of arc, the position line would be 22 minutes of arc and, therefore, 22 nautical miles *towards* (i.e. in the direction of) the azimuth of the celestial body. If the sextant elevation had been 49° 45', the position would be moved 20 minutes of arc, equating to 20 nautical miles *away* from the AP position line. The creation of a single

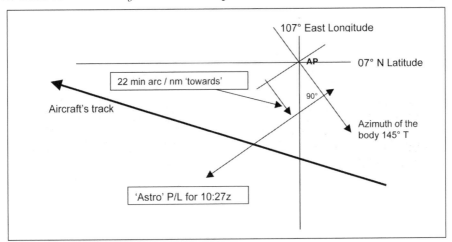

Figure 1: The St Hilaire or Intercept method of plotting celestial position lines.

astro-position line, using the first example data given above, is illustrated below.

Including extracting the necessary data for a three-star fix from the Air Almanac and Admiralty Tables (the latter in 1953 superseded by the easier and quicker HO249 – AP3270), the elapsed time taken for a navigator, working on his own, to take three star sights, complete the calculations and plot the results, could perhaps be eighteen to twenty-four minutes. A single sun sight would probably take six minutes. If two navigators worked as a team, the time taken could be reduced by a quarter, perhaps more.

When flying on an east–west track during the daytime – as for example, between the northern tip of Sumatra and the east coast of Ceylon (Sri Lanka) – the azimuth of astro-shots on the sun taken when the sun is still to the south of the equator (as in December 1952), between roughly mid-morning and mid-afternoon local time, would be on true bearings between about 130 and 220°. Sun position lines are by definition at 90° to the sun's azimuth (for reasons already explained), and on this leg they mostly gave a rather shallow cut across the aircraft's east–west track. Hence, while sun sights would then be useful for helping to maintain the intended track, they would at that time of day be less useful for obtaining an accurate check on the aircraft's groundspeed or its position 'along track'. On the other hand, if you consider taking off from Ceylon (Sri Lanka) at sunrise to fly directly east across the Indian Ocean, for the next three to four hours the azimuth of the sun will be between approximately 090°T and 135°T azimuth. Position lines on the sun will in this case, at that time of day, provide good groundspeed and distance along-track checks, but not for another two to three hours will they provide good information on whether the aircraft is maintaining its desired track. By day, therefore, while sun shots are relatively quick and easy to take compared with those on stars, their usefulness varies according to the time of day and the direction of the track along which the aircraft is required to fly relative to the sun's azimuth. On the other hand, at night (provided stars are visible), a navigator can choose to sight whichever stars or planets are at azimuths that are most advantageous for his navigation needs at a particular time. At night, the usefulness of the moon for astro – like the sun by day – will vary according to the orientation of position lines most required by the navigator.

For those who don't already know, I should perhaps mention an important characteristic of the 'North Star', Polaris. This is situated more or less vertically over the earth's geographic North Pole. Conveniently, this not only means that it gives a ready indication of the direction of true north, but conveniently its arc of elevation is virtually the same as the latitude where you are standing – or flying. The latitude of Knutsford, the town where I live, is 53° 23' N; so if I were this evening to locate Polaris in the sky and measure its arc of elevation using a sextant, with a few small corrections I would expect this to measure close to 53° 23' of arc in elevation. This can be very useful and save a lot of calculation. However, the latitude of Singapore city is 01° 22' North. Hence, in the night sky, Polaris is barely above the northern horizon – so low, in fact, that navigators flying in that area couldn't use it for astro-navigation. It wasn't until we were a little way south of Hong Kong that Polaris could be used on a night flight; by then, it was usually past dawn on a typical overnight transit to Kai Tak. Effectively, therefore, Polaris only came into play on West Coast Weather patrols to the west and south of Korea. But still, you had a great many other stars to choose from!

Bearing in mind all the other activities a navigator was required to undertake every hour to ensure accurate and safe navigation (frequent drift-taking, MPP construction, three-drift winds, periodic checks of compass accuracy using the astro-compass, making variation changes to the VSC, checking safety heights, etc.), navigation over ocean areas was mentally demanding and a constantly busy time for the navigator. He not only needed unquestioning co-operation from other crew members, to launch flame-floats for drift measurement, for compass readings, etc., but he also appreciated the offer of an occasional cup of tea or cold drink, and something to eat! Apart from an occasional trip to the toilet (downstairs in the nose section) or in winter, to warm up for a few minutes in the galley, the navigator spent most of the nine to twelve hours' flight time sitting at his table or standing on the platform beside it, looking out through the astrodome.

Coastline ranging using the bubble sextant

If the ASV search radar was unserviceable (rarely), or if we were flying at medium altitude, for example to the east of the coast of French Indo-China, I would occasionally use the bubble sextant to measure the angle of depression on the coastline or on a known range of hills or mountains. By referring to a table in the Astro-Tables and entering it with the depression angle, the aircraft's height and the height of the ground on which the sight was taken, I could read off the distance from the aircraft to the coast or hills.

The accuracy of watches for navigation in the 1950s

Time-keeping accuracy was important for both DR and astro-navigation. We are now accustomed to inexpensive wrist watches losing or gaining no more then a few seconds *in several weeks*. In the 1930s, 1940s and early 1950s, watches were hand-wound clockwork-powered, with a balance wheel for timing accuracy. Battery-powered, tuning fork and, later, transistorized and then quartz watches had not been invented. The timing accuracy of electronic watches has improved the accuracy of the average-priced watch by a factor of between 30 and 300. In 1952, a transistor suitably sized for use in watches had not been commercially developed. Navigators were issued with a so-called navigator's watch that supposedly had better than average time-keeping accuracy. Even so, in practice they typically gained or lost five to ten seconds *a day*. We had to calibrate them and check them frequently against the Greenwich Observatory time signal. Astro–navigation required accurate timing as well as accurate measurement using a sextant. Hence, navigators almost invariably had to apply a correction for the known inaccuracy of their watch when timing the start and finish of astro-sights.

Medium-frequency DF loop
A navigation aid I have not yet mentioned is the medium-frequency (MF) receiver and the associated loop antenna. These could sometimes provide bearings at 100 to 300 miles from an MF radio beacon; occasionally more from a high-power radio transmitter. When describing preparations for the ferry flight to the UK, I recounted how, when air-testing RN303 with F/O George Chesworth on 12 December 1952, I had 'swung the loop' over a small island off the north coast of Malaya. The R1155 super-heterodyne radio receiver operated between 75 kHz and 18.5 MHz in five bands. The highly directional loop antenna could be rotated through 360° against a graduated azimuth scale. At a reading of 360° the antenna mounting and azimuth ring were aligned at right-angles to the nose and hence to the fore-and-aft axis of the aircraft.

To use the antenna as an aid to navigation, the navigator would select a suitably located MF radio beacon and tune to its frequency (given in an information booklet) on his R1155 radio receiver. If a tone signal was audible at that frequency he would check that it was emitting the correct two–letter (digraph) call sign in Morse code. There was then a meter with left and right needles that compared the phase of the electromagnetic (EM) waves being received through the left and right sides of the loop antenna. The navigator would rotate the loop about its vertical axis until the left/right needles indicated that the loop was aligned at right-angles to the arriving EM wave front. The indicated loop bearing of the beacon in azimuth was measured relative to the aircraft's fore–and–aft axis. Since the aircraft's fore–and–aft axis defined its course (or heading), by adding the relative bearing shown on the scale of the loop to the course, and then applying whatever azimuth correction was shown on the loop swing correction card, the navigator could calculate the True bearing of the MF beacon *from* the aircraft (i.e. loop relative bearing + True course = MF beacon True bearing from the aircraft). By plotting the reciprocal of that bearing from the latitude and longitude position of the beacon that the navigator would have plotted on his Mercator navigation chart, he would have obtained and would be able to draw a single position line for the time at which the loop bearing was taken. A measuring error by the navigator of plus or minus one degree, and a bearing measurement error by the equipment of plus or minus 1.5 to 2.5 degrees might be expected. At a distance from the radio beacon of 120 nautical miles, this would typically result in a position line that would probably be within five to seven miles of the aircraft's true position.

The MF DF loop could also be useful as a letdown aid. If you had an MF beacon at or close to your planned alighting area and you needed to descend safely in 'instrument flight' (IF) conditions, through cloud or in darkness, to reach circuit height safely, you could follow a prescribed terminal approach pattern (TAP) relative to the MF beacon. The navigator would use the loop antenna to position the aircraft overhead, then give the pilot the first course to steer to follow the TAP descent pattern and use loop back-bearings to maintain the correct track. The navigator would then ask the pilot to alter course as necessary while descending the aircraft at the required rate (in feet per minute). At a given altitude, about half-way through the descent, the navigator would tell the pilot to turn, usually to port, onto a near-reciprocal course, when the navigator would again use the loop antenna to home the aircraft, giving the pilot course changes as necessary, towards the radio beacon. The pilot would level out at the minimum altitude permitted by the letdown procedure (perhaps 1,500 ft) and be homed to overhead the radio beacon. By this time it was to be hoped that the ground or alighting area would be in sight. This was the technique I considered using and might have used when, as I described in Chapter 3 on 27 March 1953, we had lost both VHF communications and our ASV radar *en route* from Kai Tak to Iwakuni. Unfortunately, because of lightning or night effect interference, uncertainty about the cloud base at Iwakuni and high ground in the vicinity of the airfield, I ruled it out as unsafe.

Even though a radio beacon's transmission might be weak, it might still be possible to obtain a bearing by using the 'aural' facility. This allowed a navigator to *listen* to the audible strength of the incoming signal. The equipment was so arranged that, on 'aural', when the loop was pointing directly at the signal's direction of arrival (i.e. its bearing), the audible sound of the signal reduced to nil – this was called the 'null'. So by moving the antenna to left, right and back again repeatedly about the null signal, you could interpolate the beacon's most likely bearing on the azimuth scale. However, because the received signal was in the first place weak, the bearing accuracy might not be quite as good as when it was strong enough to use the visual (needles) method; nevertheless, it was better than no bearing. The navigator, recognizing a possible degree of inaccuracy, would apply a suitable band of error to reflect this.

There were three MF emission problems that crews even today have to be aware of. The first is called night effect. The Heaviside Layer is a band of ionized gas 90–150 km above the earth. This is affected by the solar wind according to the earth's orientation in relation to the sun, and therefore according to the time of day. At around dusk and dawn for a period of two hours or so, the Heaviside Layer increases or decreases its height above the earth's surface according to a predictable cycle. During these dawn and dusk periods, movement of the 'D' region (as it is called) within the Heaviside Layer, unfortunately refracts and thereby distorts the transmission path of MF EM waves, including those transmitted by MF radio beacons used for loop direction finding (and more modern ADFs). The effect is to refract, unpredictably, the arrival path of wave fronts at the loop or ADF antenna; hence, the navigator or pilot will unknowingly measure a false bearing at the antenna. This effect is not easily detected by a crew. Hence, it had to be assumed that MF DF bearings received by a loop antenna taken an hour or two before or after dawn and dusk could be erroneous. At such times they should not be used, or only with caution – for example by taking bearings at short ranges from the beacon when any bearing errors would not translate into such large geographical position errors.

The second emission problem was 'meaconing'. This can result when taking bearings on broadcast radio stations. Sometimes a broadcast station may transmit signals from two sites that are geographically separated by a considerable distance. Hence, bearings taken by an aircraft on such transmissions can be the sum of two emissions rather than one emission. This can produce a false bearing.

I was taught a salutary lesson on 4 February 1966, when navigating a Vickers Varsity (WF425) between Stradishall and Malta while attending 153 Navigation Refresher Course at No. 1 ANS Stradishall. I was navigator of one of a stream of four Varsities, spaced at 30 min intervals. We refuelled and then took off from Nice about an hour before dusk to complete the three-hour second leg to Luqa, in Malta. The aircraft had no search radar. Our route took us south and then east-south-east from the southern tip of Sardinia towards Malta. The aircraft was equipped with a (then) modern MF ADF (rather than the older loop antenna in the Sunderland). For most of the time it was cloudy, and as it was winter, it soon became dark. There were few navigation aids other than MF beacons on Sardinia. I obtained a fix from two VHF bearings from Cagliari airfield as we passed to the south of it. On the final leg to Malta, I was using what ADF bearings I could muster, including a broadcast station in Sardinia, as my main – or sole – means of fixing. About an hour before we were due to reach Malta, I was surprised to be told by the pilot that he could see lights on a coast just about to pass under the aircraft's nose. I think we were flying at about 7,500 feet.

I concluded this could only be the western tip of Sicily, which should have been about thirty miles on our port side. Other Varsities in the stream apparently also found themselves well off track to the north. On arrival at Luqa, I learned from their Met office that an unexpected strong southerly wind had developed that afternoon, which had not been forecast. Moreover, I and navigators in the other Varsities had obviously been misled by inaccurate ADF bearings – that had resulted in significant fixing errors. These were made worse by wrong assumptions about the probable wind velocity forecast in that area at our altitude. What I found most salutary was that a projection to the east of the track on which we had actually been flying would, at about our ETA overhead Malta, have put us not far from the vicinity of Mount Etna, the height of which is 10,910 feet!

The third MF loop problem was that bearing accuracy could be badly affected by electrical activity from thunder storms. As I described in Chapter 3, these can render loop antenna bearings unreliable as a letdown aid at a time when you might be most in need of them. This was usually evident because the needles would hold steady for a short while and then sway to one side and then the other. This happened to me on 27 March 1953 when I needed to use the loop to let down at Iwakuni when we had neither VHF radio communication nor radar. As Iwakuni is surrounded by high ground this left me with a serious dilemma.

Position line bands of error and most probable positions (MPP)

A position line can be defined as a line on the earth's surface, of infinite length, above which the aircraft is theoretically located according to the information on which the position line is based. This does not take account of inaccuracies in the method used to obtain the position line – hence the need to apply 'bands of error'. Position lines obtained from astro-sights on a celestial body when using a bubble sextant were usually given a 50% band of error of eight to ten miles. However, a navigator might decide to increase the error band if the aircraft was flying in turbulent conditions.

Because of likely inaccuracies in position lines (errors from some navigation sources are greater than others) navigators bounded position lines with bands of error according to certain rules, depending on the source of the position line. When two or more intersecting position lines were used, the navigator would construct an ellipse of 'uncertainty' within the error bands. A wind velocity vector was then applied to the aircraft's air position (obtained from the API – described later), and the consequent DR position would be compared with the fix ellipse and the bands of error, to derive a probability-weighted 'most probable position' (MPP).

Figure 2 illustrates a navigator's plotting chart with position lines (H for Astro, L for Loop bearing) and appropriate bands of error; air positions from the API are shown as (+); wind velocity (W/V) vector (distinguished by three arrows), DR position (a triangle); DR position circle of error; ellipse within bands of error of two intersecting P/Ls, and the most probable position (triangle and MPP) are taken, transferred or recalculated for one common time, 14.06 Zulu (GMT) in this case. Having obtained an MPP, the navigator would then 'DR ahead'[3] and alter course either to regain track, or towards the destination or next turning-point. The DR ahead process is shown later.

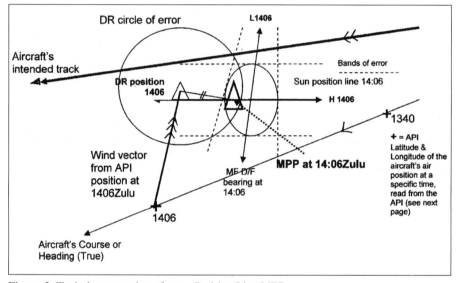

Figure 2: Typical construction of a two Position Line MPP.

The direct-reading compass (DRC)

The most important navigation aid or instrument aboard the Sunderland was the direct-reading compass. The master unit was suspended on gimbals in the rear fuselage away from electrical and spurious electromagnetic influences. A Sunderland crewman on intercom on the starboard side of the rear fuselage would read out the magnetic course indicated on the master unit to the navigator in his station on the flight deck. This would be done hourly or more frequently. The DRC, electrically driven, 'hunted' back and forth by less than a degree relative to the detected magnetic north.

The DRC sent electrical signals to repeater indicators in the navigator's and pilots' stations (one is seen on the API in the next section). Magnetic variation and deviation (compass error) corrections were applied electrically by the navigator through the variation setting control (VSC) so that the remote compass indicators on the flight deck showed the aircraft's true (rather than magnetic) heading (or course). Unlike the pilots' P10 compass, the major advantage of the DRC was that it was designed not to be affected by accelerations and was capable of withstanding quite severe aircraft manoeuvres without its accuracy being significantly affected. The most important requirement was to 'swing' all the aircraft's compasses (according to a set procedure) preferably on the ground on a non-magnetic compass base, or otherwise in the air, apply any necessary corrections (using special keys), and then draw up and display correction cards for the two pilots and in the navigator's station, on the flight deck.

As well as compass deviation corrections, navigators had to apply the correct magnetic variation setting to the aircraft's compasses manually, throughout the flight, according to the approximate geographical location of the aircraft and the value of variation isogonals at that location. These were printed on navigators' Mercator plotting charts (e.g. an isogonal of 7° W would indicate that Magnetic north was 7° in azimuth greater than True north at that location). The navigator applied these values to the variation setting control (VSC) in his navigation station. Variation could have any value, east or west, as indicated on the navigator's plotting chart. The isogonal also had a year date beside the variation value and the amount of change in variation, increasing or decreasing, per annum. Whatever the value, it was important to update the variation setting on the VSC continually, because (for example) a one-degree error in heading would result in an accumulating lateral distance error of about one mile for every thirty minutes flown. The frequency with which variation settings required to be updated were greater when flying around Japan and Korea (compared with Singapore) because values were higher and isogonals were more frequently crossed in the course of a sortie.

Air position indicator (API) and air mileage unit (AMU)

The second most important navigation instrument in the Sunderland was mentioned when discussing bands of error. This was the analogue air position indicator (API). The API is shown on page 3 of the colour section. Note the DRC compass repeater and the latitude N/S and longitude E/W air position counters on the right. The knob at the bottom allowed the navigator to set the parallel lines either side of the main DRC-driven pointer, to the navigator's desired course. This enabled the navigator to check that the pilot was steering the course he had given him to steer. The single pointer between the parallel arrows was the aircraft's actual course (heading). The accuracy of the DRC course repeater was periodically checked against the DRC master unit. Latitude/longitude API counters were reset using the knobs to the right of the N/S and E/W counters. The API received direction inputs from the direct-reading compass (DRC) and distance in air miles flown, from the air mileage unit (AMU), which in turn had received inputs from the aircraft's pitot and static system. The API gave the navigator a continuous readout of what the aircraft's position in latitude and longitude would have been if the aircraft had been unaffected by past and present wind velocities. This was extremely important information. It was, of course, subject to input errors from the air mileage unit, the direct-reading compass, and from any errors by the navigator in applying variation and deviation corrections; but these, hopefully, were small. It was also subject to errors in any latitude/longitude resets applied by the navigator during flight; for example, when a navigator had earlier reset the API to a 'fix' or MPP, any error difference in latitude and longitude between the navigator's 'fix' or MPP position and the *actual* latitude and longitude of the aircraft at the time of the fix/MPP and the API reset would inject and carry forward a similar error to the API position shown.

At take-off, the API was set to the latitude and longitude of the flying boat alighting area (or airfield for landplanes). It was therefore especially important for the navigator that the aircraft's compasses were accurate (achieved by 'swinging' and applying corrections) and by applying variation and deviation error corrections at the right time throughout the flight. Once into a sortie, the navigator was advised to reset the API only to reliable 'fixes'. The most reliable fixes were a radar fix or a pin-point, i.e. visually passing immediately overhead a position whose latitude and longitude were accurately known. However, Sunderland crews in the Far East could only infrequently obtain pin-points when flying over ocean areas – indeed, none apart from an occasional small island or reef. Nevertheless, the API was the most valuable instrument after the direct-reading compass.

The astro-compass Mk II and astrodome
Another important instrument that helped navigators keep a regular (once an hour) check on the accuracy of the aircraft's DRC and other compasses was the astro-compass. The astro-compass was attached to a removable frame that could be mounted in the astrodome. The astrodome, located immediately beside the navigator's table, was an optically corrected Perspex half-sphere, about 30 inches (76 cm) in diameter (see page 4 colour section). To use it, the navigator stood on a retractable platform with his head inside the Perspex dome whenever he wished either to take astro–sights using the sextant, or to use the astro-compass. Before take-off, the astrodome in its frame was secured to the fuselage roof. When removed it could be stowed to allow access to the upper surface of the wings, fuselage, tailplane and tail fin while the aircraft was at its mooring. In an emergency it provided an escape

exit from the flight deck. When removed, the aperture also served as the crew's main access to the upper surfaces of the aircraft for refuelling and mounting the mooring light, for pre-flight checks, and to gain access to the auxiliary power unit in the starboard wing root.

For use, the astro-compass mounting frame was attached inside the astrodome mounting exactly aligned to the fore-and-aft axis of the aircraft. The astro-compass was not a 'compass' in the usually accepted sense; it did *not* have an inbuilt north-seeking magnetic element. It had two graduated rings that could be rotated around vertical axes, each ring being marked in degrees of azimuth 001–360. The upper ring could be tilted at any given or required angle of elevation. In essence, the navigator calculated the local hour angle (or azimuth) of the sun for a given time and set it on the top ring's graduated scale. Above the upper graduated ring was a tilting screen with two vertical lines engraved on a white background and a vertical bar that would cast a shadow onto the screen when pointed directly towards the sun. The navigator aligned the sun's shadow (by rotating the bottom ring and graduated scale) so that the shadow lay exactly between the two parallel vertical lines on the screen at exactly the time for which the navigator had calculated the sun's azimuth. The angle of the aircraft's true heading was then the azimuth shown on the bottom ring. This was compared with the heading shown on the aircraft's DRC master unit and other compasses, assuming variation and deviation had been correctly applied to the DRC. The navigator then applied any necessary corrections to the aircraft's course to eliminate any compass error.

The navigator also used the astro-compass for compass accuracy checks at night by using it to directly sight a planet, star, or the moon. Direct sighting was necessary since such bodies do not cast a strong enough shadow to be visible. Any difference between the expected and actual azimuth would be due to compass error, for which the navigator could then make allowance. Finally, I have already indicated earlier in this Appendix that the astro-compass could be used to take back bearings on flame-floats and smoke markers dropped into the water when at low altitude in order to measure the aircraft's drift.

The ASV Mk VIC search radar

The Mark V Sunderland was the first Mark to be fitted with the split scanner ASV Mk VIC radar. Although the specification of this radar was optimized for ship and submarine detection, it proved extremely valuable for navigation. This capability was especially welcome because of the dearth of quick-fixing aids in the Far East in the 1950s. The Sunderland's ASV Mk VIC centimetric search radar had a 360-degree plan position indicator and (from memory) a maximum range on a rugged coastline (i.e. one that would give a good radar return) of seventy-five miles or more. Fifty to sixty miles was probably a more usual range on an average coastline. Detection ranges against ships were typically fifteen to thirty-five miles, depending on the vessel's size. The antenna installation was unusual because it had two rotating dish aerials (contained within cupolas), one on the underside of each outer wing, outboard of the wing-mounted floats. Together, these gave 360 degrees of radar coverage, which was very advantageous when patrolling and for navigation. It also meant that if one antenna failed, you still had at least 180 degrees of radar cover, albeit only to port or starboard.

Because the technical specification of the radar was optimized to detect ships and submarines, it had a comparatively long pulse length and wide beam width when compared with H2S radars designed for navigation and for target identification and 'offset' bomb-aiming. It was, none the less, good enough for coast shape recognition, ranges and bearings, and for navigating along and between coastlines up to forty miles distant. There were many occasions when in bad weather it was possible, at a height of 250 to 1,000 feet, to map-read a Sunderland from Iwakuni using the ASV radar and occasional visual sightings on the coastline or islands, southwards between the islands from Iwakuni and then westwards along the length of the Inland Sea to Shimonoseki and into the Tsushima Strait. Similarly, we were able to navigate our way back to the Iwakuni alighting area in very poor visibility, whether it was daylight or after nightfall. It was also invaluable for finding and penetrating the outer reaches of the entrance to Kowloon harbour before the white-painted cliff came into view.

When within radar range of land, the ASV radar was a boon for navigators. The Mk VIC plan position indicator was in a radar 'tent' located forward of the navigator's station; that is to say, immediately at his back because the navigator, seated on the starboard side of the aircraft, faced to the rear. Thus, it was easy to move quickly between the navigation table and the radar PPI in circumstances such as I have just described when the ASV was being used as the primary navigation aid. Also, when close to land, one of the signallers would normally be sitting in the tent, optimizing the performance of the radar and following the aircraft's position on a map; the navigator and signaller would then work as a team, constantly keeping track of the aircraft's progress by reference to maps and the radar screen. In this way we maximized flight safety, which must always be at the forefront of every crew's mind. However, for much of the time on most sorties and routes, potentially useful points of reference for navigation using the radar were either beyond the aircraft's radar range or below the radar horizon. ASV radar was our primary ship detection aid on Korean patrols.

The radio altimeter

Although not a navigation aid in the strict sense, Sunderland navigators were mindful that safe navigation is three-dimensional. The two pilots had a radio altimeter which they used typically below 1,000 feet, especially over the sea and when an accurate local QFE/QNH might well not be known. The radio altimeter was accurate down to very low altitudes (a few feet above the sea or land surface). It measured height by transmitting downwards a modulated radio signal which when reflected by the sea or ground surface provides the pilot with an accurate read-out of the aircraft's actual height. Thus, height measurement was not reliant on prior knowledge of the local barometric pressure (a difference of 1 millibar equals 30 feet in height). There was a high scale which Stuart Holmes, a former pilot on 88 Squadron, tells me was seldom selected, and a low scale which extended to 400 feet but was normally used up to 300 feet above the sea surface.

When flying on weather data-gathering and reporting sorties over the sea at night, the pilots would let down to 100 feet using the radio altimeter, and when steady at 100 feet according to the radio altimeter, they would reset the co-pilot's barometric altimeter to 100 feet and read off the resultant barometric sea level pressure in millibars. The navigator would record the latitude and longitude, the time of the pressure reading, and the pressure in millibars, which later were reported (together with wind velocity, cloud amounts, bases and tops, visibility, etc.) by VHF radio to those requiring it, typically US Navy Task Force 77 operating off the west coast of Korea. Our weather measurements in the Yellow Sea supplemented the US Navy, US Marine Corps and UN Air Forces' (mostly USAF and RAAF) own information. These weather reports were useful when planning the following day's air operations, as no weather data were available from the Communist Chinese mainland, whence most weather systems came.

Loran

In the Far East there were no quick-fixing navaids such as Decca or Gee. The only hyperbolic position line navaid was Loran (I think it was Loran 'A'). Loran ground stations emitted at low frequencies (LF), producing a sky wave, and a shorter-range ground wave that followed the curvature of the earth. It had a maximum range of several hundred miles from the transmitting stations. It was slower to use and much less accurate than Gee or Decca. Loran stations were variously sited in Japan and one at Pusan. The system in the Sunderland allowed you to use only one 'chain' at a time, giving only one position line; you had to retune to another station and transfer position lines, by time and distance, to construct a fix or MPP. It could take fifteen minutes to set up the Sunderland's Mark of Loran receiver properly; I always tried to complete this as soon as possible after take-off, especially in winter. When flying in poor weather around Japan and Korea, it was time well spent, as Loran could be very useful, especially if the ASV gave any trouble and when out of ASV radar range of land in the Yellow Sea. However, the angles of intersection between the position lines of different chains when in the Yellow Sea were rather shallow, and adjacent co-ordinates were widely spaced. Hence, towards the periphery of Loran cover, position lines were subject to wide bands of error. Nevertheless, Loran was a useful standby.

VHF DF

In some geographical areas, when flying in support of UN Korean operations in the Tsushima Strait, south of Korea, we could call for bearings from a number of USAF VHF DF stations (e.g. Kagoshima Dog Fox). I recall that on one sortie we were flying to the South of Korea and were tuned to the VHF DF net. Our port beam gunner reported that a USAF F80 Shooting Star fighter was approaching us, and eventually it flew in formation, with flaps extended, about fifty yards off our port wing. We then heard what must have been the F80's pilot calling up the DF station and saying, 'I'm flying alongside what looks a like a PBM (Mariner) but with four engines. I don't know what it is, but it's a big white son-of-a-bitch!' The Sunderland initially had only a single 4-channel VHF set, although I think we eventually persuaded the 'powers that be' to fit a second for operations from Iwakuni. One channel was always set to 121.5 International Distress. I think the others were tuned to 116.1, 118.1 and 119.7 MHz. The only other communications transmitter/receiver was the signaller's HF transmitter and receiver (T1154/R1155), which was used almost exclusively for communication by Morse code, though occasionally some rather poor-quality double side-band HF voice was possible. On operations into and from Iwakuni, RAF Sunderland aircraft always used the call-sign prefix WATCHMAN, followed by the aircraft's side-letter (e.g. WATCHMAN CHARLIE) (see page 5 colour section).

The Dalton computer

The Dalton computer was a double-sided calculating instrument carried by each navigator. It measured about 8 inches by 6 inches and was an inch deep. You couldn't safely fly any sortie without one. One side was a multi-function circular slide rule designed to enable navigators to solve any time and space problem, and, for example, to convert indicated or rectified air speed to true air speed at any altitude and ambient temperature. You could also use it to calculate an ETA, point of no return, or critical point (see page 3 colour section).

On the other side of the calculator was a graduated 360-degree rotating ring, and a movable blind with drift angles and speed lines behind a transparent Perspex screen. On this side you could convert two drifts or three drifts, with or without a groundspeed measurement from the drift recorder, into a wind velocity. Alternatively you could draw a forecast wind vector on the Perspex screen and calculate the course required for any track, or the true air speed required on any heading for a required groundspeed. You could calculate the aircraft's drift angle on any course at any true air speed, and calculate the groundspeed. It was a very compact and cleverly designed, manually operated calculator, and the first piece of equipment you learned to use in basic navigation training. It was essential for DR navigation. It was an excellent piece of kit – replaced in the mid-1950s by a lighter and slimmer device made of plastic and aluminium.

The Douglas protractor
While not specific to the Sunderland, mention must be made of the Douglas protractor. It was designed by the late Rear-Admiral Sir H.P. Douglas RN, Superintendent of Charts, Hydrographic Department, Admiralty, London. Millions of these must have been used by navigators over the past sixty years. It is a simple, square (about 5 inches) Perspex device to lay off, read or plot courses and bearings, use as a parallel rule, measure the departure between two positions, plot position lines, and other uses. My left hand is seen resting on one in the photograph on page 8. Well done, Admiral Douglas; we will for ever be indebted to you!

The navigator's log and chart
On each flight, navigators had to try to work to a laid-down activity schedule. This was to ensure that aircraft were navigated safely and to a high standard. Logs and charts for every sortie were handed to the squadron navigation leader at the first opportunity after landing. In the 1950s, the type of chart most commonly used for plotting was the 1:1,000,000 or 1:2,000,000 Mercator projection. The main feature of the Mercator, which is a cylindrical projection, is its ability to represent lines of constant true bearing or true course (called rhumb lines) as straight-line segments. All lines of latitude are parallel, as are meridians of longitude, and both are at right-angles to one another. One of several advantages provided by the Mercator projection for air navigation is that it allows a navigator to draw a straight line track between two geographical places shown on a chart, and fly a single (rhumb line) course between them. Although aircraft will then fly rhumb line tracks – these are slightly longer than an equivalent Great Circle track – the disadvantage of flying slightly farther between any two geographic locations is outweighed by the plotting and steering advantages afforded by a Mercator projection.

The Mercator charts used by Sunderland navigators had a latitude/ longitude grid and showed only coastlines, major spot heights (in metres), major rivers, a few towns and very little else. The outline was coloured green or red. The positions of navigation aids, airfields, aircraft tracks and ATC or airway boundaries had to be drawn onto the chart by the navigator (by reference to RAFACs and planning documents, etc.), according to need.

The squadron navigation leader examined all logs line by line to see whether all the necessary safety checks had been carried out at the required interval. On the chart he measured the accuracy of the navigator's plotting and calculations, against what he had written in the log. Marks, usually out of 100, were awarded for 'activity', 'accuracy' and (I seem to recall) 'application'. Comments were made on the general standard of navigation and on any matters that the navigation leader felt were warranted, praise as well as advice. Any errors were highlighted. In this way, the navigation leader, aircraft captains and the squadron commander were made aware of any significant weaknesses; navigators were then helped to improve their techniques and accuracy. Safety was extremely important, as the lives of a whole crew rested on the performance of the navigator, as well as on that of the pilots.

Air signallers, flight engineers and air gunners, too, all had their part to play in achieving a high standard of navigation and air safety. Leaders of the other aircrew specializations monitored the performances of their aircrew categories in various ways, and addressed any apparent weaknesses by further training. Annually, navigators received an assessment: Below Average, Average, Above Average or Exceptional. This was awarded by the squadron commander, based on information and a recommendation provided to him by the navigation leader and the navigator's aircraft captain. The assessment was entered into the navigator's flying logbook as a permanent record. Log and chart marking and navigator assessment was time-consuming, as I found out myself from January 1954, when I was appointed the navigation leader besides carrying out my duties as navigator of one of the squadron's five aircraft.

DR ahead procedure

'DR ahead' is the term used to describe the actions the navigator takes when he wishes to make an alteration of course towards the next planned turning-point, or to the position where the navigator wishes to regain the originally planned track.

The reader is reminded that in most instances it will have taken some minutes to construct and plot a 'fix' or most probable position. Some fixes or MPPs took longer to plot than others. For example in most instances a pin-point could be plotted within a minute, but pin-points were few and far between when transiting ocean areas. It was more common for a navigator to be constructing a fix or MPP from MF bearings and/or celestial position lines. Unless, for example, an MF bearing was taken by a second navigator at the mid-time of a celestial sight that was being taken by a second navigator – in which case both position lines would have the same effective time – it would be necessary to move (or transfer) the first position line, up to the time of the second or last position line, before a fix or MPP could be constructed. This process would involve the navigator moving the first position line on the plotting chart along track by a distance equal to the aircraft's ground distance covered during the time difference between the times of each position line and the effective time of the fix or MPP. That transfer process and construction of the resultant fix or MPP could take anything from two to perhaps ten minutes.

The navigator then had to plot, as accurately as possible, the DR position where he predicted the aircraft would be, say, twelve minutes after the effective time of the fix or MPP he had just calculated. He would then draw a new, required track from that DR position to the next turning-point (B) along the route, or alternatively, towards the position in which he wished to intercept the originally planned track. This whole process was and is known as 'DR-ing ahead'. This was achieved using either the air plot or the groundspeed and track methods. The former was more accurate because it took into account any alterations of heading the aircraft may have made (for example, to avoid a rain storm) between the time the fix was taken and the planned time of the DR ahead. This is illustrated in Fig. 3, in which it is assumed that a navigator has required twelve minutes to complete the construction of a most possible position from two celestial sights and an MF Loop bearing, and to construct a DR ahead position based on the resultant MPP and wind velocity vector. Position lines are normally annotated by the effective time of the position line and also by a letter to indicate the 'navaid' used to obtain the position line (e.g. L = loop antenna; H = astro). In addition, position lines that have been transferred in time are marked with a double arrow. Likewise, an intended or actual track of an aircraft is normally marked by two arrows close together. In this example, because the two position lines at 1406 and the third transferred position line, form a very small 'cocked hat', the centre of the 'fix' has been accepted as the MPP at 1406.

Topographical maps
In the Far East, among the most popular topographical map was the Airways series of American maps, an example of which is shown below (Map 227). This was the map we always had with us when operating from Iwakuni. There was a larger-scale version available which was superior for map reading. This is the second of the two maps and is shown on Map 228. It is of Tsushima Island, in the Shimonoseki Strait off the southern coast of Korea, to the west of Kyushu and Honshu Islands.

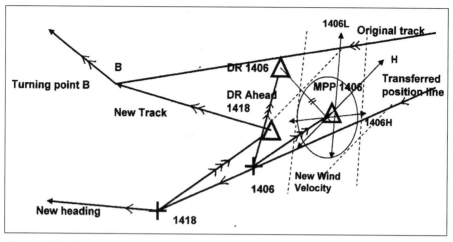

Figure 3: DR Ahead Procedure (illustrative only).

The navigator's bomb-aiming role and equipment

In the nose compartment a Mark 3 low-level bombsight (stowed in a box when not in use) was mounted by the navigator on a bracket in front of the bomb-aiming window, as and when required. To the right was a bomb-release button on a lead. The LLBS was a simple yet accurate device. It had a square, stabilized ground-glass screen. This was attached to a lever which the navigator could raise and lower to view the target through the glass screen. An electric motor rotated a cylindrical drum about a longitudinal axis. The drum had horizontal slots in the body, and a light at the centre. This shone through slots which were arranged in such a way that when viewed by the navigator through the glass screen, it appeared as an image akin to the illuminated rungs of a ladder, continuously moving downwards. The navigator could swivel the sight to left and right to aim it in azimuth so that he could always view the target (a submarine, towed target or smoke float) through the illuminated 'ladder rungs', even though the pilot might turn the aircraft or jink to the left or right.

To the left of the 1st pilot's seat (see colour section page 6) was a panel on which the pilot selected the appropriate weapons and fused them by a switch. The panel was electrically linked to the navigator's bomb-release button in the nose compartment. A forward-throw computer, also electrically linked to the LLBS in the nose, and was located to the right of the co-pilot, who set the weapon type, stick length, intended attack height and speed, agreed between the navigator and the pilots. The pilot in control would turn the aircraft to aim it towards the target, allowing for some deflection depending on the direction and speed of travel of the target submarine relative to the aircraft's direction of approach and distance to run. The pilot would open the bomb doors and run the electrically driven bomb racks out beneath the port and starboard wings. The pilot would be reducing height or diving to about 100–150 feet above the sea. The navigator would call for corrections in heading that he thought necessary to straddle the target with a stick of weapons. The aircraft should if possible track across the submarine at an angle of 45–60° to the target's course. Normally, a 100 yd overall stick length of four or six depth charges would be dropped, ideally an equal number entering the water either side of the hull (i.e. two or three to port and to starboard). The navigator would constantly view the target through the glass screen, where he would see the illuminated rungs of the 'ladder' continuously moving downwards. Viewing the target through the ladder 'rungs', the navigator would steer the sight with one hand to keep it over the target as the pilot jinked and manoeuvred either to follow the navigator's directions or to throw a retaliating gunner on a surfaced submarine off his aim (the bombsight design was such that the navigator would still be able to track the target, regardless of the pilot's manoeuvres); at the same time the 'nav' held with the other hand an electrical lead with a bomb-release button at its end.

As the two pilots made the necessary weapons selections and forward-throw settings, the speed of rotation of the drum of the LLBS would automatically be adjusted to the correct speed for an accurate weapon drop. When the target was distant, the sight's illuminated 'rungs' would appear to the navigator to be moving faster, downwards, overtaking the target; but as the aircraft gradually closed with the target, the vertical sight-line from the LLBS to the target gradually depressed, and the target image would appear to be speeding up and getting nearer and nearer to matching the downward speed of movement of the bombsight's illuminated ladder 'rungs'. The navigator, watching intently, at the same time giving the pilot any course corrections in azimuth over the intercom – 'Left, left' – 'Steady' – 'Steady' – 'Right – Steady' – waited for the instant when the apparent speed of movement of the target was *exactly* the same as that of the moving ladder. At that moment, the navigator would squeeze the bomb-release button and call 'Bombs gone' over the intercom. A stick of (for example) four depth charges in a 100 yd stick would instantly be released by the electromechanical release units (EMRU) on the bomb racks at whatever interval would equal the required spacing between each depth charge (i.e. about half a second between the release of each of four weapons at typical Sunderland speeds).

If the navigator had judged the weapon release instant correctly and the pilot, aided by the navigator, had flown the aircraft directly over the submarine, towed moving target[4] or smoke float, the stick of weapons would straddle the target, the first and last weapons being equidistant from it. Using an overall stick length of 100 yards, or sometimes 50 yards, the ideal result would be a 50–50 (or 25–25) straddle – that was the navigator's and pilots' aim.

I thoroughly enjoyed using the Mk 3 LLBS. To be almost certain of straddling the target, whether with a 100 yd or 50 yd stick length, I always asked the co-pilot to set the forward-throw computer to a speed that was 15 kts higher than the aircraft's estimated groundspeed on the attack run to the target. I had found by experimentation that I could then be quite sure that the *moment critique* had arrived (i.e. the target and ladder speeds were *identical*) before I pressed the bomb release. This 15 kt speed addition allowed me a fraction of a second in which to decide whether the proper release time had 'arrived' or not; it seemed to suit my natural eye-to-brain-to-hand co-ordination and prevented me from overshooting the target, or undershooting it through the anxiety of avoiding the more common 'overshoot'. The benefit of doing this was (certainly in my case) confirmed by my bombing results at several armament practice camps and when practice bombing on other occasions. Other navigators may have used a similar technique.

Summary

This Appendix has provided a summary of DR navigation, and of navigation and bombing equipment and techniques used in Sunderland aircraft in the 1950s. Aircraft performance, engine settings and fuel consumption of the Sunderland Mk V were summarized in Appendix 2. To supplement information in this Appendix, and in various chapters of the main book, Appendix 4 will take the reader on a tour of the crew stations and other parts of the Sunderland Mk V. This will show exactly where most of the navigation equipments just discussed were located in the aircraft.

Notes

1. The descriptions of DR navigation techniques and navigation aids and equipment are written so as to be understood by those with no previous experience of navigation or flying as a crew member, and by those who have never been on the flight deck of an aircraft. They are not drawn from official sources.
2. Plan position indicator. This gave a plan view of the sea or land surface, below, throughout 360° in azimuth.
3. To 'DR ahead' after having obtained a fix or MPP, means that a navigator would predict, based on the latest positional and wind velocity information, where the aircraft would be in (say) three minutes' time, and within that time he would calculate the new heading (course) that he should tell the pilot to turn onto in order to head towards the next turning-point or regain track. He would also calculate the new ETA.
4. Sometimes we were fortunate to have an RAF Marine Craft RTTL available at a sea bombing range or in the open sea that would tow, at a separation distance of something like 1,000 yards, a metal and wooden target frame. When towed at about ten knots this caused a small jet of water to be thrown into the air above the target. This looked similar to the wake caused by a submarine's periscope or snorkel. This was the best type of target for training, as the Sunderland crew then had to judge the correct lateral deflection when approaching the target in order to straddle it. It most closely simulated an attack against a real submarine.

A Tour of Sunderland Mark V, ML796

Introduction

This Appendix takes the reader on an internal conducted tour of Sunderland Mk V, ML796. The author was given permission by the Imperial War Museum to photograph this aircraft which is on display at Duxford. It is the best-equipped Sunderland at any museum that I am aware of. All except two photographs in this Appendix were taken by me. This aircraft, which was the first production Mark V, entered service in February 1945. The second Mark V off the production was ML797; fortuitously this was the aircraft that flew the last official RAF sortie by a Sunderland, on 20 May 1959. This took place at RAF Seletar, Singapore. The last Mark V off the production line, on 14 June 1946, was SZ599. The author navigated that aircraft from the Short Bros & Harland base at Wig Bay, Loch Ryan, north of Stranraer, to Seletar in February/March 1953. This tour of ML796 begins at the navigator's station (see colour section also).

The navigator's station

The navigator's main work station was on the upper deck, on the starboard side of the aircraft facing aft immediately forward of the main spar. The navigator had a second station in the aircraft's nose from where he operated the Mark 3 low-level bombsight (discussed in Appendix 3). In UK-based aircraft there was also a navigator's GPI table aft of the 1st pilot's seat. This was not fitted in Far East aircraft. The navigator's main table was about 3 ft 6 in. (105 cm) wide and 2 ft (60 cm) deep; it formed the lid of a box which was about 6 in. (15 cm) deep, within which to store maps, charts and navigation instruments. The 'nav' had a swivel chair, bolted to the floor.

Above the nav's desk is the R1155 radio receiver. This was used mainly to tune into and obtain bearings from MF radio beacons by means of the DF loop antenna. In the Atlantic Ocean in the 1950s the R1155 was also used to obtain Consol position lines and fixes. Mounted above the R1155 was a Loran 'A' receiver. The other module to the right of the Loran is a Gee Mark

1 set, not fitted to Far East Flying Boat Wing (FEFBW) Sunderlands. To the right and below the R1155 radio receiver is the air position indicator (API), including a direct-reading compass (DRC) repeater. Above the API are an airspeed indicator and a barometric altimeter. Unfortunately, the

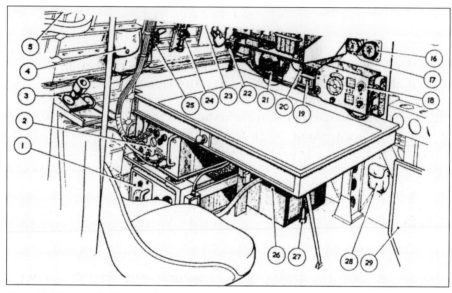

Figure 1: Navigator's Crew Station.

Key:

1. Gee receiver unit #
2. Loran receiver
3. Drift recorder
4. Stowage for WFA
5. Air temperature gauge
6. Dinghy manual release
7. Gee/Loran antenna
8. Gee indicator unit *#
9. Loran indicator *
10. Lamp and switch *
11. Visual indicator R1155 *
12. Loop lamp and switch *
13. DF loop control *
14. Altimeter *
15. MF receiver R1155 *
16. Airspeed indicator
17. Clock #
18. Air position indicator
19. DR compass control
20. Switch unit
21. Variation setting control
22. Press to transmit switch
23. APU fuel cock control
24. Lamp and dimmer switch
25. Storage for WFA plug
26. Air mileage unit
27. Intercom. socket
28. Clothing heating plug
29. Navigator's astrodome
     platform in stowed position

Note 1: * denotes Items 8 to 15 in the above table that are not shown in the figure above the table.

Note 2. # in the above table indicates equipment that was not fitted to Far East Air Force Sunderland aircraft.

This diagram from AP1566E was kindly made available by Tony Burt.

magnetic variation setting control (VSC) and the loop antenna are not fitted in ML796. The VSC was close to the API. The loop antenna, 360° scale and cursor were fitted to the starboard side of the rear of the astrodome hatch, outboard of the left/right DF needles indicator. There is a porthole window, high up to the navigator's left shoulder and above the drift recorder, through which the starboard inner engine and wing root are visible. Also, high up in the roof on the starboard side behind the navigator's seat was the Gee aerial tuning unit, not fitted in FEFBW Sunderlands.

To the left, on the aircraft's starboard wall, is the drift recorder (sometimes called the drift sight). Stowed above it (not shown) was the wind-finding attachment (WFA). The astrodome, in the fuselage roof immediately to the right of the navigator, was accessed by standing on a platform beside the navigator's table in the central gangway. Just below and to the left of the astrodome (when facing to the rear) are the left/right (LR) direction needles for aligning the null point of MF radio bearings received through the loop antenna. The navigator's 'crash' position was sitting on the floor – or strictly speaking, the closed hatch that led to the stairway into the galley and lower deck – facing aft to the rear of, and with his back to, the main spar.

This photograph shows the navigator's excellent view from the astrodome. The photograph is taken looking towards the tailfin. The pitot-head mast can be seen towards the right of the picture. The navigator had a view overhead throughout 360° in azimuth apart from a small interruption on a relative bearing of about 120° relative to the aircraft's nose where the loop antenna cupola interrupted the line of sight. This was not a serious disadvantage. *Author*

The ASV radar station

The ASV Mk VIC radar station was surrounded by a 'tent' (made of black material). It had a flap entrance. The station was forward of the navigator's station on the starboard side, the operator facing forward. This was manned by one of the air signallers, and sometimes by the navigator. It contained the control unit and ASV Mark VIC plan position indicator (PPI).

A Rebecca Mk II was also fitted in this station, probably above the ASV. I am uncertain where Eureka ground transponder beacons were located in the Far East. There may have been one at RAF Butterworth, and possibly at Changi and Tengah. There were none at Kai Tak and Iwakuni. A beacon approach beam system (BABS) was at some point installed at RAF Seletar. My logbook confirms that Sunderland crews carried out practice BABS approaches at Seletar, though I never remember using BABS through necessity.

The flight engineer's station

The flight engineer's station was to the rear of the main spar on the starboard side, with the engineer facing aft. He had a control panel in front of him where he could make all the fuel tank selections. He had fuel contents gauges, fuel pressure warning lights, cylinder temperature gauges, oil temperature gauges, oil pressure gauges, propeller and wing de-icing controls, indicator lights and flow control rheostats, vacuum pump selector cocks, fuel cock controls, carburettor air intake heat controls, de-icing selector cocks and hand-pumps, the APU refuelling pump and cock, and oil dilution selector switches and push-button. He monitored fuel consumption in conjunction with the navigator, and calculated the air nautical miles per gallon of fuel consumed, and the safe endurance of the aircraft at any time. An air mileage unit was fitted in the engineer's station. He generally monitored the ongoing serviceability of the aircraft's equipment, especially that associated with the airworthiness of the aircraft, flight controls, and the engines and propellers (see colour section page 5).

Further information on fuel burn rates and other aircraft performance matters are to be found in Appendix 2.

The wireless operator's station

The HF radio (or W/T – wireless telegraphy) operator's station was on the port side, to the right of the navigator but facing forward. The radio operator had a T1154 HF transmitter and an R1155 receiver (identical to the navigator's receiver). The radio operator could wind out a trailing aerial from his seat; this was a cable that could be extended a hundred feet or more below the aircraft. The radio operator's station was occupied by one of the three air signallers. The T1154/R1155 radio equipment was first introduced into the Sunderland and other heavy aircraft during the Second World War. The transmitter required skilful tuning. Communication was nearly all by Morse

The 1st Lieutenant of USS *De Haven*, Hal Smith USNR, who was in charge of the captain's gig sent from the ship to the stricken Sunderland RN302, to find out what assistance was required. (*Hal Smith*)

The photograph of RN302 on the right was taken by Lt Hal Smith. Ballast had been placed on the port outer wing to counter-balance the loss of No. 1 engine which had fallen into the sea during the heavy landing on a swell of 6–8 feet. (*Hal Smith*)

Captain T.C. Sigmund USN, captain of USS *De Haven*, is seated at the head of the officers' ward room table. Lt Hal Smith is in the background reading a magazine and must have been on the second lunch sitting on that day. The crew of Sunderland RN302 were made most welcome aboard USS *De Haven* until we disembarked at Sasebo, Japan. (*Hal Smith*)

RAF marine craft moored alongside the pier at RAF Seletar. No. 1124 MCU and the MCRS supported three Sunderland squadrons: Nos 88, 205 and 209. (*Courtesy of the RAFSA*)

N-Nan of No. 295 Squadron moored at Seletar, Singapore. Note the careful alignment of the propeller blades when the aircraft is moored. (*Courtesy of the RAFSA*)

RNZAF Sunderland Q-Queen on the step at about 75 knots and shortly to be airborne at Seletar. Note the twin ADF and additional HF aerial mast. This aircraft may have been on a delivery flight to New Zealand. (*Courtesy of the RAFSA*)

'L' Love of No. 205 Squadron moored at China Bay, Sri Lanka. (*Courtesy of the RAFSA*)

W-Whiskey over Seletar trots. (*Courtesy of the RAFSA*)

Above the Navigator's table the Loran receiver can just be seen on the left and a Gee Mk 1 Receiver (fitted only in UK-based aircraft) is on the right. Below is the R1155 radio receiver with the Air Position Indicator lower on the right. The Variation Setting Control is missing. The right-hand photograph is the Drift Recorder. The vertical periscope sight (minus its sponge rubber eye protector) is central. To the right is the drift measurement screen and to the left, the groundspeed calculator. Its location on the starboard side of the aircraft, beside the navigator, is shown in the lower left photograph. The Drift Recorder is described in Appendix 3.

The Loop Aerial Left/Right Needles indicator (right-hand photograph) indicated to the navigator when he had correctly aligned the loop antenna with the direction of arrival of an incoming radio signal from an MF beacon. Above it is a small red night light.

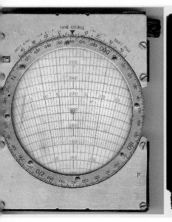

On the left is the Dalton Computer (this can be seen by my left elbow on p. 8). It was an essential and invaluable aid to every navigator enabling him to carry out all the necessary heading, track, drift, speed, distance, temperature, pressure, altitude and timing calculations and conversations.

The left-hand photograph shows the Air Position Indicator. The DRC repeater is the left-hand circular dial with North at the top. The centre of the three parallel pointers is the actual True heading being flown; the two outer pointers are set by the navigator to the heading he asked the pilot to steer. This gave the navigator an immediate indication whether the pilot was maintaining the required heading. The counters in the right-hand windows indicate the aircraft's 'air position' North or South and East or West in degrees and minutes of Latitude and Longitude. The two knobs to the right were for re-setting the Latitude and Longitude. The right-hand photograph is of the Loran receiver. The navigator tuned to the required Loran Chain and read off values which were then plotted onto a Loran chart. The resultant position was then transferred to the navigator's plotting chart.

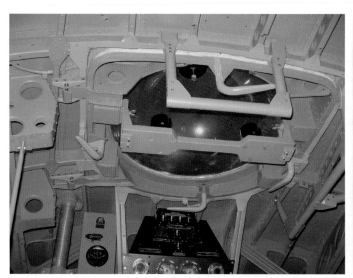

The left photograph is a view of the astrodome from the flight deck, looking aft. The Engine Start panel can just be seen aft of the dome at the bottom of the photograph. To the left can be seen the DF Loop Left/Right needles shown on the previous page. The vertical aluminium tube to their left is the axis mounting of the DF Loop Antenna to the bottom of which was fitted a 360° scale and cursor, used by the navigator to measure the bearing in Degrees Relative to the aircraft fore and aft axis. Secured by two wing nuts, a wooden Astro Compass mounting frame is below the astrodome. It was removed when not in use and when astro sights were being taken using a sextant. The sextant was suspended from the centre of the dome to steady it. The astrodome was removed and stowed to give access to the top of the aircraft before and after flight, and as an emergency escape exit. The photograph to the right is the ASV Mk 6C mounted in the radar operator's station. A Rebecca II radar indicator was positioned beside the ASV indicator.

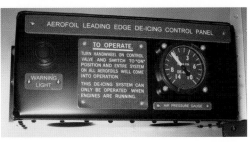

Above is the wing leading edge de-icing control panel. On the left is the Engineer's main control panel. Just out of view are the oil dilution selector switches an push-buttons. Below, in rows, are the fuel contents gauges, fuel pressure warning light switch and warning lights, the cylinder temperature gauges, the oil temperature gauge switch and gauges, the (vertical) oil pressure gauges, the propeller de-icing motor indicator lights and de-icing flow control rheostats, and the two vacuum pump selector cocks. On the horizontal panel are two carburettor intake heat controls (centre) and the fuel cock controls (7 either side).

Right is the W/Ops station showing the T1154 wireless transmitter. The frequency coverage was from 200 kHz to 5.5 MHz in three bands: yellow, red and blue. The maximum output was 70 watts for W/T Morse and 17.5 watts for speech. It was valve operated and required careful tuning. On the left is the R1155 Receiver, identical to that in the navigator's station. An Aerial Control Unit is above the T1154. A Crystal Monitor Type 2 is above the R1155.

Below left is the W/OP's Trailing Aerial drum holding 100 feet or more of cable. Below right is the Navigator's Ground Position Indicator (not fitted in FEFBW aircraft). This projected an illuminated arrow onto a chart below, continuously indicating the aircraft's position and heading.

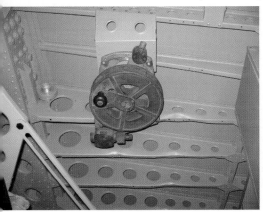

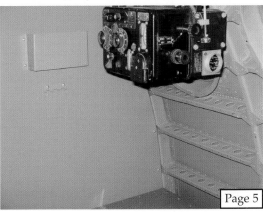

This photograph shows the first pilot's seat and main flight instruments, primary flying panel and aircraft controls. The P10 magnetic compass is between the first pilots legs near the rudder pedals. Weapon selection switches are just out of sight to the left of the pilot's seat.

The co-pilot's seat is on the right. The Weapon Forward Throw analogue computer can be seen to the right of the pilot's seat. This was connected to the navigator's Mk III Low Level Bomb Sight in the aircraft's nose station.

The flight deck viewed from between the navigator's and wireless operator's stations. Part of the ASV Mk VIc radar indicator is just visible to the right of the picture. Normally, this would be hidden within the operator's tent to limit extraneous light shining on the PPI screen. The pilots' central pedestal which houses the four throttles, fuel mixture and propeller pitch controls can be seen straight ahead.

Above left, are roof mounted controls between the pilots' seats. Nearest is the rudder trim tab control, with elevator tab controls on the left and right side. The red and green levers are the port and starboard master fuel cocks. The red and green handles farthest forward are the fuel jettison controls. The right photograph shows the throttle, fuel mixture and propeller pitch control levers.

The left photograph shows the nose section including the ammunition boxes and four 0.303-inch fixed forward-facing machine guns. The mooring bollard (left) is stowed. A Mk 3 LLBS was mounted in front of the navigator's bomb-aiming window in the aircraft's nose. The right-hand photograph is a view upwards into the nose turret that contained another two Browning machine guns.

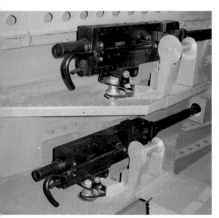
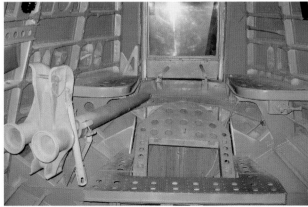

Two port-side fixed-mounted Browning 0.303-inch machine guns are shown in the left-hand photograph. The right-hand photograph shows the mooring bollard. In flight the Mk 3 Low Level Bomb Site was positioned in front of the window, slotted onto a bracket. The sight and a weapon-release button were operated by the navigator.

The left photograph shows the Ward Room, looking aft. Bunks to port and starboard are either side of a gate leg table with folding leaves. The stairway through the door leads to the flight engineer's station at the rear of the flight deck and main spar. The right photograph shows the galley primus stoves. The porthole is in the starboard hatch that opens and secures upwards; below it is a bin to stow the sea drogue. A similar hatch and stowage was located on the port side.

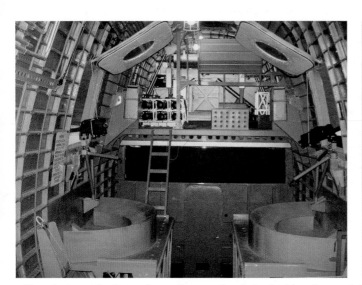

The photograph above shows the rear fuselage, looking forward. The port and starboard 0.5-inch Hispano canon were mounted beside the open hatches. The right-hand photograph is of the rear fuselage. Below on the left, the starboard bomb-door is closed. Bottom right, the port bomb-door is lowered. Electrically-driven carriers suspended from rails, ran weapons from the bomb-room outwards beneath the port and starboard inner wings for release into the sea.

code, typically at 18–22 words per minute (the definition of a 'word' is 5 letters), and was therefore rather slow compared with voice or teletype; however, it had the advantage of being able to be heard in poor communications conditions, and could be encoded and abbreviated. HF W/T was used mainly to receive actual and forecast weather reports and to transmit position, ship and submarine sightings, and weather reports. It provided long-range communication, typically up to 1,000 or 1,500 nm provided a suitable frequency was used. Crews were generally required to report their position, hourly, mainly as a safety check (see colour section page 5).

The first and co-pilots' stations
The first pilot's seat (see colour section page 6) was on the port side at the front of the flight deck, forward of the navigator's GPI station (not fitted in FEFBW aircraft) and the radio operator's station. On the left-hand wall were the auto-pilot controls and the weapon station selector and fusing switches. In front of the pilot were all the usual flying and engine instruments. The co-pilot's seat was to starboard, forward of the ASV radar station. The co-pilot had a weapon forward-throw analogue computer that fed the Mark 3 low-level bombsight, located in the nose and operated by the navigator. Onto this device, the co-pilot set the weapon type, stick length, height and speed, in conjunction with the navigator/weapon aimer. Because the pilots had control of weapon selection, fusing, bomb doors and bomb trolleys, they could if necessary drop weapons from the flight deck, aiming 'by eye'.

The pilots' communications and other equipment included a four-channel VHF transmitter receiver, barometric altimeters, a radio altimeter, gyro indicators, DRC compass repeaters, a P10 magnetic compass and a standby or emergency compass.

The Sunderland normally had only one button-selected, four-channel, crystal-controlled VHF set. This might have been the TR1143. One button (channel) was set to the Distress frequency, 121.5 MHz. Preset frequencies will almost certainly have included common-use frequencies such as 116.1, 118.1 and/or 119.7 MHz. Mainly because of communication demands when deployed to Iwakuni for Korean War operations, at some date during the summer of 1953, aircraft had a second four-channel set installed. Only one VHF set was fitted until at the earliest the end of March 1953.

Access to the lower deck
Access to the lower deck, galley, wardroom, bomb room, toilet and bomb or depth charge aiming position, was by either of two stairways. The main one was beneath a hatch and stairway ladder immediately behind the main spar (to the right of the flight engineer). A second set of stairs was accessed via a sliding hatch in the flight deck floor, just to the rear of the throttle and pitch lever pedestal, between the pilots.

Lower deck nose compartment, fixed guns and gun turret

To the rear of the nose section compartment on the lower deck was the main entrance door to the aircraft, on the port side. The only door on the starboard side was in the tail section. A toilet with a door was at the rear of the nose compartment on the starboard side. There was a hand-pump-flushed toilet and a small wash-basin. Forward of the entrance door and toilet were a winch (removed in the picture), the anchor and the bollard stowage. There were four forward-firing 0.303 in. machine-guns fixed-mounted in the nose of the aircraft, two on either side. These fired straight ahead. The pilots directed fire from them by pointing the aircraft in the direction of the target, correcting their aim by observing the splash impact of shots in the water. There was a rotating FN gun turret in the aircraft's nose, usually manned by one of the air gunners and armed with two 0.303 in. machine-guns. This had a field of fire of about 110 degrees in azimuth to port and to starboard, as well as up and down. The turret could be retracted about three feet into the nose compartment, on rails, using a crank, chain and cogwheel arrangement (see colour section). This space was big enough to allow two crewmen to stand upright on the decking in the nose with the bollard erected. For mooring, a special ladder was temporarily attached to the outside of the fuselage on which one crewman would stand with the 'short slip' rope to 'catch' the buoy when the pilot approached it during the mooring process. A second man then quickly secured the short slip around the bollard. There were other mooring and unmooring technicalities and procedures that I will not attempt to describe here. The task of mooring and unmooring was skilled, and was shared among members of the crew. In the latter stages, you had to put your hands and arms into the sea, which was very cold in winter in Japan and Europe.

The navigator's bomb aiming station

The navigator's second station was in the aircraft's nose compartment below the gun turret. The navigator was responsible for visually aiming and releasing depth charges (and practice bombs) against submarines on or just below the sea surface. On the very front on the aircraft's nose, there was a flat window about 15 in. (37 cm) square, facing directly forward, through which the navigator could sight and aim at the target when attacking a surfaced or partly submerged submarine. This window could be opened while on the water, and *was* opened to give access to the buoy's pendants during the mooring and unmooring process. From this position, the navigator could speak to the pilots by intercom. A description of the use of the LLBS during attacks when aiming and releasing practice bombs or depth charges is given in Appendix 3.

The aft upper deck

The upper deck aft of the flight engineer's station was a radio and radar equipment bay (and was the roof of the 'bomb room'). Also installed there were motors that drove the wing flaps and bomb racks. Other stores, such a marine markers and sonobuoys, could be stowed there in racks.

Beam gun stations
To the rear of the equipment bay was a ladder leading down to the port and starboard 0.5 in. cannon positions, each with a large hatch, about 3 ft 3 in. (1 m) square, in the fuselage side. These opened into the fuselage and were then latched to the roof when open in flight. The two cannon could then be swivelled on their mountings, the barrels protruding out of the aircraft to port and starboard. They had 'stops' to prevent the gunner from shooting the aircraft's wing and tailplane. Each was manned by an air gunner or one of the other crew members. There were two large bins on the upper deck to port and starboard, just forward of the guns, in which belts of several hundred rounds of 0.5 in. ammunition were stowed, and from which the ammunition was fed directly to each gun. There was a well into which spent cartridge cases fell.

Rear fuselage and tail gun turret
Walking aft down a narrow wooden slatted gangway on the floor towards the tail, you would pass, first, a door in the starboard wall of the aircraft (this could be used to access the aircraft from a dinghy or to launch an inflatable dinghy onto the sea). Further aft on the left was the DRC master unit, suspended from a bracket attached to the starboard side of the fuselage. There was also a small hatchway and camera mounting on the floor, for a rear-facing camera, to record weapon impacts on the sea surface. This could also be used to mount a flare chute. At the very aft end of the fuselage were doors with a small glass porthole, leading directly into the tail gunner's rotating Frazer-Nash turret, armed with four Browning 0.303 in. machine-guns, the gunsight and ammunition stowage bins (see colour section page 8).

Rear door, mid-fuselage lower deck and bomb room
Retracing our steps forward, we pass on the starboard side before reaching the beam gun station, the inward opening rear door. This was not often used because access into and from the aircraft was much easier via the front port side door in the nose.

Walking forward between the port and starboard beam gun stations, and down some stairs, you pass two rest bunks (one to port and one to starboard) and thence through a central door to enter the bomb room. Here up to eight 250 lb depth charges or many more practice bombs (or a Lindholme gear or other search and rescue containers) could be loaded onto, and suspended from, carriers with electromagnetic release units (EMRUs) attached to electrically driven bomb rack trolleys suspended on rails attached to the roof of the bomb room. Large bomb doors (seen later) in each side of the fuselage, just below each wing root, were attached to frames, EMRU-latched to each side of the fuselage in the bomb room. These were so arranged that, when the pilot pressed the Doors Open switch on the flight deck, it allowed the bomb doors to drop under their own weight, guided by their retaining frame.

The port and starboard bomb racks could then be motored outwards from the bomb room, suspended from rails mounted in the under surface of the port and starboard wings until they were in the slipstream inboard of the inner engine cowlings and clear of the fuselage. Bomb door opening and motoring of the racks, outboard and inboard, were electrically controlled by the pilots from the flight deck. The bomb room and wardroom had both full-length doors and additional waist-high doors that were latched closed for take-off and landing. These provided compartmentation and added rigidity to the airframe during take-off and landing, but were often open in flight for ease of crew movement.

The galley, drogue stowage, hatches and ladder to the upper deck
Forward of the bomb room was the galley, with two small primus ovens, rings and storage cupboards (see colour section page 8). Beneath the two large hatches in the port and starboard side of the fuselage were stowage bins to hold canvas drogues. Each was attached to the airframe by a strong hawser and shackle. Pilots would signal to the galley, always manned by two crewmen while mooring, when they required to deploy one or both drogues to slow down the aircraft while taxiing towards the buoy. Drogue signal switches (port and starboard) on the flight deck activated individual drogue lights in the galley; illumination of these was acknowledged by drogue operators in the galley. The use of one or more drogues was usually necessary when there was little surface wind, or difficult wind and current conditions. Slowing down the aircraft considerably helped the initial mooring process. A crew member looped one end of a slipline (or 'short slip' – a length of rope) over the aircraft's bollard and had to pass the other end through one of the hawsers that encased the buoy's red rubber float, as it passed close to the aircraft's port bow, then quickly put two turns of the rope around the bollard.

The wardroom
Forward of the galley was the wardroom. This had two canvas bunks, each about 6 ft 6 in. long (one either side of the fuselage) and a central gate-leg table with folding leaves. The Sunderland was many senior officers' and VIPs' preferred means of air travel in the Far East. Attractions were the superior 'cuisine' (despite the basic cooking facilities), bunks to recline on, and the ability to walk around the aircraft more or less at will, to take in the view. HRH the Duchess of Kent was taken on an official tour of various Far East countries in a specially fitted-out Sunderland temporarily renamed 'Powder Puff' in 1953/4.

FEFBW Sunderland crew composition

The crew composition could vary, but in the Far East it usually consisted of ten or eleven members, as follows:

a) The Captain – Most crews were captained by one of the pilots, but one crew per squadron was sometimes captained by a navigator.

b) Two Pilots – Most were commissioned, but in 1952/54 there were still a few SNCO pilots (typically one or two per squadron). All pilots were trained to 1st pilot standard and usually rotated 1st pilot duties

c) One, and sometimes two, Navigators – Originally there was only one navigator on Far East squadrons where, in the absence of a GPI, there really wasn't a need for a second navigator. However, from mid-1952 a number of additional navigators (straight from Navigation School) were posted on strength as 2nd navigators. This was at the request of the then OC FEFBW. By early 1953, nearly all FEFBW squadron navigators were commissioned. When their tour ended, the few remaining non-commissioned navigators were replaced by officers. One of the navigators would be appointed squadron navigation leader. This could sometimes be a very experienced SNCO navigator.

d) Two Flight Engineers – most were sergeants or flight sergeants, but a few were master engineers, usually one per squadron. One of the flight engineers would man one of the beam gun positions when at action stations.

e) Three or four Air Signallers – There were a few commissioned air signallers; normally one per squadron. One would be appointed squadron signals leader. The majority were sergeants or flight sergeants, with usually one and sometimes two master signallers (warrant officers) per squadron. Air signallers could all operate the W/T and ASV radar, and one would man a beam gun station at 'action stations'.

f) One or two Air Gunners – by June 1952 all were sergeants or flight sergeants.

Tailpiece

Information in this paper is based almost entirely on the author's own recollection; I apologize for any errors. Performance data on the Sunderland Mk V are contained in Appendix 2.

Imagery

Some images of equipment which could not be found anywhere else and whose origins are not known were downloaded from the Internet. All other imagery in this Appendix were taken by the author, who is most grateful to the Imperial War Museum, Duxford, for its permission to take these photographs. The diagram of the navigator station in AP1566E was provided by Tony Burt.

Glossary of Terms and Abbreviations

Abbreviation	Definition
ACM	Air Chief Marshal; air officer rank senior to AM.
AHQ	Air Headquarters (AHQ Singapore, AHQ Malaya and AHQ Hong Kong). Assumed responsibility for RAF stations within a defined geographical area
Air Cdre	Air Commodore, the most junior air rank officer, below AVM
Air Position	The geographical position of an aircraft had it been flying through still air (i.e. zero wind conditions)
Air Speed	See CAS, IAS, RAS and TAS
Airman/Airwoman	A member of the Royal Air Force (or formerly the Women's Royal Air Force, now disbanded) who has not attained junior NCO rank
Altitude	An aircraft's height above mean sea level (MSL) or above ground level (AGL). Also used in astro-navigation to describe the angle of arc of a heavenly body measured from the horizon (i.e. the true horizontal) to the celestial body
AM	Air Marshal, the air officer rank above AVM.
ASI	Air Speed Indicator
ASV	Anti-Surface Vessel – a class of radar designed to detect surface ships, submarine periscopes, masts and snorkels. Also used for navigation. ASV Mark VI in the Sunderland Mark V had two rotating scanners, one beneath each wing, which gave 360-degree coverage in azimuth
ATA	Actual Time of Arrival
AVM	Air Vice-Marshal, the second-highest rank of air officer
Band of error	Navigation aids are assigned a 'band of error' expressed in degrees or nautical miles, normally at a 50% probability level. They enable the navigator to determine an aircraft's most likely geographical position, taking into account the possible inaccuracy of certain types of navigation aid and in dead-reckoning navigation
Beaufort scale	A scale that describes and defines wind strengths and sea states
Bombscow	A motor-driven sea-going vessel used to transport weapons and ammunition between the shore and flying boats at their moorings
Buoy	A floating device anchored to the seabed or a riverbed to which a vessel or flying boat can be tethered or to indicate a channel or obstruction
CAS	See definition of RAS. A second meaning is Chief of Air Staff

Cb	Abbreviation for cumulonimbus cloud
Course	Term used to define the direction of travel of an aircraft through an air mass relative to True North – Course (T), or to Magnetic North – Course (M)
Cpl	Corporal, a junior non-commissioned officer
Cumulonimbus	The most vertically developed of clouds; usually displays an anvil-shaped top. Associated with strong updrafts, downdrafts and turbulence; also with thunderstorms, lightning, hail, icing and heavy rain. The vertical extent of the cloud can exceed 40,000 ft
Current	Horizontal movement or flow of a water mass (sea or river)
DC	Depth Charge – a weapon dropped into the sea from aircraft such as a Sunderland to attack, damage or destroy a submarine. A hydrostatic fuse enabled the weapon to be exploded at a preset depth below the sea surface
DR	Dead reckoning (navigation). The process of plotting air positions, courses, speeds and position lines, and calculating required course/heading changes, estimating times of arrival, etc., while navigating an aircraft throughout its mission. More fully described in Appendix 3
DRC	Direct-Reading Compass – described in Appendix 3
Drogue	A strong canvas bag-like device, secured to the airframe of a flying boat; can be released into the sea by a crewman while the aircraft is taxiing in order to slow it down or improve directional control when approaching a mooring buoy
ESM	Electronic Support Measures equipment. Used to locate and analyse radar and other electronic emissions
ETA	Estimated Time of Arrival
F/L	Flight Lieutenant (or Flt Lt), the most senior of junior commissioned officer ranks
F/O	Flying Officer (or Fg Off), a junior commissioned officer, senior to a pilot officer and junior to a flight lieutenant
F/Sgt	Flight Sergeant (or FS) – a senior non-commissioned officer, senior to a sergeant and junior to a warrant officer or master
FEAF	Far East Air Force
FEFBW	Far East Flying Boat Wing. Formed in 1950 at RAF Seletar, Singapore. Commanded by a wing commander. It consisted of a Wing Headquarters and three Sunderland Mark V squadrons, Nos 88, 205 and 209, with fifteen flying boats and fifteen crews
Fitter	Describes generally a mechanic or technician qualified in the maintenance of an aircraft
Fix	Navigation term meaning the assumed geographical position of an aircraft at a stated time found by means of a visual pin-point, or by position lines obtained by radio, radar, astronomical or visual aids
Flame-Float	A pyrotechnic device dropped into the sea from an aircraft; ignites on entering the water and emits a flame. Burns for about three minutes. Used as a short-term sea marker, and to enable back bearings to be taken on it for the purposes of aircraft drift assessment

Flight Commander	A flying squadron usually has one or two flights commanded by Flight Commander(s); normally one rank junior to the squadron commander. Sunderland squadrons were commanded by a squadron leader
GPI	Ground Position Indicator, an instrument for tactical navigation
G/C	Group Captain (or Gp Capt), the highest rank of senior commissioned officers, senior to a wing commander
G/S	Groundspeed – speed over the ground or sea along an aircraft's track
Heading	Term used since the 1960s to define the direction of travel of an aircraft through an air mass relative to True North – Heading (T) – or Magnetic North – Heading (M)
Height	A term describing the vertical distance of an aircraft (in feet, or less commonly in metres) above the ground or sea surface at lower attitudes (typically below 2,000 ft). Also used to describe the vertical extent of terrain above sea level
HF	High Frequency – radio/radar operating in the 3–30 MHz band
HSL	High Speed Launch operated by the RAF Marine Branch. This type of vessel was superseded by the RTTL
IAS	Indicated Air Speed – air speed as shown on an aircraft's ASI
IFF	Identification Friend from Foe. A radar transponder fitted to aircraft to assist ground radar operators to distinguish known friendly aircraft from others
LF	Low Frequency – radio and navaids operating between 30 and 300 kHz
Loop	Loop antenna. A circular radio antenna, operating in the MF band, mounted vertically on an axis capable of rotation through 360 degrees in azimuth. Combined with a scale to indicate the antenna's direction relative to the fore-and-aft axis of the aircraft, it was used to measure the relative bearing of radio signals emitted by distant radio beacons. An aid to radio navigation in the Sunderland. Now superseded by a radio compass
Marine Marker	(or Marker Marine) Dropped into the sea from an aircraft and used for longer-term marking compared with a flame-float; burns for about fifteen minutes
Master (aircrew)	Aircrew specialization warrant officer, e.g. Master Pilot, Master Signaller, Master Engineer
MCMU	Marine Craft Maintenance Unit – a unit equipped to carry out deep maintenance of RAF marine craft. Identified by a number
MCU	Marine Craft Unit – a unit formed to operate RAF marine craft. Identified by a number (e.g. 1151 MCU)
MF	Medium Frequency – between 300 and 3,000 kHz
MPP	Most Probable Position – a geographical position (generally latitude and longitude) derived by a navigator taking into account the likely accuracy and bands of error of navigation aids used, combined with the position as determined by the aircraft's air position and calculated or forecast wind velocities
MRAF	Marshal of the Royal Air Force – the most senior RAF rank. At most, one such rank of serving officer is appointed at any time

Navaid	Navigation aid – a general term describing any type equipment or system used to aid navigation
Navigation Leader	Nav Ldr – responsible to the squadron commander for maintaining high standards of navigation within a squadron
P/O	Pilot Officer (or Plt Off), the most junior commissioned officer
Pinnace	A general-purpose type of RAF marine craft used mainly to support seaplanes/flying boats. Operated by the RAF Marine Branch (disbanded)
PPI	Plan Position (radar) Indicator
PRC	People's Republic of China
QFE	The atmospheric pressure to be set on the millibar sub-scale of an altimeter for it to read the aircraft's height above a particular airfield, and for it to read zero altitude when the aircraft is on the runway
QFI	Qualified Flying Instructor
QNH	The atmospheric pressure to be set on the millibar sub-scale of an altimeter for it to read altitude above mean sea level
QTE	The bearing of an aircraft from a direction-finding station measured relative to True North
R-1155	An MF and HF radio receiver fitted in Sunderlands and other large aircraft in the 1940s and 1950s. Usually linked to a loop antenna for direction finding, and may also have a trailing aerial
RAF	Royal Air Force
RAS	Rectified Air Speed – IAS corrected for installation and instrument errors
Refueller	A self-propelled seagoing vessel used to bring fuel to a flying boat at its moorings
RTTL	Rescue and Target Towing Launch, operated by the RAF Marine Branch (now disbanded)
SAR	Search and Rescue
S/L	Squadron Leader (or Sqn Ldr), the most junior of senior commissioned officers
Safety Height	Definitions vary. Typically, the height of the highest ground above sea level within thirty miles of an aircraft plus 1,500 feet
Sgt	Sergeant – a senior non-commissioned officer (SNCO), junior to a flight sergeant
Smoke Marker	Similar to a Marker Marine but emits white or coloured smoke rather than flame. Burns for about fifteen minutes
Sonobuoy	An active or passive acoustic sensor released into the sea by an aircraft or helicopter to detect submarines. Data detected by hydrophones within the sonobuoy system are relayed by a radio link to patrolling aircraft fitted with equipment to process incoming data which are then interpreted by specially trained crewmen aboard the aircraft. Not carried by FEAF Sunderlands
Sqn	Squadron – describes a numbered unit (e.g. No. 88 Squadron). May be a fighting or a ground support unit. Each FEFBW aircraft squadron was established with five Sunderland Mark V aircraft and five aircraft crews

Step	A sharp change in the contour of a flying boat's hull just aft of the aircraft's centre of buoyancy when at planing speed. This helped to break the suction between the surface of the sea and the hull. 'Unsticking' the aircraft on take-off was most difficult under calm water conditions.
Squadron Commander	Sunderland squadrons were commanded by a squadron leader. Most squadrons today are commanded by a wing commander
Swell	Sinusoidal motion of the sea due to the effect of past strong winds. Characterized by its long wavelength. Since the sea surface, superimposed on a swell, may be calm or slight, this can make it difficult to estimate the height of the swell from an airborne aircraft. A swell presents a particular danger to flying boats while alighting or taking off, and also to landplanes forced to ditch in the sea. The preferred direction of alighting or take-off is parallel to the crests and troughs
T-1154	An HF transmitter fitted in the signaller's/WT operator's crew station in Sunderland Mk V flying boats in the 1950s
TAS	True Air Speed – the speed of an aircraft relative to the air mass in which it is flying. In zero wind, TAS equals groundspeed. TAS is derived from RAS (often now referred to as Calibrated Air Speed) with corrections applied for ambient air temperature and air pressure. For example, flying in an ICAN standard atmosphere, an aircraft cruising at an RAS/CAS of 125 kts at 10,000 ft altitude will have a true air speed of 145 kts
Tide	The flow of a river from its source towards the sea. Tidal speed, or current, can be affected by past rainfall upstream
TOT	Time on Task (patrol) or Time on Target
UN	United Nations. Sunderland operations around Korea were mounted in the name of the UN under the Taccom of the USN
VFR	Visual Flight Rules (see also VMC)
VHF	Very high frequency – 30–300 MHz. This was the main voice communication frequency band in use in the 1950s. Now supplemented and, for military aircraft, superseded by UHF, between 300 MHz and 3 GHz
VMC	Visual Meteorological Conditions. Defined in terms of horizontal visibility and distance from cloud. Conditions permitting flight according to defined Visual Flight Rules (VFR)
VP	Abbreviation used by the US Navy to describe maritime patrol aircraft
W/C	Wing Commander (today abbreviated to Wg Cdr), the senior officer rank above squadron leader and below group captain
W/O	Warrant Officer (or WO), the most senior rank below a commissioned officer. Equivalent to a Master (aircrew)
W/V	Wind velocity – the vector defined by the prevailing speed of movement of an air mass and its direction relative to true north
Waves	Horizontal movement of a sea surface due to present wind and tidal conditions

WFA	Wind-Finding Attachment – a device used by Sunderland navigators to calculate the local wind velocity. Described in Appendix 3
White horses	A term describing white foam caused when a sea wave breaks. With experience and reference to the Beaufort scale, the strength of the wind at the sea surface, and the likely height of the waves, can be estimated with a fair degree of accuracy by observing the number and appearance of 'white horses'
Wind lanes	Visible lines or 'lanes' on the sea surface caused by the disturbance effect of the prevailing wind. Can be seen at low altitude from an aircraft. The stronger the wind, the more pronounced the wind lanes become. Extensively used by maritime patrol navigators and pilots to check surface wind direction

Phonetic Alphabet 1952–4

A – Able	B – Baker	C – Charlie
D – Dog	E – Easy	F – Fox
G – George	H – How	I – Item
J – Jig	K – King	L – Love
M – Mike	N – Nan	O – Oboe
P – Peter	Q – Queen	R – Roger
S – Sugar	T – Tare	U – Uncle
V – Victor	W – William	X – X-ray
Y – Yoke	Z – Zebra	

Index